DAWN
WATCH
IN
CHINA

DAWN
WATCH
IN
CHINA

By JOY HOMER

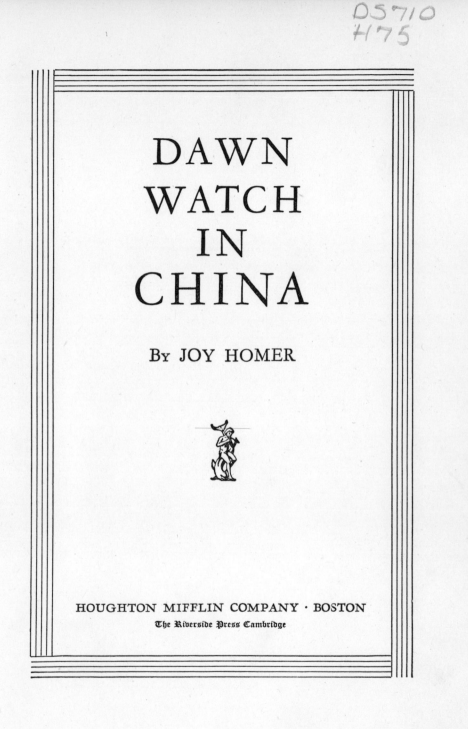

HOUGHTON MIFFLIN COMPANY · BOSTON
The Riverside Press Cambridge

The Riverside Press
CAMBRIDGE · MASSACHUSETTS
PRINTED IN THE U.S.A.

TO
MY HUSBAND

CONTENTS

(1)

THROUGH THE BLOCKADE
INTO FREE CHINA

MR. SUN at my elbow murmured: 'Those very black objects you of course see. Quite near the shore. *Pu pu pu!* ... to the left. I regret that they are mines.'

I stared out over the boat's rail, and I too regretted deeply that they were mines.

'Last week three ships were erupted,' said Mr. Sun pleasantly.

We were silent for a while, watching our prow glide toward the mine fields. The wide glassy mouth of the Kao River lay quite beautiful beneath the sun in mocking peace. I could not have guessed what lay in the land beyond that estuary. The bare brown mountains and quiet water gave no hint of the terror and beauty that was ahead. Behind us loomed a fleet of high-sterned fishing junks, heading into the wind beyond the inland passage. To our right a village clung to the cinnamon mountain cliff and its bandit tower sat upon the hilltop. A few miles up this estuary lay the little gray-walled city of Wenchow, port of the China Coast. Until the dynasty of Ming she had been called the 'Deer City' because there had once come to her gates a white deer bearing a flower in its mouth. Here was to be my first entrance into Free China.

A three-year longing had led up to this moment; three years of private struggle with Chinese history and background. I had

always known that I would go there. A good many things in the
world needed doing. In China, for instance, there was need for
money and need for news.

China had always been my first love. For the past three years
travelers returning from the East had brought me tales of a new
China. The gradual consolidation of the Kuomintang or National
Government under Chiang Kai-shek was only part of the story
which began at the turn of the century when the deepest foundations of Chinese culture were summarily uprooted and the intellectual life of the nation turned topsy-turvy. Sun Yat-Sen's revolution was more than a political upheaval. It brought with it the
rebellion of youth against the oversophistication of their country's
learning. Students began to return from the newly fashionable
'foreign' universities, their minds whirling with Ibsen and Tolstoi
and Marx. Characteristically, they threw over their own sacred
institutions without bothering to separate the wheat from the
chaff. Family traditions went up in flames. So did the iron structure of classical education and corrupt officialdom. Western customs of dress and marriage were flaunted by students in the faces
of their horrified elders.

Gradually the strange ways of the West were turned into more
constructive channels. Under the leadership of the Generalissimo
and his remarkable wife, our own broadest ideal for democratic
government and social reform began to find concrete expression
in the East. First came the righting of old wrongs, the gradual
elimination of squeeze and graft, the gradual dismissal of corrupt
officials, the not at all gradual consignment of the opium addict
to a clinic and the opium-seller to his executioner. The rotten core
of Old China would not be cleaned out in a day, or even a decade.
But the purge was under way.

Even more constructive programs went into effect. New schools
and universities, many of them mission-born, began spreading out
over the country. Farmers' credit societies were formed with

government loans as part of an agricultural co-operative movement. Mass education for the working class became the rule rather than the exception. A modern medical program started its battle against superstition and the old Chinese traditions of medicine. Inaugurated by Madam Chiang, the New Life Movement began to teach the people western methods of sanitation and good health, improved farming and livestock, inoculation, education, Spartan tastes among the wealthy — all that the Chinese most needed and were most reluctant to adopt. The capital at Nanking became a hotbed of reform and revitalization. Young people the country over were wild with the new spirit that was springing up in the land. They were ready for any sacrifice.

All this story lay hidden in obscure articles and mission reports, and in the tales of my friends. The newspapers came duly forth with Chiang's kidnapping, the winning over of the Communists, and the growing resentment against the encroachments of Japan. At the outbreak of the war they filled their columns with stories of the great Shanghai battle. From that moment, reports became as military and as bloodthirsty as possible; and as trivial. The months went on, and now not even the obscure articles told the story of what was happening to this young New China. No one knew. Apparently it was struggling on out there behind the Chinese lines. But how? What had happened to the students who had followed their government out into the West? Was there still such a thing as the New Life Movement? What of the new standards of medicine? How much effect was the whole great westward trek of the people having upon old medieval West China? Was the war changing the people's way of living and way of thinking? Were they now uncontrollably bitter against Japan? Would their new-found determination to strengthen themselves and their nation be the first casualty of the war? The answers were not known. There seemed to be only one way to find out.

I went to China. The final leave-taking was not, after all, as easy as I had expected; for during my last three weeks in New York, a certain gentleman by the name of Bill (who now happens to be my husband) suddenly, and gaily, made himself a part of my life. But my job in China was already accepted, the tickets bought; and the work had to be done. So it came about that in early October, 1938, exactly two months before I sailed into Wenchow harbor, the great Interdenominational Church Committee for China Relief sent me to the Far East as their press correspondent to gather accurate news and raise relief funds by a series of articles, stories, and photographs to be published in America. But Shanghai, my first port of call, knew little detail of the sweeping changes that were rampant in the West. It did not even seem to care. I was met on every side with generalizations. Oh, yes, the colleges had all moved out to Chengtu and places like that — wonderful trek, wasn't it? They'd heard about the Industrial Co-operatives, of course, but they wouldn't know how many there were or that sort of thing. Well, the morale was supposed to be pretty good out there in the West, but that was probably all tommyrot. You couldn't believe the Chinese reports these days any more than the Japanese. The food situation? Dammit, how should they know?

For three days I sweated blood in Shanghai, inspecting the ruins, visiting leper colonies and refugee camps, seeing children dead on the streets, and getting nowhere. The agony of Shanghai was an old and tragic story. The constructive news lay buried in the interior, out there in the West where the Chinese Government was fighting for its life.

On the third day, Charles Boynton, missionary *extraordinaire* and man of parts, called me into his office.

"Miss Homer, I thought you might like to meet Doctor Brown. He's just in from Wuhu. Superintendent of the hospital there and about to start into Free China. You're trying out a new route, aren't you, Robert?'

There was a gleam in the eye of Mr. Boynton. It was a Machiavellian gleam and it needed no interpretation. I solemnly shook hands with the unsuspecting Robert Brown. He was a broad-shouldered, straight-backed man, with the military carriage and lean, blunt features of an army general, rather than a mission doctor.

'Really a new route?' I inquired mildly.

'New for this war,' Doctor Brown said. 'At least it's never been tried.' He made an effort not to sound too proud.

'Where are you bound?'

'Doctor Brown is taking in some relief doctors to the Nanchang hospital behind the Chinese lines,' explained Mr. Boynton. 'After that ——'

'Nobody knows' — Doctor Brown almost licked his chops. 'The trip will take us three months at least.'

It was high time for the blow to fall.

'How about me?' I asked ambiguously.

'Yes,' added Mr. Boynton with malice. 'Take her along. Teach her the ropes. She needs something to write about.'

For the space of a second Doctor Brown stared at us in congealed horror. Then his sense of humor overcame his better judgment. He grinned, and it was a healthy grin.

'Why not?' he said.

It was as quick as that.

The next day we conferred over a map like two scheming generals. Instead of reaching Free China by the usual circuitous route via the French Indo-China railway to Kunming, we were to cut straight into the heart of China by the little port of Wenchow. Lying some five hundred miles south of Shanghai in the province of Chekiang, the city, like most of the southern coast, was still in Chinese hands, but officially under Japanese blockade. The harbor had been mined. Now rumor had it that coastal boats and junks were sneaking through the mine field with monotonous regularity and carrying on a lively and supposedly forbidden trade with the little city. From Wenchow there was a bus route to Kinhua, the provincial capital; and from Kinhua a railroad led straight inland to Nanchang.

'What then?'

'Perhaps on to Changsha or the south,' said the doctor. 'Even to Chungking if we can get there. Anyway, the route will show us a section of China right along the fighting zones where no one but a few missionaries has been since the war began. You'll have to rough it some.'

His warning turned out to be a flagrant understatement.

We were to leave the following Saturday aboard a coastal steamer bound for Wenchow and affiliated 'closed' ports. During the next few days I streaked about Shanghai in violent confusion, trying to buy myself a traveling kit, continually losing my way, and inflicting upon those about me a strong case of nervous fatigue. The outfit, when I finally assembled it in my room one night, was peculiar in the extreme. It consisted of assorted trousers and heavy sweaters, mostly black, ski boots and jacket, a typewriter, a vast bulk of moving-picture and other camera equipment (I was to be photographer as well as reporter), notebooks and sharpened pencils (but no sharpener), and two lonely dresses. Evidently I considered the interior a dangerous and informal place. On the whole I was right. But from the day that I left Shanghai, I steadily cursed my shortage of attractive clothes.

So on the morning of December 3 we steamed slowly out through the yellow Yangtze estuary and turned south into the China Sea. We were off on our three-months trip. But eight months were to pass before I saw Shanghai again.

Our craft was thoroughly improbable. Her name sounded German, but she was run by the Chinese; for only the Chinese would have had the unabashed gall to take her on the open ocean. About two hundred feet over all and almost as high, she was built to be a river launch and drew only nine feet of water. She might have been a Hudson River night boat out of a Lackawanna ferry. Fortunately the sea was glassy during those three luxurious days to Wenchow, but even the slight ground swell rolled her onto her beam's end. Every time she dipped her imponderable superstructure toward the waves, my insides welled up within me.

We ran between the islands, sometimes only a few hundred yards from the coast. The bare moth-eaten mountains rose steeply from the sea and stuck their round heads out as islands. They were yellow-brown as camel's hair. No trees or rock or village relieved their monotony, for China kept herself well hidden here. They were the homeliest mountains I had ever seen, and I thought them beautiful. So much for my state of mind.

There were six in our party. The young Jewish doctor and his technician wife were destined for the big Methodist Hospital at Nanchang. They were refugees from Austria without a penny to their name, and they were scared and bitter, still not quite sure of the power to start life over again. Another recruit for the journey was Ida Pruitt, an American woman, the brilliant, unconventional, China-wise daughter of Peking missionaries, who was following the trail of the Industrial Co-operatives into the West. A fourth member of the party, a young Chinese doctor, was also bound for the Nanchang hospital.

As for Robert Brown, his reputation in China was public property. He was something of a hero: supposedly the first American to stay at his post during the Japanese occupation of Wuhu in the early months of the war. On the days of shelling and street fighting, he had calmly driven through the devastated streets in his battered Ford with a pint-sized American flag flying from its snout, to bring in carload after carload of young women to the hospital compound. Later, he had saved his hospital and the three thousand refugees camped within its protecting walls from the

Japanese by refusing, at bayonet point, to give them the keys to
the compound. He was unofficially titled the best medical admin-
istrator in China, sent out now on a difficult job — to co-ordinate
the mission and Chinese Government medical work behind the
lines. His nickname throughout the country was 'Skipper,' and I
proceeded to take prompt advantage of the fact. He was fifty-one,
possessed of a sense of humor and an Irish wife, whom I had met
in Shanghai and liked at once. I suspected that he was vain, and
I was right. I also suspected that he was a fairly simple, uncom-
plicated soul, inclined toward sentiment and excessive heroics;
and in this I was partly wrong. When I watched the way in which
he talked to the Chinese, and saw his hands touch them when they
were sick, and sensed the love they held for the man, I was then
beginning to know him.

The only other passenger on our boat was Mr. Sun. He was a
friendly little man, rather incongruous in whipcord breeches and
expensive leather jacket. Oddly enough, he was the Chekiang
guerrilla army's envoy to Shanghai. When I asked him inanely
if the Japanese were aware of his title, he grinned and grinned.

'I see that my men are supplied with what they need,' he explained not very clearly, and thereafter smiled in reminiscent
amusement every time he caught my eye.

Now, as we stood by the ship's rail and watched the mines grow
larger, he turned to me again.

'You will think that we are nearly defeated,' he said soberly,
'and you are not right. You will see very quickly how it is other-
wise.'

I knew what he referred to so abruptly. Only a few weeks ago
had come the almost simultaneous fall of Canton and Hankow,
the latter after months of unexpectedly stubborn resistance. No
one knew just what the immediate future of China was to be. I
had found Shanghai suffering from an acute pessimism known
locally as 'the Shanghai mind,' convinced that the surrender of

Chiang Kai-shek was only a matter of days or weeks. They had put up a good fight, the Chinese, but they must realize by this time how hopeless it all was. Their government had moved far up the Yangtze to Chungking. But already the Japanese were pressing on, west and south of Hankow. It was a crucial moment for China.

I turned to Mr. Sun.

'You intend to go on fighting?' I asked.

'We intend to go on fighting,' he said, and his halting repetition made the answer strangely moving.

Far ahead of us the gray walls of Wenchow crept into sight around the river bend. I stared at them, wondering what lay beyond. While I wondered, and while I watched spellbound the gradual unfolding of the graceful little city and the toxic beauty of her five guardian pagodas, we slipped quietly through the mine field.

And that was that.

A small junk drew alongside and took us in to shore. A moment later and we were bouncing and swaying in rickshas toward the mission hospital in the heart of the town. I stared bug-eyed at the scene. It was my first glimpse of a wholly Chinese city, and my mind grew drunk with the detail of it. It was typical of nearly all the cities we visited south of the Yangtze Valley. The streets were of dirt, or occasionally of flat stones set close together but often deeply pitted. I was surprised to find them quite clean. The few avenues were broad enough, but the others no more than alleyways, winding and secret and just wide enough to permit the passage of a ricksha. The wide streets were lined with stores, most of them built of wood. At night the fronts were boarded up tight, but during the day the boards were taken out and the entire store front left open to the street. A strange and wonderful conglomeration of merchandise hung in profusion from the walls and rafters. Butcher shops displayed rows upon rows of flat varnished ducks in

preparation for the February New Year. Grocery stores were
laden with mandarin oranges in gay pyramids, sacks of pomeloes
and water chestnuts, dried melon seeds, and bunches of nameless
white roots. Clothing shops hung their rafters with second-hand
trousers and padded jackets and — proud above all else — long
'foreign' underwear. Brass shops shone with pots and lanterns.
Silk markets with vast cavernous interiors displayed their bolts
of incredibly beautiful silks and satins. Leather stores hung belts
and shiny boots and satchels from a hundred hooks. Drug shops
put forth a gruesome display of medicinal snakes and spiders in
great glass bowls. A single 'department store' of impressive size
sold things 'foreign' with special emphasis upon cheap but streamlined alarm clocks, thermos bottles made in Japan, old-fashioned
sweaters and American shoes, bottle-openers, flashlights, and the
various shiny gadgets that are Western civilization's most profitable contribution to China. Sprinkled in between these shops were
the restaurants and teahouses, overflowing almost onto the street,
their square wooden tables and stools virtually hidden by the
swarm of men — coolies and farmers and rich men — who
hunched happily over their tea and talked of many things.

Through these shopping streets moved oxcarts, laden donkeys,
water buffaloes, black pigs, and incredible scrawny chickens.
But almost blotting out the animal life was a solid wedge of humanity. The wedge was bumping, colliding, laughing and swear-
ing, intensely and happily aware of all that went on about it.
Our ricksha boys threaded their way through the mess at a dead
run. Their special warning call, a low meaningless bark, magically
cleared a path before us. The crowd flowed by on either side.
There were peddlers and itinerant barbers, the tools of their trade
across their shoulders; young students looking incredibly wise in
their long sober gowns; coolies with lithe muscles and brown flesh
bright with sweat, padding along with heavy loads on bamboo
poles; women with babies strapped to their backs; sleek-headed

young girls with bobbed hair, dressed in long gay-colored gowns; ancient matriarchs and old gentlemen with humorous eyes; beggars in rags crying their open sores; slim young soldiers in uniform; and children strenuous in padded jackets and trousers with small bare behinds.

The people moved slowly but in violent and constant emotion at everything about them. They seemed never to stop talking as they glided on about their business. To my ignorant ear the arpeggio of voices seemed the aimless talk of the Banderlog. Their faces, even more flexible than our own, changed with every breath. I had thought that the people of China were supposed to be inscrutable! It did not seem possible that the sober-faced Chinese of American tradition could be so temperamentally and violently alive, or so clean and somehow civilized. When they were not laughing they were cursing, and when they were not cursing they were telling enormously funny stories. Never had I seen a crowd enjoy itself so thoroughly! Emotional, fundamentally happy and fundamentally hot-tempered, these were the people of South China.

To turn out of the main streets with their holiday crowd into the quiet little alleyways was to close a sudden door on a blaring carnival. Here were peace and an almost unnatural stillness. Most of the residential houses were low and built of gray brick or stones. Homes of the better class lay enclosed in their own compound and showed little of themselves to prying eyes. The narrow dirt alleys were lined with these compound walls of restful gray brick, set with gatehouses and gay red or blue or shiny black wooden doorways. The tiled roofs of the houses tilted impudently upward. Occasional trees leaned outward from the compounds and shaded the little streets; but South China cities are too crowded to allow for much foliage. Bell towers and drum towers thrust their graceful curves of tile and gargoyle out above the city. Grinning lions stood guard beside the temples of bright stone and low curly roofs. Sometimes a door into a courtyard would open and we could glance in and see the bound-footed grandmother leading her grandchild slowly across the cobbled yard, a coolie lighting a cigarette in an archway, in another corner the fat *amah* beating her wash with a stiff board.

That afternoon the old city gathered us in and the people of South China smiled at us as we rattled by.

The war had been kind to Wenchow. Though its harbor had been mined, it carried on a constant stream of commerce with the outside world. Rumor had it that Japan was keeping the port open to permit the influx of Japanese goods into Free China. Had Wenchow's sufferings been acute, it might have resented this fact more angrily. But life so far had been good. Never had commerce been better. Only the stream of refugees from the Hangchow district to the north disturbed the city's little fleeting period of prosperity. Knowing that it could not last forever, the people were wisely making plans for the future. We watched the children learning to run in orderly ranks, so that they might be the first to escape the city when its turn to be bombed should come. Instinctively that laughing, brawling crowd in the streets realized that their peace could not go on. The city knew her fate. A few months later her death began in the first sweeping air raid. A year after that, the port was summarily and efficiently closed to all shipping by order of the Japanese navy. I wonder a little what it looks like now. I wonder if the children ran fast enough.

The river, we were told that afternoon, was the only gateway into the interior, since the road had been destroyed to hinder a possible Japanese attack. So at four-thirty the next morning we were on our way. Rickshas carried us from the mission to the waterfront. There was a suspended hush in the total blackness of the streets. The city was poised in an almost unnatural silence. Our rickshas seemed to fly single-file over the unseen cobbles, with only the creak of a wheel to break the city's slumber, the

calls of the coolies hallooing back and forth to one another, and
the soft pad-pad of their feet as they rode the shafts. The stars
were still bright and close above the narrow archways and dark
up-curled roofs, for dawn had not yet begun.

In the waterfront office where we were to negotiate for a launch,
to take us upstream, the big room was alive with dim moving
figures, all talking at once, all gargling and spitting and probably
cursing into the darkness. There were to be other passengers that
morning, apparently several dozen of them. It was well we had
started early. As I sat in huddled misery on my blanket roll, a
coolie came up to me and by multiple gestures and earnest conversation indicated that I was to follow him. He led me over to
his ricksha, which was tipped on a horizontal plane, and showed
me how to curl up quite comfortably on the foot-rest with the
seat as a pillow. I did so gratefully and finished my night's sleep,
while he hovered about me like a solicitous parent. When I was
shaken awake some time later, I found that he had covered me
with his own very warm and very grimy jacket. An offer of a tip
threw him into a blushing rage. It was quite a while before I
learned when to offer tips in China.

Sampans ferried us out to our launch, a small but businesslike
craft with two infinitesimal cabins. Along the waterfront, the city
was bawling into life as dawn and noise came up together. The
street hawkers and traveling barber shops swung into action
alongside of the pigs and the chickens and the chanting coolies.
The harbor was scuttling with movement as listing junks swung
into the wind, patched sails taut, and sampans went stormily
about their smaller affairs. A freighter flying a European flag
weighed anchor and stood out to sea. The sun was rising gaudy
red above the city wall as our own engines purred into life beneath
us and we began moving slowly and chuggingly upstream.

We sprawled ourselves on the after hatch and stared back over
the stern. That vague clamor in our wake now resolved itself into

a heavy junk and three sampans, all tied to our labored craft in one long happy chain and riding smugly in our wake. Within them sat dark masses of smiling humanity — the day's passenger list. It waved to us cheerfully. Astern of us the gray-walled city gleamed below the sun and the harbor water threw sparks into our eyes. On their five promontories shaded with trees, the five spidery pagodas of lustrous stone watched over the city and the river mouth and gave back the sun's redness.

That morning Skipper presented me with my first lesson in Mandarin. By disregarding the characters altogether and concentrating solely upon the spoken language, I was able to rattle off fifty useful phrases by the end of the day. I, who had failed my various language tests of the past as regularly as the rising sun, was learning to speak Chinese! In three or four months I could carry on small, inaccurate conversations about routine subjects. Actually I never learned more than four thousand words and phrases; but I could at least make myself understood, glean over half of what was spoken around me, and, most important of all, do my own interviewing. To any self-respecting missionary this was all pretty infantile. The missionaries, spending a year and more on the language before they began their work, could read, write, and speak with some elegance. They filled me with such terror that I dared not utter a word of Chinese in their presence.

Curiously enough, those exasperating creatures known as 'tones' — traditionally the most difficult factor in the Chinese language — became for me the easiest. A Chinese sentence is more than a sentence; it is a musical phrase with tune and rhythm. My own small brain is so constructed that it cannot memorize the simplest French verb, but music it can absorb like water. Wherefore my atrocious Mandarin was at least spoken in a near-Chinese accent. Certainly I did not regret the exhausting hours I spent on its study. Only after I was able to understand the chatter of the people about me, speak to them myself without benefit of interpreter, and absorb their opinions and ideas all day long and every day, was I able to go beneath the surface of China and gather more than the superficial evidence meted out to the usual writer. Without that knowledge of the language, I should never have dared to write about modern China, who does not give herself away.

During the morning I scarcely noticed that the river was narrowing and the mountains closing in upon us. At noon we reached a landing place where, we were told, we must now transfer to sampans. It seems they were the only craft able to negotiate the approaching rapids. By this time the string of parasitic sampans attached to the stem of the launch had been augmented by dozens of their fellows, progressing under their own square sails, and piled high with merchandise recently landed at Wenchow and bound for interior cities. Some fifty more now joined us at the landing. They were jaunty little boats, these sampans, with rakish white sails, lean lines, and a round igloo mound of matting covering the boat amidships. We lay stretched under the matting with our heads sticking out foolishly toward the stern. Two boatmen in the bow poled us through the shallow water, while another handled the tiller in the stern and punted almost with the same motion. The latter gentleman had a habit of poling too vigorously and falling backward into the water — a performance which happened fairly often and which he seemed to enjoy.

By this time there were well over a hundred sampans with sails to the wind, all poling gaily and laboriously over the shallow rapids. Rivalry was high. Once they raced for a certain narrow opening in the gorge, and proceeded to jam up in one of the most agonizing traffic snarls I have ever seen. Our boats were wedged in gunwale to gunwale, while the boatmen yelled and heaved and finally dissolved in hysteria, some of them lying helpless on the boat or in the water and holding their sides.

All this time, the mountains were hedging in closer to the

stream. They were bare mountains, terraced in places with green grain and expressive with shadows made by their own dark shapes. By now the valley had become a gorge. Sun turned the shallow water a luminous emerald green that might have been touched in by a child's crayon; the occasional trees, now winter red, made abrupt daubs of twisted fire on the slopes and promontories; always within sight was a many-colored temple or joss house squatting upon a high place; these and the blue sky and the white impudent sails of a hundred sampans against the green river under the red trees — all these were the stage-props of a single countryside of China which I was never to see repeated.

Late in the afternoon we arrived at the village where the motor road had its beginning. Busses were lined up and waiting for us, already jammed with perspiring passengers; but Skipper and I were given a short reprieve by the sudden appearance of our guerrilla friend and fellow passenger, Mr. Sun, who promptly installed us in his military and highly camouflaged car and drove us on to Lishui.

The road wound in serpent curves above the stream. From here, the river was an even brighter green and the square little sails of the sampans a blinding white. In the shallows stood long-legged cormorants, intent upon nothing in the world but fish. Now and then we passed through a village perched upon the terraced mountain-side. The houses were of straw matting with low thatched roofs as fragile as blown hay; the one dirt road was cluttered with hens and children and lean black pigs.

At Lishui we were arrested as spies. It was our own fault. The rest of our party, coming through by bus, had calmly taken photographs along the route without a word of explanation. By this time, our guardian Mr. Sun had gone on to Kinhua and was no longer here to speak up for us; moreover, the officer in charge of the little town's garrison was away. So we suddenly found ourselves at the Lishui bus stop surrounded by small excited soldiery, with bayonets poised, thrilled beyond measure at their catch. They were new recruits, and they half-suspected that we might be Japanese. Explanations helped us not at all; we had taken the forbidden photographs, therefore we must be dangerous. They stood in a circle about us and everyone talked at once. We soon discovered their quandary. There was no jail in town, and now that they had captured us, they did not know exactly what to do with us. We suggested that perhaps the bus station might do. Just the thing, they decided. A moment later we were herded into the bus station and our baggage was laid out for inspection, while most of the citizens in town peered over our shoulders in starry-eyed excitement. They were especially spellbound over my feminine underwear, which was solemnly passed around for inspection. Though convinced we were spies, they were apparently quite fond of us.

In the midst of the baggage inspection, the officer in charge of the troops arrived. At once apologies flowed like water. Everyone, including ourselves, bowed in prostration and complete humility. The soldiers responsible for the mistake were duly forgiven. They looked ready to burst into tears. But a few moments later I came out of the station unexpectedly and saw them gathered across the street almost doubled up in helpless laughter. I was yet to understand the workings of the Chinese sense of humor.

I spent that night on the floor of a lightless, running-waterless mission residence. At four the next morning we were up and on to Kinhua by bus. With a terrible *joie de vivre*, our busses were scheduled to start as soon as they were full. Consequently everyone rushed for places in the dead of night.

Along that winding dirt road was a stream of humanity that never seemed to end. Recruits for the army, we were told; long ragged lines of countrymen and coolies with heavy loads of equipment across their shoulders. They were a pretty depressing lot, still dressed in their own nameless faded blue garments, bare feet caked with dust. They shuffled along the road edge in patient endless file, and most of them smiled at us as we passed.

Skipper muttered: 'Poor devils, do they know what they're in for?'

There was another human trek along that road which puzzled us for some time. We must have passed over five hundred men with heavily loaded handcarts bound in the direction of Wenchow. We learned later that they were refugees from the region of Hangchow who had arrived at Kinhua without money enough to reach the coast. The provincial government at Kinhua had solved the problem by employing these men to carry loads of goods to Wenchow for sufficient wages to tide them over. It was a system which killed several important birds with a single stone; it had to date saved over eight thousand men from death on this one stretch of road, and it had quickened the constant stream of foodstuffs and commodities destined for Wenchow and forever jamming up in the interior cities. The system was by this time in full swing throughout the province. Any refugees without enough money to buy rice, women as well as men, could reach their relatives in such-and-such a city or seek a new home in this-or-that village merely by hiring out as part of this human freight train. The whole problem of commerce and communications, so urgent in time of war, had speeded up in Chekiang, thanks to the wise use of starving man power. Goods do not travel fast by refugee-back, but they reach their destination. And even this in China is a major triumph. Apparently there is no question of goods being confiscated by the refugees to whom they are entrusted. Here one who is not a professional bandit is an honorable man; and it will take more than simple hunger and even more simple death to turn him into a thief.

Banditry itself, in Free China, had almost died out as a profession since the outbreak of war. All the best bandits had joined the army and learned for the first time the joys of a full

stomach. They made exceedingly patriotic guerrillas. But a few
still lingered on the wilder terrains. Shortly before we reached
Kinhua, over a stretch of flat, wild country, we rounded a turn
and saw a band of twenty or thirty men grouped in the center of
the road with guns and clubs poised. Perhaps they were only
an unruly band of recruits that wanted a lift; but their intention
was plain enough. The bus slithered to a halt, and instantly the
men were at the door trying to pry it open. When they found it
locked they sent up a howl. At that moment the driver retrieved
his courage and started up the bus with a jerk that sent the
clinging figures flying in various directions. I looked back and
saw several of them raise their rifles. But some thread of fear or
conscience held them back. Instead they began picking up large
rocks from the roadside and hurling them through the windows of
the laboriously grinding bus. For a moment glass and rocks were
plentiful in that crowded interior. Strangely, no one was hurt.
I noticed the man sitting diagonally behind us. He had read his
newspaper throughout the episode. When the last rock crashed
through the window beside him, landed in his lap and liberally
showered him with glass, he was quite annoyed. I saw him look
up with a slight frown, brush off the offending glass, and return to
his paper.

At Kinhua we again ran into our friend Mr. Sun, who was turning out to be a valuable acquaintance. He had, he said, arranged
for Doctor Brown and me to interview the Governor of Chekiang,
who was anxious to talk with us. Governors, on the whole, are inaccessible, and we were pleased. Since Kinhua had taken the
place of Hangchow as the capital of Chekiang Province, and since
its own devastating raids had begun some months before, it
must now keep the headquarters of the Provincial Government
well hidden from even the ordinary citizen. We were driven far
out into the country in the Governor's battered little car, with
such an air of conspiracy that I expected to be blindfolded almost

any moment. The headquarters were well camouflaged, all right. They were lodged in the last place one would ever think to look for them; all of which is adding insult to injury, since I cannot, of course, say anything more about them.

Even more impressive than the interview was Governor Wong himself. He was a big man, dressed in simple uniform without insignia, direct, decisive, and alive with enthusiasm: the antithesis of the traditionally oversubtle and overeducated Chinese official of the past. In spite of myself, I was impressed with his intelligence and vision. Was this the typical military governor of a Chinese province? If so, the country had come a long way from the old smiling, scheming officialdom of the past. The man was young, under forty. He knew where he stood and he knew what he was doing. More than anything else, he was sincere.

It was no scoop, this interview; but it gave me for the first time the universal war cry of 'Free China' that I was to hear repeated a thousand times and more in the months to follow. Out of the seventy-five counties or *hsien* in Chekiang, fourteen had been lost to the Japanese; but in each of these lost *hsien* were Governor Wong's own officials, controlling most of the territory and the destiny of the people. His mobile guerrilla units were operating throughout this occupied zone. Puppet rulers set up by the Japanese were mainly old discarded officials blacklisted by the Chinese, and only a few were able to visit their respective counties and stay alive.

It surprised me that the Governor spent most of his time telling us about the industrial and economic progress in his province instead of dwelling upon his admittedly successful military coups. He seemed to be full of home industry and the way the province was turning out for the first time its own paper, butter, small arms, sweaters, and dozens of other oddly contrasting commodities. Experiments were being made in useful substitutions, he said; the seed of the wax tree, for instance, was being used as oil for lamps in order to save on fuel. A good part of this home-industry program was carried on by refugees, with wages from the provincial government.

'Like your W.P.A.,' he said casually, and I jumped. 'Besides our freight service that you have already seen, we employ these troubled people to do repairs, make new roads; we teach them industrial weaving. There is much progress here, you can see. That is why the people wish to continue fighting. We in Free China are prepared to fight for another five years. Our expenses are low because we have no occupying army to finance and because we can make our own small arms so easily. And we wish to fight, because the longer we fight the more we can learn. The war is improving the government. It is strengthening the people. I have been able to do more in these eleven months than in my previous two years' term, because I am wiser and the people are strong. After the war we shall have a better country here than we have had before.'

It was propaganda talk, of course, and full of the usual Chinese overoptimism. I felt only skepticism and a sneaking admiration for the man's courage as I listened to him that afternoon, squatting on a stool before the square table of his bare little reception room. Later, when I had observed and watched and wondered at what I saw, I was to remember this first interview and smile at my own disbelief.

That evening, Rewi Alley turned up at the mission home where we were staying. It seems strange to anyone who has lived in Free China that there should be still people in the world who do not know about Rewi. He has become that much of a national figure, all in the space of a single year. He is a big-boned, red-haired New Zealander with a homely, vivid face, and the enthusiasm of a dog and the shrewdness of a fox. When I met him there at Kinhua, he and the young Chinese official K. P. Liu were promoting the now famous institutions known as the Chinese Industrial Co-operatives. We sat talking for some two hours in

the late afternoon sun while I received my first groundwork in
the study of this movement, which is today transforming the
life and thought of Free China. Later at Paochi I was to study it
from first-hand observation. Now I merely listened and reserved
judgment. Meanwhile Rewi persuaded Ida Pruitt, who lived and
dreamed co-operatives and who had come to Free China expressly
to find and work with him, to return via Wenchow to Hongkong
and set up a promotion office there. Our party had already begun
to narrow down.

The next night we took the train from Kinhua straight west
to Nanchang, a twenty-four-hour run. There was a thin moon
out when we started for the station. Something strange about
that cold winter moon. Our ricksha coolies were nervous. They
ran as if the Devil were at their heels, and perhaps he was. As we
drew near the station we heard the train begin a shrill, childish
whistle. The engineer knew something of moonlight raids and
was anxious to be under way. The Kinhua railhead was uncomfortably near the Japanese lines to the north, and already there
had been eight hundred killed in the city. We picked our way
through the ruins of the station and out onto the tracks. A raid
the week before had made three direct hits on the station, leaving
only two walls and a bit of roof still standing. But typically it
was still selling tickets in the débris-littered waiting-room. The
big old ruin stood patient, like a Hollywood still of the Great
War, upreared against that convenient moonlight. Out on the
platform dark forms moved restlessly back and forth about their
business and spat into the night. There were no lights, only the
swinging red of an occasional lantern. Once a flashlight began
an aimless search from a train window and flicked across the lip
of a bomb hole beside the tracks. We instinctively spoke in low
tones, almost as if the bombers might hear us. We slept that
night in our clothes, with shoes and flashlight well within reach.

The following day was cloudless and full of sun, too hot and lazy to have any dealings with a war. Winter and violence died away together in that peaceful air. It is always strange in China that one moment there can be war and terror and the next such absolute peace. We laughed at ourselves, and leaned far out of the windows to watch the land slide by. The soil was red and the low hills gleamed with neatly terraced rice paddies. At every station the train stopped for ten minutes while the stationmaster telephoned ahead for news of the whereabouts of Japanese planes. Sometimes we would get out and walk up and down the platform in the peaceful sun. Once we noticed that our engine and some of the cars were jagged with rents and bullet holes.

'Have you had any raids lately?' asked Skipper.

'Four days ago,' said the engineer. 'They held us up for twenty minutes,' he went on, and snickered.

We smiled with him. The sun was hot. The whole world was at peace. War? What war!

Late that afternoon we reached the railhead near Nanchang. Because the front lines were only thirty miles away, the Chinese had torn up the rails some forty miles east of the city. Arrangements had been made by wire for an army truck to meet us and take us into Nanchang, but when we stepped out on the platform there was no truck in sight. Thanks to a breakdown, it did not appear for over five dreadful hours. The sun had deserted us by this time, and the December evening was asserting itself in no uncertain terms. We piled on all our spare clothing, but the wind whimpered over the flat dusty land and sieved through our heavy coats as if they were made of cheesecloth.

The small station was alive with restless humanity. At a continuous row of stalls and tables along the edge of the platform the refugees were trying to sell their goods and personal belongings. In front of this noisy row of auctioneers stood another oddly quiet gathering of people. These, too, were refugees waiting in silence for the transport train that would take them

out of the danger zone into what they must have thought would
be safety. Several hundred of them gathered there: old men and
small babies, brown-faced farmers from the north, women with
bound feet and dusty faces, children with smaller children on
their back, sick children, and children wet to the skin. It was not
a pretty group. In that blind winter wind, most of them were
dressed in one thin, usually light blue, cotton garment, fortified
with additional rags and bits of cloth. A few more prosperous
wore padded clothes, but even they were stiff with cold. Most of
them had straggled into the station on the morning of the previous
day, without money for rice. Still they waited wordlessly. They
had been on the road, many of them, for weeks. Now the free government train would take them south on the last lap of their
journey. The women nodded and smiled to each other.

The children were numbly patient. Even the babies did not
cry very much. I remembered with a start that these were not
necessarily the very poor, who were used to suffering. The poor
in most cases had had to stay behind and brave out the Japanese
occupations. These were the well-to-do farmers and shopkeepers,
the small-business men and professional men, the skilled laborers,
even in a few cases the wealthy; until now, the thought of going
without a meal or suffering from cold would have seemed as
absurd to them as it would to us. It was their first experience of
this kind. On the road, they had gradually sold off the few
valuables they had been able to bring with them. Self-respecting
citizens with an enormous weight of pride in their hearts, they
were now reduced to the rôle of beggar. And still they chatted
together quietly. They were not aware of themselves as tragic
heroes. It took all of their thought and energy to keep alive.

One family, I noticed, had purchased a little rice. The occasion
called for celebration. So they gathered the whole crowd about
them and began dishing out the rice to most of the two or three
hundred refugees on the platform. Three mouthfuls each was

the quota. As I sidled over to watch, they noticed me for the first time and called out a casual greeting.

'*Hao pu hao, Hsiaochieh?* (How are you, little sister?)'

I said oh, I was fine, thank you. And hoping to help them a little, I said in my atrocious Mandarin:

'It's pretty cold today, isn't it.'

But they did not take the hint. They were not at all interested in the cold. They were interested in me. Speaking slowly so that I could half-understand them, they began thrusting questions at me.

'So you come from America, Hsiaochieh!'

'That is a very beautiful country, is it not?'

'But why did you come all this way?'

'Aren't you homesick?'

Finally the young woman who was dishing out the rice took an enormous rice bowl in her hand and began filling it to the top and overflowing with the precious white kernels. Holding it out, she called over to me:

'Come, little sister, sit down and have some rice with us, and please tell us *all* about America!'

She stared at me in puzzled hurt when I haltingly refused. I might as well have slapped her in the face.

A young mother near us was carrying her ten-year-old son. Once she started to put him down, but his legs buckled under him and she took him into her arms again.

Skipper casually edged nearer until he was standing beside them.

'Excuse me, T'ai T'ai,' he said. 'Your son is afflicted with malaria, is he not?'

'It is the malaria, Hsien-sheng. But we cannot leave him in a hospital and go on without him, for we might not be able to find him again. And we are without money and food here until we can reach my sister's home in Kian.'

'He is very sick, T'ai T'ai. Perhaps we could make him well again at the foreigners' hospital in Nanchang. Will you not leave him?'

But the woman shook her head stubbornly and bitterly. 'We cannot lose our son. We cannot leave him behind.'

The boy was already out of his head, shaking with malaria chills and yellow with jaundice. Skipper opened his bag and began dosing him with quinine. He spoke to me in English:

'The boy is already dying. I don't think we could save him anyway.'

The rest of our party crowded around, and both the Chinese and Austrian doctors with us opened their kits to see what they could contribute. The crowd was not long in catching on. There were few who were not in need of medical treatment. Some of them were already past help. In a moment the station platform had been turned into an impromptu clinic.

'Elder Brother is very sick with the dysentery, American Doctor. You will perhaps make him well again?'

'My grandfather is over by the station but he is too weak to walk. Please, Hsien-sheng, come quickly!'

It was a natural and thriving little clinic, without hesitation or embarrassment on the part of anyone. They were too far gone to be afraid. Old wounds were bathed and bound, quinine flowed like water. I watched the gentleness of Skipper's hands and the unconscious grin on his face and listened to the quiet courtesy of his speech. I began to understand why the Chinese loved him so instinctively.

Three hours later the refugees' train steamed into the station, bound for Kian and the south. Five minutes after that every boxcar and coal wagon was piled high with yelling, laughing people. Their journey was almost over. In the south of the province they would be safe. They could start life again. They sprawled on the roofs of the cars, leaned waving from the doorways, half-mad with joy. Among the last to climb aboard was the young mother who had started our platform clinic, still clutching her little yellow mummy of a son. The cheering of the crowd seemed to hang upon the air long after the train had rounded the curve and disappeared.

Two days later word came to Nanchang that the refugee train had been bombed and machine-gunned with heavy slaughter only twenty minutes' run from Kian.

When we were all thoroughly congealed, the truck arrived, and the night air was filled with greetings and apologies. We piled ourselves and our luggage into the back of the truck, and it started out bumpily and without headlights toward Nanchang. The front was uncomfortably near. Once we saw the glow of a burning village far out in the night. As we rolled finally through the streets of Nanchang, we could just make out the blind ruins standing up against the paler sky. The city had been bombed with mechanical regularity since the beginning of the war. Once the headquarters of the Chinese aviation corps, it had suffered for its military importance. That night, with the Japanese only thirty miles from the city, the people were waiting patiently for the end.

It was midnight when we drew up before the gates of the big Methodist Hospital compound. We wondered what we would discover here at the hospital, that had been struggling along for three months without regular doctors. We soon found out when we pounded on the door of the mission residence and watched the faces of the staff as we presented them with two new doctors and a technician.

'For almost three months,' said a young American teacher, 'we've been praying for a doctor. Just one doctor. We've prayed ourselves hoarse, and I think we've all been perfectly sure that a doctor would somehow materialize out of the clouds or something.'

Midnight supper that night was full of laughter and wisecracks and general celebration. The next morning in the little hospital chapel, missionaries and cooks and coolies, and a good many townspeople as well, gathered for a special service of thanksgiving for their new staff. By the afternoon, word had gone out through the city that once again there were doctors in the foreigners' hospital, and the compound swarmed with sick and wounded.

I was surprised at the hospital itself. Somehow I had always pictured mission hospitals as rather primitive and makeshift affairs; anyway, not like this great brick building with its shining equipment and sunny wards. Unfortunately it was located only a few hundred yards from the Japanese bombers' pet objective, a bridge that spanned the Kan River. A few days before we arrived, a bomb exploded fifty feet from the hospital wall, wounding four patients and showering the missionaries and staff with glass.

'It's the night raids I don't like,' remarked one American girl who was filling in as a makeshift nurse. 'They always bomb that bridge at night. The last time they did it, I got under the bed.'

During the week we spent at Nanchang, interviewing governors and mayors and other dignitaries and inspecting the ruins of the city, I lunched several times with four young Chinese officials; and for some reason I cannot get them out of my mind. They were extremely modern young men, educated at Yale and Columbia. They called themselves the Four Horsemen, very sarcastically, and they worked harder than necessary so that they would not have time to think. Their wives were back in their home towns near Shanghai, either alive or dead or perhaps raped. As for them, they moved as the government moved; when the Japanese took Nanchang, they would move again.

They had a small victrola and two or three ancient records, and sometimes we danced sedately in their officers' quarters.

It was the first time that they had relaxed in so long that they were a little awkward. It went to their heads, and they laughed quite close to hysteria. It was too good to be true. They perched on stools around their lunch table, dressed in khaki civilian uniform with high collars, young, brown-faced, trying to be gay. They drank my health a dozen times a meal and sang 'Old Eli,' laughing at themselves. They were so typical of China and her tragedy that they left me too bitter to weep.

It was here at Nanchang too that we came to know Marshal Shang Chen, at that time vice-commander of the entire Ninth War Zone and one of China's best men. As it happened, he had just become a Christian. Three weeks before he had been baptized in the little mission chapel. Like so many Chinese officials, he seemed almost too genial and smiling, too happily childlike for a commander; until we happened to see him giving orders to his men, and sensed something as hard as steel within him.

One day he lent us his car and waved us off upon a special tour of the front lines north of Nanchang. It was something we had definitely planned on doing, Skipper to study medical and stretcher facilities, myself to observe anything I pleased and write about it. Fronts were not open to foreigners, even in China, and we shook hands with ourselves more than once on the journey out. The lines above Nanchang constituted one of the few fronts in all this war where the system of trenches typical of the World War was in use. Some weeks earlier, the Japanese driving south had been halted on the north bank of a small river; the Chinese had hastily dug trenches on the south bank and installed artillery. There the Japanese drive had bogged down, for the region was mountainous and the river a swift one and not easy to cross. Nanchang had been granted a temporary reprieve, though the Chinese were well aware that their enemies could force the river crossing whenever they felt that the sacrifice

of men justified it. No one knew upon what hour or day or
month the attack would come.

For two hours we drove through a deserted countryside. There
was an occasional empty farm, nothing more. Progress was slow,
for the road had been half-destroyed to prevent the passage of
Japanese mechanized units, and was systematically mined every
half-mile and ready for complete destruction on the day the
Japanese should cross the river. The terrain was dotted with
barbed wire and machine-gun emplacements, deserted now but
ready for defense. As we drew near the lines, surprisingly the
countryside came to life. Coolies with heavy loads on their bamboo poles bobbed unemotionally along the road headed for the
trenches; stretcher-bearers passed carrying the wounded toward
the rear. I almost laughed when I looked across into a big pasture
and saw a crowded market in full swing with several hundred
country people happily trading in their foodstuffs to the army, all
jabbering and laughing and talking at once. Apparently not even
a front has any privacy in China.

Once we stopped at a dressing-station belonging to the Chinese
Red Cross (an entirely Chinese organization), and watched emergency dressings being applied to the severely wounded. There
were no dramatics, no conversation of any kind; there simply
wasn't time. The Chinese doctor in neat white Red Cross jacket
went swiftly and in silence from stretcher to stretcher, bathing
and disinfecting the ugly wounds and putting on temporary ban-
dages. The men watched him without emotion. They seemed
not to suffer pain at all.

Half a mile from the river, the road ended. Here at a deserted
and very ordinary little bamboo-and-straw farmhouse was located
the staff and officers' headquarters, so perfectly camouflaged that
enemy planes ranging overhead for the past few weeks had not
paid it the slightest attention. The rich crops and wet paddies of
rice were deceptively peaceful. So were the lotus leaves lying

sprawled on the quiet pond before the farmhouse door. With much bowing and scraping we were introduced to General Kao, the garrison commander in charge of this sector, who promptly invited us for lunch. We wondered what food they could find out here, where everything had to be brought from Nanchang on coolies' backs. We soon found out when course after course began appearing on the table, beautifully cooked in delicate sauces and spices. Skipper and I looked at each other with large eyes, but said nothing. The officers' fare we knew was simple enough: rice and a little vegetable. How much trouble and pains had these preparations cost them? How had they known about our coming? And so we feasted there in state, half a mile from the Japanese lines.

Midway through the meal, without any warning at all, the big guns began a throaty roar. I jumped visibly and lost face. But the conversation flowed smoothly on; no one seemed to notice the bombardment. I was longing to get out of there and see what was happening, but Chinese courtesy was complete and adamant, and I had to sit there murmuring low nothings while, as I afterward learned, the Japanese shelled an artillery emplacement on the very hillside where we lunched. What I had taken to be the roar of cannon had been the bursting of shells.

After lunch, we walked the remaining distance to the trenches. The bombardment was still in progress and the earth shook and rumbled. But the shelling stopped while we were still a safe distance away. Once in the trenches, we were shown about as politely and nonchalantly as if we were being guided through the British Museum. We inspected dugouts and machine-gun emplacements. We peered out over the firing step at the Japanese lines across the river, a few hundred yards away. We chatted with the soldiers, and trotted through the winding trenches feeling ridiculously like tourists. There was some desultory shooting which I suspected was merely rifle practice, and occasionally a

machine gun chattered near by. It was by all odds the most
orderly and well-behaved front! I was surprised to find the
Chinese soldiers, far from the ragged troops I had expected to see,
a well-uniformed and well-disciplined lot.

'It is very nice here,' explained an officer, with what I considered undue optimism. 'At night we cross the river and raid the
Japanese lines. We destroy their trucks behind them and they
never catch us. In the day they throw shells at our artillery but
they never hit them. It is very nice, you see.'

I agreed with him. It was not bad at all. But how long would
this vacation last? Four months later, when the Japanese closed
in on Nanchang from all sides, crossed the Kan River, and
finally took the city, perhaps it was not quite so nice. Not many
Chinese survived that crossing. Even today I wait instinctively
for news of these men, of the little camouflaged farmhouse, of the
peasant market-place down the road, of my friends the Four
Horsemen in Nanchang. It still seems queer that I shall never
know.

Three days later we took the night train straight west toward
Changsha. Skipper had business to attend to at Liling, a small
city halfway on the journey. By this time we were accustomed to
reach our destinations at the most inconvenient possible moments,
and it seemed quite natural that the train should dump us onto the
Liling platform at one in the morning. The station was far outside the city; there was no question of finding a proper place to
sleep. The single room inside the station was already occupied
with a hundred-odd refugees and soldiery sleeping huddled on the
cement floor, so we spent the remainder of the night pacing the
platform fast in order to keep warm. Even here in Central China,
the winter nights held a damp, insidious cold against which there
was no defense. A drizzle of rain soon had us chilled to the bone.

Once far down the platform we saw a glow of light and strolled
over to investigate. Crouching before us were the figures of a

woman and her child, each of them dressed in a single ragged cotton garment held together with bits of string. The girl was pot-bellied from eating bark and much water. She was too weak to stand. The mother might have been beautiful, for she had the high cheekbones and perfect almond face of China's loveliest women; but her skin was too tight and her eyes sunk deep. Squatting there in the fine rain at two in the morning, with their primitive lantern beside the track, they were sifting through a pile of ashes disgorged by some passing engine, searching for bits of precious coal that they might sell for a few coppers.

As we drew near, they saw us and shrank back. Skipper spoke to them very casually.

'The coal is hard to find, is it not?'

'It is hard to find, Hsien-sheng.' The woman watched us, wary as an animal.

'Is your husband not about?'

'My husband has been dead three days. When we left our shop at Hankow before the Japanese came he was sick even then with the dysentery. He walked all this way carrying our child and he did not tell us anything. So then he died. We have no money, you see, and the coal is not enough. The child has been sick and there is no money to buy rice.'

'How long since you have eaten rice?' Skipper asked.

'My husband sometimes bought us rice. It would not matter now, but the child is sick. She cannot go farther. It would be better if she could die.'

She spoke unemotionally, not conscious of drama, nor aware of this as a hard-luck story at all. Skipper took some bills out of his purse and started to hold them out, but the woman stared at him in sudden strange fury and backed away.

'It is all right, T'ai T'ai,' he told her gently, using a term of respect. 'It is only for the child.'

But the woman merely stared at the ground in silence and bitterness. Skipper laid the bills quietly down beside the track and we moved away. The girl, who had been sitting on the ash heap holding her swollen stomach, looked at us impersonally and went back to her coal.

That night, after visiting the hospitals in the city, we were back at the station looking for transportation to Changsha. Like most of China's trains since the war, those on this line were inclined to be haphazard. Sorry, yesterday's train hadn't come in yet, might be in tonight. Would we care to wait? It might leave for Changsha as early as midnight, six hours hence, which would be very fortunate. Just then a long, dark troop train began to whistle and show signs of moving on. Yes, it was going to Changsha. In thirty seconds we were installed in a boxcar filled with straw and Chinese troops. Happily we sprawled on the straw amid the khaki knees and elbows and we slept.

It was three in the morning when we pulled into the once proud city of Changsha, capital of Hunan Province. It had been burned (according to the 'scorched earth' policy) by the Chinese garrison some three weeks before, when it looked as if the Japanese, driving down from the north, would capture the city at any hour. Actually, the enemy had been almost a hundred miles away and the premature burning had been a colossal blunder, the unnecessary destruction of one of the most beautiful cities in all China. Politics may have had something to do with it. There were rumors of sabotage and mutiny within the garrison. It was certainly true that after Chiang Kai-shek himself arrived in the city to stop the destruction and call the commanders to task for the horrible mistake, the setting of fires still went on for two or three days, apparently unchecked.

The true story of the burning will never be known, and perhaps it is just as well. For jealousy is not a pretty thing when it calls for the razing of a great metropolis and the burning of her people. True, most of the population was evacuated beforehand, but some hundreds of wounded soldiers, not removed in time, were caught like rats and burned alive. Even now, three weeks later, the fire still smoldered and flamed in rice factories and storehouses. The night air that swept through the open door of the boxcar was foul with the smell of wet, burning wood. The whole city, lying under a thick blanket of rain, stank of it.

With a coolie to carry our bags, we started through the charred streets, dead black in the downpour of rain. An hour later, even before dawn broke, we reached the gates of the famous Yale-in-China Hospital. Refugees were huddled under the lee of the gate, which did little to protect them from the rain and the December cold. A few of the more fortunate were crouched beneath a piece of bedding; the rest sat as they were with their knees against their chests and their backs against the gate. One child was coughing hideously and monotonously. My heavy clothes made me feel a little cheap.

While we were reviving at the breakfast table of the mission residence, a young Chinese soldier flung into the room. We learned later that he was quite a famous general, though he wore no insignia or special uniform. He was bursting with news. Apparently he had just come from a council meeting of the Generalissimo and all his highest commanders in a village just outside of Hengyang. The most important meeting of the whole war, the young man told us urgently. The entire Chinese army was to be reorganized on a guerrilla basis. Every soldier in China was to be taught the guerrilla tactics of the Eighth Route Army, and every guerrilla was to be a member of the Generalissimo's regular troops. There would be three divisions in the army; a third of the men would be fighting on the field, while another third was kept in reserve and still another third in training.

'Entirely new system, do you not see?' cried the general in English. 'Such unity we have not had before never yet! It will cause the army to pull as one man. There will be no more fighting

in the open and so much death. We will learn to strike and disap
pear. Watch us! You will see how important is this meeting. And
those in Chungking have not even yet been told.'

He was scarcely out of the room when Finance Minister Ying of
the Hunan Provincial Government came to call. The elderly
gentleman was feeling quite complacent that morning over the
state of his provincial finances. Only yesterday, he told us, he
had been in a desperate situation. A week before it had been announced that all families who had lost their homes in the fire could
apply on this day at his offices and receive a compensation of five
dollars per person. Morning revealed a crowd of approximately
eighty-seven thousand homeless people gathered outside his
finance bureau. It was, he said, an extremely bad moment. How
could he give out the money without causing a riot? How could
he keep that much cash on hand in the presence of such a hungry
mob? Well, he said, he just turned to his Bible. He was always
one to take his Christianity seriously. Now he merely opened his
Old Testament at random. The first verse to meet his eye read:
'Fear not. Take the men of war with you.' Two hours later he
came before the multitude with $435,000 in cash and at least half
the provincial guard, armed with machine guns and, according to
Minister Ying, looking very sour.

'There was not so much as a single outbreak during the day,'
he told us piously. But I noticed a gleam of something very like
unholy mirth in his eyes.

Later that morning we walked for hours through the dark ruins
of Changsha. The American hospital, safe in the suburbs, had
escaped both fire and repeated bombings. But within the city
walls, nine out of every ten houses had been gutted. Fire does not
leave much in China. There was a thick scattering of bricks.
Occasional solitary walls thrust up black distorted shapes, their
windows staring at the sky with dead eyes. The streets showed
mile upon mile of silent death. There was nothing left that was

familiar and man-made, but only the twisted and grotesque, the gaping belly, the gray corpse of a city.

Already, before the flames had died, the people were beginning to return. They were raking through the piled-up bricks, salvaging pieces of blackened kitchenware, smiling and talking among themselves. We learned later that over fifty thousand had journeyed back to build their homes again upon the old sites. Near the outskirts of the city had sprung up hundreds, perhaps thousands of mat sheds, the traditional home of the poor, made entirely of woven straw matting. They were perched up in long flimsy lines on top of the charred débris. Round about them people were setting up shop in blackened doorways. Families were hard at work piling up the scattered bricks into high walls, laying matting across the top, and moving in again. There were no signs of mourning, but only intense work and planning and excited conversation. Before the day was out, a municipal official was showing me a detailed plan of the new city that was to rise upon the ruins of the old. And I wondered then, and have never ceased to wonder, at the strange resilience of these people.

It took only one look inside the Yale-in-China Hospital to know the horror and misery that went on beneath its cheerful front. It was the one hospital or medical clinic of any kind left in the city. Here were the war wounded who had been saved from the fire; here were civilian wounded from the constant raids, adults and children who had been caught and burned three weeks before. The clinic was lined with sick and the floor crowded with them, though they waited quietly and without confusion. A sense of orderliness filled the hospital. There was good discipline here, as in every mission hospital I was to enter. The medical school connected with Yale-in-China had moved farther west to avoid the Japanese drive. Only one doctor could be spared to remain behind. He was Phil Greene, our host at the mission home, long-legged, middle-aged, and in constant enjoyment of life. With a

handful of nurses to help him, he was carrying over ninety in-
patients and an enormous clinic virtually single-handed. No one
knew quite how he managed it, least of all Doctor Greene himself.
But there were no heroics; only hard work and not very much
sleep.

Once I watched him operate. Without enough money to heat
the main theater, he had turned an adjoining wash-up room into
an operating room. The cubbyhole, heated by a wood stove with
the pipe going out the window, barely allowed room to move
about without touching the sterile instrument table. Here, with
one nurse to help him, I watched one of the greatest surgeons in
the East amputate the leg of an old coolie. It was a queer performance. I had been commandeered for want of an extra nurse
to hold the horribly infected leg. As surgeon's assistant, to do all
the complicated suturing and tying of bleeders, there was only a
young English teacher connected with the mission. He had not so
much as witnessed an operation until a few weeks before. The
tiny room was hot and filled with the terrible stench of infection.
Without slowing up his work, Phil Greene casually explained each
process to his assistant, each muscle to be cut and vein or artery to
be dissected out and tied. The old coolie, under local anesthetic
and perfectly conscious, held his breath and said nothing.

Afterward I wandered out into the hall and breathed hard to
get the smell out of my system. As I passed an open door, a little
way down the corridor, someone called out:

'Hello!'

I went in. There was only a young Chinese girl, lying flat on
a bed in the semi-darkness. Her hair was a thick black mop over
a thin face, and the starched white hospital gown made her look
curiously chaste. I must have appeared surprised, for she said
quickly:

'I am from Singapore, you see, so I can speak English.'

'What happened?' I asked. 'Is it very bad?'

'Oh, no, not very bad. But they have taken off so much of me! My leg, my hand. It is very funny, I quite miss myself!'

I stumbled around, not knowing just what to say.

'In a raid?'

'Yes.'

Again that awkward silence. Again it was she who helped me out.

'There were many of us came up from Singapore together. Haven't you heard? Sixteen of us at first. All girls, and we were trained by Madame Chiang herself.'

'How swell!' I said inanely, feeling and sounding like a schoolgirl.

'It was what you call war work. Dressings for the wounded and helping the refugees and teaching them to weave and make things and teaching the people to read and write. It is very important and you must know all about it, of course. She trains us, Madame herself, for several months, and then we graduate and are ready.'

'Yes, I've heard all about you, and it sounds wonderful. But will you be in here much longer?'

'Oh, no, not so much longer. I have been here so long, it is not bad now. If they would only not have more raids! They tell me I am the only one of my sixteen friends who is alive.'

'The only —! But ——' I fumbled again, not knowing what to say to this girl of my own age, and scared of saying the wrong thing. 'Was it really worth while, your coming from Singapore like this? When it has cost so much?'

Unexpectedly she laughed at me. Not with me, but right at me, with honest amusement in her voice.

'My friends would do it quickly again! It is too bad you cannot ask them and see.'

I stared at her.

'You must know,' she said with almost a grin, 'that we do not

want to die. We came here to teach and to help China and to
dress wounds. But we came to die also. It is not so serious and
so terrible, all this!'

I straightened up, and catching her mood for the first time,
smiled with her in relief, feeling the sudden banishment of melodrama and bitterness from the room. There was something
significant here, but I was too new to China to catch its meaning.
I wondered only that death could seem so untroubled and somehow natural.

When we left Changsha a few days later, it was still only a
burnt-out shell of a city. Today it is a boom town! Contrary to
all expectations, the Japanese failed to take the city. The people
flocked back to rebuild their homes and hope for the best. Then
in October, 1939, the Japanese a hundred miles to the north began a furious drive on Changsha. They approached almost to the
city walls, and once more the population fled to the south. But
the Chinese had learned their lesson. There was no burning this
time. The Chinese armies, circling around to the rear of the
overconfident Japanese, closed in behind them and cut in between
their three divisions, which had failed to maintain proper communication with one another. The result was slaughter and
one of China's greatest victories. The Japanese were driven
back a hundred miles to Yochow.

Changsha is still free. Several hundred thousand people are
hard at work there. The ruins have been cleaned up. Small,
cheaply built homes are springing up like mushrooms. Commerce and trade is good. Some day the city will be rebuilt along
lines of great beauty. Ask the Chinese. They will tell you that
after the Japanese have been disposed of, Changsha is to become
the loveliest city in all of China.

$$(2)$$

THE EMBATTLED SOUTH

AGAIN we took the train, this time due south along the notorious Canton–Hankow railway, both terminals of which were in the hands of the Japanese. It was typical of the Chinese that they should continue to use the center section of the railway with blithe and stubborn efficiency, in spite of almost daily bombings. Our next stop was Hengyang, and as usual we found ourselves tramping the extra miles into the city at early dawn, across the swaying bridge of sampans that forded the Siung-Kiang, and up to the Methodist Mission door. Missions were part of our business: Skipper to reorganize their medical work, I to write about them, along with all else in China that was significant. By this time I was accustomed to finding a mission hospital a well-equipped and large-scale affair, doing a job that in America would be called spectacular and heroic and would be written up in the papers with suitable pictures. I was not even surprised any more at the missionaries themselves. Somehow I had imagined missionaries, when I had imagined them at all, as rather middle-aged and prayerful creatures, long of face and filled with right-eousness, who went dashing about after converts. After meeting some fifty-odd specimens, I still wondered subconsciously when I was to meet a missionary. Surely not these doctors and nurses and teachers, who were just like most of the doctors and teachers

I had known in America! They were casual, almost impious!
Many of them were my own age, a hard-headed, highly trained
crowd, well dressed, well groomed, and apparently having a whale
of a time right in the middle of bombings and a very disagreeable
war.

Hengyang was a city of horror. Twelve thousand wounded
soldiers hurriedly evacuated from Changsha and sent south had
arrived in this town, already overburdened with streams of
refugees from the north. The hospitals were soon filled to capacity, and there were still seven thousand wounded to be cared for.
We found them lying about in 'receiving stations' — empty
temples, houses, mat sheds — stretched out on concrete or dirt
with a single strip of matting beneath them and a single *pei wo*
over them; thousands upon thousands who had gone for as much
as six weeks without medical attention and with very little food.
Thin young kids, they were dying of disease, most of them; and
the lightly wounded were dying of slow starvation. The dysentery
patients, with no one to move them or care for them in any way,
lay where they were in their own dried filth. Most of the wounded
still wore their summer uniforms of cotton shorts and shirt;
wounds received months before festered and grew worse. The
mission doctors, already white from overwork, did what they
could. But their strength was almost gone.

No, it was not the fault of graft or heartlessness; the city and
its authorities were sick with the burden of suffering. It was the
lack of doctors, the sudden crisis, and the too few hospitals.
To some extent it was lack of foresight and proper medical facilities. When we arrived, there was campaigning in the streets and
the training in of volunteers to work in the receiving stations.
In other wars China had scorned and even feared her wounded
soldiers, thinking them no better than bandits and a menace to
the country. Though the social status of the soldier was even now
little better than before, nevertheless here in Hengyang an or-

ganization calling itself Friends of the Wounded Soldiers was collecting thousands of dollars a day from the sorely pressed citizens. Was China learning militarism? Or was the sacrificial spirit of this war teaching her compassion?

The faces of the wounded in the receiving stations were eloquent as we passed: curiosity, surprise, amusement, everything but self-pity. Most of them grinned at us, and some of them nodded and bowed. In their eyes, we were a particularly juicy sideshow. One of the authorities with us explained to them casually that we were Americans, and the result was electric. Everyone talked at once. Those who could walk crowded around us, and bowed and scraped and smiled until it seemed their faces would break. The stiff covered figures on the floor were calling out frantic greetings and questions:

'Truly from America?'

'Are you not our long-time friends?'

'What are you doing here?'

'Did you know that America was helping us?'

One brown, half-naked little soldier was tugging insistently at Skipper's elbow. 'They tell us you are a doctor and I can walk, but my friend over here cannot walk and will you come please?' All in one breath.

We let ourselves be led to the far end of the room where his friend lay. The boy — he could not have been more than fifteen — was dying fast. His breath came and went in long shuddering sighs. But he was conscious, and he looked at us solemnly and shyly. Kneeling down, Skipper felt the thin wrist and uncovered the already blackened wound. There was nothing to be done. The boy might die with any passing second, and the knowledge of it was in his eyes; he was longing to let go and be afraid of what was happening to him, but the people all around and these two foreigners would not let him do it. Skipper picked up an extra *pei wo* from the adjoining empty mat and laid it over the soldier. Instantly the boy protested in an agonized whisper:

'No, Hsien-sheng, you must not do that. You must not! We are permitted but one *pei wo* apiece, and it would not be fair.'

The effort to speak took all his breath, and when he finished it would not come again.

The next day, news spread through the streets of a Japanese pilot who had been rescued from his burning plane some way outside of the city and who was even now being carried in to one of the local hospitals. We hurried down to investigate. Inside the hospital, we had to step over stretchers of badly wounded lying about the floors and corridors, waiting to be operated upon. And there in the operating room, stretched out upon the table, was the enemy pilot who had come to bomb the defenseless city. He was burned a crisp unhuman brown. Two Chinese doctors and three nurses were working over him; gently, almost tenderly, peeling off the charred skin, cleansing, bandaging, reconstructing his face. It was a hard job. Now and then one of the nurses ran her fingers slowly through the man's black hair, touched his forehead for a moment. When we left the room, they were still working over him, while the entire hospital held its breath agog and waited for news. They saved the man's life. And before leaving the city some days later, we heard that the Chinese wounded in the hospital were showering him with oranges and peanuts and other small treasures they had saved up.

The whole incongruous little incident failed to fit into the pattern of bitterness I had expected to find. I was curiously upset and curiously relieved.

Christmas Day came to Hengyang. It seemed queer to celebrate Christmas without home or presents. Our determination to be cheerful only made things worse. Skipper spent most of the day writing sixteen pages to his wife, Brownie, while I tried to write articles and finally just sat around and missed Bill. Air-raid

warnings during the morning helped to relieve the monotony.
But it was something totally unexpected that finally saved the
day. An American aviator by the name of Bob Lancaster, in
charge of the big Hengyang aviation machine shop for the
Chinese Government, gave a Christmas dinner to his colleagues,
the Chinese pilots and mechanics across the river at the air field.
The present consisted of eight little suckling pigs. So we sat
about the yard of the machine shop, watching them turn slowly
over the great fires on their individual spits, and come out at last,
head, tail, hoofs, and hide a delicate golden brown. The skin was
like Melba toast and the white flesh as soft as ice cream. I cannot
talk about those pigs today without drifting into the mood of a
sonnet sequence.

We chewed in solemn meditation. All around us were the
mangled remains of fighting planes and the black, oily motors of
bombers and pursuit planes, most of them assembled and ready
for use. A big silver two-seater stood near us with its nose in the
air.

'That's a Japanese plane,' said Bob Lancaster. 'Came down
in a raid here about a month ago and we've almost got it in shape.
It's in the Chinese air force now.'

'How do the Japanese planes rate with the rest?' I asked.

'Only fair. They seem to be made of pretty flimsy stuff.
Those Russian motors over there have stood up well, and the
American motors are the best of the lot. Everyone seems to think
Russian machinery must be fifty per cent junk, but they're almost as good as our own. I suppose you know that the Russian
flyers that are being trained over here have sunk a lot of Jap
boats along the Yangtze. It's all hushed up, of course. The
Chinese pilots have been doing damn good work too' — and he
laid his hand casually on the arm of the flyer sitting next to him.
'Ask Ma Tze, here. He's brought down three Jap bombers in the
past month.'

The Chinese pilot grinned self-consciously and looked in another direction.

Bob went on: 'Only a few of the Chinese that started flying in this war lived longer than those first days at Nanking. Ma Tze's one of them. All his friends are dead.'

Ma Tze suddenly turned to us, his brown, square face very serious.

'You must not think it is unfair,' he told us urgently. 'Naturally I expect to be killed and I am scared almost all of the time. But the Government will give my family ten thousand dollars if I die in action, and that is wonderful, more than I could make in my whole lifetime, for I am only a middle school man. And they pay me two hundred dollars a month, which is ten times my ordinary pay. You see, the Government plays square with us. Why should I complain of dying?'

Bob translated this to me, and we fell silent, for there was nothing we could say. He told me later that Ma Tze had taken on the job of observer in the nose of a bomber, the most dangerous job of all. If the plane fell and began to burn, there was no way for the observer to get out and he was roasted alive. If it nosed into the ground, he was pulverized.

As we rose to leave, I noticed what seemed to be a plane made of ordinary wood, the same size as a pursuit but built like a toy without engine or parts. Major Wong, in charge of the air field, explained in perfect English:

'They are the dummy planes. Surely you have heard. We place them side by side on our air fields, and the Japanese bombers come and waste their bombs and also do not hit our regular planes, which are hidden in the bushes. It is very excellent.'

'Like that time last month,' added Bob. 'The dummies saved a whole Chinese regiment. Those Japs had gotten on to the troop movement somehow. They've got a devilish spy service, and so have we. Anyway, a squadron of bombers started out for a regiment that was on the march, and those Chinese might have been dead right then for all the chance they had. But the bombers flew over our field and we had a batch of about twenty dummies lined up just waiting for them. And damned if it wasn't too much for them. The leaders simply turned in midair and dived, and the whole squadron wasted every bomb they had blowing the things to bits. Gave the regiment plenty of time to get under cover. Cute little things, those dummies. The Japs are always growling about them. They claim the Chinese are insincere.'

That night we went to a Christmas pageant that was being held in the only theater in town. It was quite a show. The place was so jammed it was as much as our lives were worth to squeeze up onto the balcony, which I fully expected would collapse before the end of the evening. There must have been a thousand come to hear the Christians of the city perform. The decorations were cheap but magnificent. One interminable play after another blazed and died on the stage. Chinese entertainments are five-hour affairs. The plays were for the most part modern and somewhat lacking the spirit of Christmas, but they were loudly cheered. The acting was so good that it had me on the edge of my seat. In the old Chinese drama it was perfectly correct to converse loudly throughout the play, and tonight was no exception. The audience clapped heartily when the villain met his frightful end; they laughed loudly when the heroine committed suicide; the rest of the time they chatted comfortably with their friends. Later there was carol-singing, in parts and very beautifully done. Just to top things off, Santa Claus arrived upon the stage, bent and humped and witty. He grew tired of giving out presents and began throwing them out into the crowd. The stampede that followed threatened to wreck the theater. Finally the cast began to steal presents out of Santa's sack, and the audience in protest tried to climb up on the stage and had to be hauled back. And we left. More and more did I approve of the Chinese. No nonsense about them. They just had an extremely good time.

Two days after Christmas we were on our way again. Skipper and I both wanted to see the headquarters of the Chinese Red Cross at Kiyang, which was on the road due south toward Kweilin. After voluble negotiations, we arranged to ride in an ambulance that was driving down. The regular driver and myself took turns at the wheel. It was all I could do to keep the enormous top-heavy thing from going off the road, which was not much of a road at that.

Lunch and a few hours at Kiyang gave us just time enough for a satisfactory interview with Doctor Robert Lim, head of the organization. This Red Cross was wholly Chinese. It was known to be doing perhaps the best medical job in all of China. With headquarters in the rear, it sent out medical units including doctors, nurses, anaesthetists, and stretcher-bearers into the front lines and the base hospitals to work under the regular army doctors. Nearly all the Red Cross personnel were a well-certified lot. It must have taken a good deal of courage for them to bury their pride in their pockets and work under the Army Medical Corps, which, according to Skipper, was the one really corrupt institution left in China. The standards that governed army doctors had long been non-existent; a man could take a three-months Red Cross course and be eligible as superintendent of an army hospital. Few army doctors were capable of performing major operations, and the death rate among their patients was horrible. Only the Red Cross units saved the situation from complete chaos. One might instinctively protest, 'But why not remove the army doctors, or at least raise their standards of training?' A good deal has already been done along that very line. But it cannot be done all at once, for this is China. If the army doctors were made to lose face, they would resign in a body; and China needs even these men now. Meanwhile the Red Cross and mission doctors bury their pride and do a thoroughly heroic job. The International Red Cross, with American and British funds, still donates the equipment, medicines, and supply trucks; and the Chinese Health Administration under Yale medical graduate Doctor F. C. Yen has gradually stiffened the army requirements and the morale and training of all China's medical workers. But the wounded still swamp the hospitals and drive the doctors close to madness. It is a tragic thing to be wounded in China's war.

From Kiyang, the ambulance took us still farther south to Lingling and parked us there for the night. By this time we were suffering from an acute overdose of missions, and voluntarily put up in a local Chinese inn. There is something wonderfully sheltered and intimate and timeless about a Chinese inn. It is a haven for wayfarers in the oldest sense of the term. Generally the downstairs room is an impromptu restaurant filled with square wooden tables and stools, where a traveler can buy a good meal at any time of the day or night. Upstairs are the bedrooms, small and cosy with plain wooden furniture. The only heat in the room comes from a *ho pan* or open brazier filled with hot coals. The beds are of wood, without benefit of mattress. A straw mat over the boards, a Chinese padded *pukai*, a fancy canopy overhead, and the traveler climbs into bed exactly as he did in the days of Marco Polo.

The next morning we became hitch-hikers. Without visible means of traversing the last two hundred miles to Kweilin, we stood patiently by the side of the road and hoped for the best. The cold was bitter, but we dared not leave the roadside for fear of missing our chance; it was well we stayed, for at about two in the afternoon an ambulance supply truck bound for Kweilin passed and picked us up. For the next ten hours, Skipper and I bounced around in the back of that truck and cursed our aching bones. Shortly after midnight we pulled into Kweilin, and spent the next two hours looking for a place to spend the night. Ap-

parently the city was quite literally full. Finally we remembered
the American Baptist Hospital, and the nurse in charge gave us
rooms for the night. Had we found a room in another part of the
city, much that happened the next day would have been different.

Five hours later we creaked out of bed and set about seeing
Kweilin. Never had I dreamed of a city so crowded. What we
began to sense in refugee-laden Hengyang we now saw for the
first time in all its confusion — an entire nation on the move.
Long before leaving New York I had heard rumors of the vast
trek of the Chinese from the Japanese-occupied coast out to the
West. Kweilin, capital of Kwangsi Province and metropolis of
the South, located a safe distance from the Japanese lines, was a
natural bottleneck for the drifting population. It is an over-
powering thing, a human migration. Perhaps nothing in history
can compare with this wholesale uprooting of families from their
homes, and the vast sweep of population toward the fertile plains
of West China. The official figures state that about a hundred
and fifty million people took part in the stubborn march, to take
up their lives again in the free provinces.

They were here in Kweilin, about three hundred thousand of
them, streaming along the streets, working in offices and shops,
filling each inn and mat shed and empty lot to capacity, swelling
the city to twice its normal size. There were men and women from
every province in China. Some of them were helpless refugees;
some, workers who had deliberately left their homes in occupied
territory to come out and give their services for Free China.
Pushing our way through the narrow, cluttered streets, we
rubbed shoulders with refugee nurses and doctors, bankers and
lawyers, merchants and beggars and thieves. For months they
had been sweeping in by the thousands and the tens of thousands,
most of them by foot. They had turned the once peaceful city
into a melting-pot for all China. Here at my elbow would be a
shopkeeper just arrived in town, with his goods piled onto a

wheelbarrow and his children on top of his goods; here a professor from a famous university, now living in one room with his wife and two children; over here would be a talkative young Chinese student, just graduated from the University of Wisconsin and returned to do propaganda work for his government; next to him a homesick little nurse working twelve hours a day in a government hospital, who had heard nothing from her parents since their town was captured sixteen months before. Here was a once prosperous farmer from the north, now living on ten cents per day government dole. Here was a schoolteacher come to organize local help for the wounded soldiers, a beggar fresh from the country, a bewildered shipbuilder without money, a bewildered financier with too much money. This was Kweilin, overburdened with humanity, a brawling, laughing, weeping city.

Other towns may boast their thousands of refugees; but only Kweilin can boast of its caves. The city is literally surrounded by queer old fangs of mountains, found nowhere in the world beyond the borders of Kwangsi and Kweichow. Seeing them for the first time, crowded in about the city wall, I realized that the grotesque round-headed peaks of Chinese traditional paintings were based not upon imagination but upon fact. Kweilin lay, as it were, in a sort of lower jaw, with molars and incisors all about the edge. It was admirably suited to a subterranean existence. For these mountains were virtually honeycombed with caves, echoing caverns, some of them ten miles in length. And in their friendly interiors was enough room to house several Kweilins. The city had quite literally turned the clock back and sought an underground existence as the best defense against Japanese bombs. Cave-dwelling started here about a month before we arrived, when a rumor crept about that the Japanese were planning to level the city. Capital of Kwangsi Province, the home of Generals Pai and Li, pet bogeymen in the eyes of Japan, and the headquarters of some remarkably effective anti-Japanese propaganda, Kweilin was born to be a thorn in the side of Japan. The rumor was, of course, exaggerated. At last report, only a little more than two thirds of the city has been destroyed.

The first raid, three weeks before, had brought heavy casualties. Since then the people had learned to use the caves with all the instinct of prairie dogs. Thereafter there were few civilian casualties, for the simple reason that there were few civilians around to be killed: all but a scattering of people had virtually retreated underground. We were informed on that first morning that about one third of the population waited until the alarm rang before fleeing to the caves; another third shouldered its belongings and children and left the city at ten o'clock every morning, remaining in the caves until after the raiding hour; the still more cautious third was simply living in the caves, with occasional forays into the out-of-doors. There was nothing haphazard about the arrangement. Inhabitants of city blocks were assigned to certain specified caves during raids, much as passengers on board ship are assigned to lifeboats. And there was more than enough room for everyone.

We called on those caves, before we left the city ten days later. Many of them had been fitted with electricity and sanitary facilities. Loudspeakers had been installed, and schools for children and adults were carried on day and night. Stores and restaurants of every kind had sprung up among the stalagmites and stalactites, so that a shopping tour could be conducted quite nicely within the safe confines of a single cave. Many of the larger caverns had been divided up into private apartments which were leased out on a monthly rental basis. Generals and aristocrats had their own private caves. One cave had even been turned into a maternity ward; the Chinese, unable to resist any sort of joke, had named the six babies so far born there during raids 'Cave One,' 'Cave Two,' 'Cave Three,' and so on. Most successful of all were the anti-Japanese propaganda classes which were carried on every day before thousands of interested citizens, while outside, only a few hundred yards away, the Japanese dropped indignant bombs upon their city.

I can never talk about Kweilin and its caves without sounding like a raconteur with a strong imagination. The fact that every word I say is true only makes the story appear so much more absurd. Those caves might be a whole lot funnier if they were not so deadly efficient.

The American Baptist doctor in charge of the big brick hospital showed us about that first morning. The raids were beginning to tell on him. After the last bad one, he had finally ordered both patients and staff to evacuate the city at the sound of an alarm. As in most of China's cities, the authorities were informed about the movements of Japanese planes well in advance, and there was at least a half-hour of warning before the planes would appear over the city. Kweilin was particularly unpleasant during a raid, since the city is absurdly small in circumference — less than half a mile across — and indiscriminate bombing had been the rule for the past month. Already a wide swath of ruin had been cut across the city.

'It's been hell,' said the mission doctor, sounding not at all like a mission doctor; and we stared up at the hot sun-filled sky. It was a perfect day for a raid. A film of fish-scale cloud was across the sky; a strong wind. A wind! It was to bring terror before the day was out.

At one-thirty in the afternoon the *ching pao* or air-raid alarm wailed out over the city: one long, high shriek and then an undulating siren call. Instantly Kweilin sprang into life, with sureness of purpose but without panic. The streets became jammed with people carrying their children and prized possessions in their arms. Most of the women were smiling and chatting among themselves. It was fortunate that they did not know then what was to come. No one seemed to quicken his pace, but in ten

minutes the city was almost deserted. The calm mountains gave
no hint of the swarming life within their caves.

Skipper and I had one thought in mind — a high place and a
good view for pictures. With childish bravado, we stayed inside
the city. Finally we installed ourselves upon the tumbledown
city wall that surrounded the place like a vice. As it happened,
we chose the riskiest spot in the city from which to view a raid,
for the circumference of Kweilin was small, and shrapnel flies
upward. But we were still in the show-off stage, and that day we
learned our lesson.

For about ten minutes we waited atop the mound of wall with
cameras poised. Then in the dead stillness the *ching ching* or
'urgent alarm' sounded its scared siren. We held our breaths.
The silence lay tenuous as mist upon the waiting city. No clock
ticked off the seconds. All living things were stilled to listen,
feeling death draw nearer, straining to grip the menace and shake
it loose from this unnatural hush.

All at once a young coolie just below us against the wall, the
only human being in sight, yelled out:

'*Lai la! Lai la!* (They're coming! They're coming!)'

Far off, so faint we could not be sure, there was a new sound,
a low hum in the east. It might have been the quiet, drowsy
strumming of a summer's garden. Around us, the world and the
mountains with their burden of patient men and children gave
no sign of having heard. The humming grew into a deep drone,
wavering, still far away. Then too quickly that low drone became a roar. The anti-aircraft from the hillsides about us began
their frantic plopping, sharp and nervous. The sky filled with
white smoke puffs. But though we stared and stared upward, we
could see no planes. Yet the bombers were over the city. The
air shook with their deep growl. And still we craned and could not
find them. There was something chilling about the clear blue
sky and those unseen planes. Something was wrong!

Suddenly Skipper pointed to a spot directly overhead.

'A bunch of them are up there. They're coming over us!'

He sounded worried, but the significance of what he said missed me completely. Straining my eyes, I made out the tiny crosses in the heavens. They were flying at ten thousand feet. They looked like toy planes, transparent as the shed skin of an insect.

The next moment the air whined to the scream of falling bombs. I wanted to drop flat on my stomach, but my feet would not move. Split seconds crawled by. Then, two hundred yards away in the direction of the hospital, a volcano erupted in brown, heavy coils. Others followed with the sharp crackle of ripping cloth, spouting directly toward us in a straight fast line. They beat at our faces with noise and scruff. Houses just below us sprang outward, thrusting their bellies into the sunny air. A hundred feet away an explosion burst our ears and spread its arms above us. The concussion jerked my finger, snapped the poised camera. The next bomb would be ours. It would... It ...

It did not come.

We stood without speaking, watching the brown smoke about us thin and settle. It was merciful that I did not remember in that moment the human blood and bone that had spat outward into this same dark pall. Over fifty bombs had exploded directly below us — fifty yards, thirty yards — and their fragments had passed us by. It was a strange, prayerful little moment. I looked down then and saw the young coolie who had called out hardly a moment before, sitting quietly against the wall with the top of his head blown off.

As our ears gradually stopped ringing, we heard once more the deep drone of the planes. They were coming back. Twenty-seven bombers circled lazily through the western sky and turned their noses again toward the city, this time a quarter of a mile to the south of us. A moment later I rubbed my eyes in disbelief. The

entire southern section of the town blossomed into flower! Over
a hundred bombs, dropped simultaneously, exploded in one great
burst of flame and shouting as a hundred globular columns,
fifteen hundred homes, lifted heavenward in instantaneous destruction.

The raid was over. But the horror had only just begun. For
now throughout the city, a queer undertone of fire was swelling
to a roar. The wind...

We scarcely heard the planes drone away into the distance.
We were running toward the hospital. Already it was hidden by
columns of black smoke that were rising in a dozen places. What
would incendiary bombs do here? I was intelligent enough to be
scared. Bombs were bad enough. But fire in these narrow streets!

By now the sky over the whole city was layered in smoke and
thin tongues of flame. The wind flayed her, and she was burning
fast. The road to the hospital we found blocked by flaming
houses that had collapsed outward, though it was not more than
five minutes since the bombs had fallen. In some way, we had to
get through. There might be patients in there; certainly there was
valuable equipment, not to mention all our belongings and money.

But by this time, the streets on three sides of the big brick hospital were ablaze. On the fourth side was an open dump, burning but still passable. Boots scattering the fire, we crossed this
space at a dead run through smoke so thick we lost each other.
The heat curled our skin, for the tight-packed tinder blocks made
three walls of flame around us. A moment later and we were
through the wooden gate in the high compound wall and standing
before the hospital. Here the air was clear enough to breathe,
but the yelling of the fire almost stole my wits away. One end
of the hospital was just beginning to catch from the adjoining
house. The surrounding flames were licking over the roof. There
might yet be a chance of saving the place, but no living soul remained in the building, and it was a big job for the two of us.

Finding the place empty, we dragged out our own bags and bits of hospital equipment and piled them by the gate leading into the burning dump where the air was clearest. As the pile grew, I was delegated to stand watch over it while Skipper went back for more. This was all very well; but the flames from the refuse outside the wall were now over twenty feet high. Then on the dump about ten feet from where I stood a delayed incendiary bomb exploded with a breath of flame and the air filled with burning fragments. The gate itself began to burn. It was our only way of escape from the place. I began to make periodic forays onto the dump to stamp out the crackling mass from around the base of the gate, and then dodge in again as my trousers and boots began to smolder. But the material from the still spluttering bomb was stubborn and hard to extinguish.

It was while I stamped about in the fire-filled dump that I was blinded. A bit of burning matter caught me across the eyes. For a moment I closed them and fought the pain of the burn. But a second later when I opened them again, I was still blind. I was totally blind! I did not know I had it in me to be so scared. All reason squashed out of me, and I began hopping about like a chicken with its head off. The fire was underfoot and I could feel it hot about my ankles, but I dared not move in any direction for fear of walking into the high flames.

It lasted for about a minute, this special little dance of mine. Then my sight gradually came back. I stumbled through the gate into the compound, and at the same moment Skipper stuck his head out of an upper window of the hospital and began to laugh. 'Having fun?' he called. If he had been within reach, I would gladly have slapped his face. As it was, he was still laughing when he came down to help me put out the burning gate.

An hour later we were still moving equipment from the hospital. The streets all about it had burned themselves out and there were no more blazing dumps to haunt me. For a while we were very nearly successful in saving the entire building. One wing had begun to blaze merrily, but by opening windows and creating a through draft, Skipper almost put out the fire. For half an hour he tramped through that burning wing, up and down staircases that were already afire, along corridors in which the walls were blazing and the wooden floor boards hot under foot; while I, too scared to stay behind, trailed feebly at his heels and suggested that wasn't it time to go out now, and hadn't he better go downstairs while the stairs were still there, and dammit how long did he expect to stay up here anyway?

Still, there was no smoke in those burning halls, and little heat. The fire flickered quietly, almost gently. I was able once to light a cigarette from a windowsill. It was a slow fire but a persistent one, and no sooner would we beat out the flames from one section of the burning wing than we would find the upstairs corridors ablaze and the patient fight would start again.

It is sometimes a small thing in moments like this that makes us afraid. Once I almost gave way to panic — when we reached the end of a long corridor delicately ringed and feathered by the flame of burning woodwork, and entered a room at random. The empty room contained a single bed, the sheets rumpled, a chair and a table. There was no sign of the fire here, no smoke, except that the window had been shattered by bombs and on the floor beneath the jagged frame was a piece of rag and the rag was on fire. It blazed there all by itself, and suddenly I was terrified. I picked it up and tried to thrust it through the broken window but I released it too soon and it fell to the floor. I stamped on it in a frenzy, but still it burned on and on. Just a piece of rag. I flung out of the room into the hot corridor, trying not to run, and left it flickering there.

The fire beat us at last; we deserted the big hospital and gave it up to its flames. With my report to the Associated Press sent off by radio, the rest of the afternoon was spent picking our way through the still blazing streets, looking for possible casualties in the path of the fire and watching the firemen fighting that great red tide. Once while I was standing beside a gutted building that was still on fire, a series of explosions almost lifted me off my feet. The building must have been an arsenal. Small bombs, that sounded like hand grenades, and belts of machine-gun bullets were bursting all at once, and the dirt around my feet began shooting up unpleasant little puffs of dust. I lost no time in getting out of there. In fact, I dived into a bomb hole near by and landed on my face in the mud. Everything that day seemed to conspire together to make me lose my dignity.

Even after dark the fire burned on. The hospital was now a black shell with blazing eyes. We could walk up to it on the windward side and look through the windows into the interior of solid flame. Almost a third of Kweilin burned that day and that night. If the people had stayed in the city during the raid, the casualties would have reached many thousands. At midnight, we limped back to the mission home that had mercifully been spared. Lighting a lamp in the kitchen, we took stock of ourselves and began smearing each other with various sticky preparations. The soles of my heavy ski boots I found to be burned through. Our last act that night, after the impromptu clinic was done, was to search by flashlight for the young coolie who had been killed in the compound below us and who must not be left out all night.

The next morning we watched the city of Kweilin virtually get up and brush itself off, after it had to all intents and purposes been annihilated. The authorities estimated and later verified that this had been the most destructive raid of the war. To every high-explosive bomb — and there were over a hundred and fifty of them — had been attached a smaller incendiary bomb which was hurled aside as its parent burst and which landed among the débris of the house to begin its mischief. The wind had done the rest. Now the people were quietly flocking back along the devastated streets, back to their own private ruins. They returned silently and without tears. At once they started in salvaging what they could from the scattered heaps of bricks. There was no complaining and no smiling; just a wordless acceptance of the thing. In the shops that were still standing we watched people come to buy, and there was no quibbling over prices. They just asked the cost, paid it, and left. The merchant himself, with disaster in his brain, sold his goods for very little. There was no jabbering or talk of individual experiences. There was far too much work to be done. Everywhere along the smoking streets men, women, and children silently raked with shovels or with their hands, searching through the hot ashes. Sometimes they found bits of kitchenware or charcoal which they might sell for a few coppers. It seemed as if everyone in the city was at work, salvaging, rebuilding, repairing, setting up shelters and mat sheds amongst the ruins.

Here on our street three children were seated on the remains of their home. They had cleared a small space of débris and they were playing marbles — good American marbles. A block away, in a building which had survived the raid, someone was practicing on a saxophone. Meanwhile the streets were rapidly cleared of wreckage, wires and electric-light poles were repaired and roads mended. Every building that had more than one wall standing was patched up into a residence or a general store. In the half-collapsed ruins, merchants calmly set up shop and carried on a thriving trade.

Across the middle of a devastated street that had been completely gutted on either side we saw a crew of workmen digging a ditch.

'Please may I ask,' said Skipper, using as he always did the politest possible language to the coolie, 'what is this that you are digging?'

The men smiled.

'It is a water main, Hsien-sheng.'

Skipper looked puzzled.

'But why a water main here?' he asked them. 'What good will it do? The houses on either side are burned.'

'But don't you see, Hsien-sheng,' they said gently, as to a nice but stupid child, 'this is to supply the fireproof houses we are putting up here next month.'

Afterward, walking back along the street, I mumbled to Skipper: 'How do they do it? After a raid like this, I mean?'

He understood what I was trying to say.

'Sometimes I think I know,' he said. 'I decided that it's stoicism or patience or just plain guts. And then after I have it all worked out, I suddenly realize that I don't know at all. You see that little printer's shop where you bought those cards yesterday morning? Nothing left of it now, but he's probably moved into another shop somewhere else and has already opened up again.'

'But what about those that didn't save anything from the fire and haven't any money?'

'Well, here in Kweilin the city government gives them money to tide them over — from ten to thirty dollars each and forty cents a day, and that's quite a lot. They can't build new homes on it, of course. See that woman over there?' and he pointed at a well-dressed young woman pushing a wheelbarrow piled high with clothing and household goods, her children, also laden down, trailing along after her down the street toward the south gate. 'That's what a lot of them will do: shoulder their stuff and start out for the next province. Others I suppose will stay and try to rebuild their homes and businesses.'

'What will they do tonight with everything burned?'

'Oh, they'll sleep in theaters or caves or drift into the country and put up in barns, mat sheds, anything. You can see how

they're already piling up the bricks into new walls. After that
they'll lay matting across the top and move in again. They
keep warm by curling up beside the houses that are still burning.
By daybreak, you watch: they'll be ready for anything!'

'Don't they know when they've had enough?' I demanded.

'No,' said Skipper.

My eyes had never quite recovered from yesterday's dose of
fire. As the day wore on they began to grow inflamed. By nightfall I was totally blind. There was no way of telling exactly what
was the matter; Skipper thought possibly iritis or infection set up
by the burn and overdose of smoke. At any rate, I remained
blind for five strange waiting days. Occasionally I could dis-
tinguish between light and dark; most of the time I could see
nothing. As a child I had learned a trick of resting my eyes by
shutting out all light with my cupped hands and, with my eyes
open, picturing the blackest objects I could think of; pianos,
typewriters, black skies of night. But no blackness in all this
world could compare with the blackness that filled my eyes and
stared back at me now. Every object of chair and table that the
thick air contained became a danger. The slightest brush of the
hand across an unexpected and unidentified surface was as horrible as the sudden touch of a snake. Perhaps to the blind the
darkness becomes friendly; I do not know. To me, in my five
days' journey through a sightless world, even with the comforting
knowledge that in all probability it would not last, the experience
was a time of shrouded nightmare. Undramatically, I think I
worried most about my make-up! Skipper took upon himself the
job of combing my hair, but it was not enough. Never have I felt
so unattractive.

During those five days, Skipper led me about like a puppy on
a leash, as we called on official after official. Since we were not
very worried about my sight in any case, my blindness became a
good joke. The American missionaries in town gave me a whole-

sale razzing. But the Chinese Government men refused to laugh.
Their laws of courtesy made them doubly solicitous, and I spent
my days in an agony of embarrassment over the whole ridiculous
situation.

Meanwhile, from the deciphering of my blindly taken notes,
those interviews with the Governor, Mayor, Transport Commis-
sioner, and others told us a good deal that was significant about
Kwangsi and the set-up in South China. In the years before the
war, the province of Kwangsi, under the leadership of the astute
General Li Tsung-jen and his even more astute colleague, General
Pai Chung-hsi, had been quietly built up into a political and
military machine famous for its Spartan efficiency. In 1937, before the outbreak of hostilities, the generals threatened revolution
and a violent break with Chiang Kai-shek. Whereupon the
pacifist-minded Generalissimo resorted to his usual unorthodox
tactics: he went alone into the heart of the enemy camp, and
without protection of any kind talked the matter over with the
two rebels in their own headquarters. The result was another
coup d'état for Chiang, and the complete winning over of the
Kwangsi faction. From that moment, the two generals became
Chiang's loyalest henchmen and most efficient co-workers in the
struggle against Japan.

So ran the story of Kwangsi. But we were nevertheless surprised to find it to be literally true. In no other section of China
did I see greater loyalty to the Central Government than here in
this once-rebel province. There seemed to be nothing temporary
about it. Admiration for the Generalissimo had driven all
thought of personal power from the minds of officials. Even
today, after the setback in November, 1939, when the Japanese
captured Nanning, the former Kwangsi capital, and brought
down the wrath of Chiang Kai-shek upon the Kwangsi armies,
the faction seems to be as strongly loyal as before. At the time
of our visit, we were impressed in spite of ourselves with the

strength of the armies, the rigorous life of the officials, and the plain intelligence with which the province and its burden of refugees were administered.

Two days after the fire, I spent an afternoon talking with Mr Hung, the manager of the new Hengyang–Kweilin railroad that had been planned and completed all in the past eleven months. His story of the operation of railroads in Free China left me dazed; but he was a serious, overscrupulous individual, and I knew he was telling the truth. There had, he said, been a near-boom in railroad building and operation since the war broke out. (How typical of China that in the midst of her struggle for exist-ence she should build new railroads!)

'We use volunteer refugee labor,' said Mr. Hung. 'It gives the refugees good jobs and keeps them from starving. But it's risky work. Did you know that there is more danger for a railroadman than for a soldier in this war? We have often lost over a hundred men a day on the Canton–Hankow line, from raids and machine-gunnings.'

Many of the engineers and foremen, he told us, were Chinese return graduates from American technological institutes; a good part of them had already lost their lives, but others would step in to take their places. In the face of all Japan's efforts to destroy the lines, China's rolling stock had not once been delayed for more than a few hours. The raids were going on every day. It is a rule, said Mr. Hung, that one or two members of the crew re-main on their train as guards during a bombing, to put out fires.

'How does the crew decide who is to stay behind?' I asked.

Mr. Hung shook his head. 'That is a question not even a manager can answer. They do not seem to argue the matter. There is only an unspoken agreement by which one man detaches himself from the group and stays behind. He will tell you that his chances are pretty good. Engines are not often hit.'

I wondered if the sacrifice of men was necessary, but there was

no doubt in the mind of Mr. Hung. The results, he pointed out, were worth it. New bridges were being built. Besides the new line between Hengyang and Kweilin, others were under way from Kunming to Szechwan and from Chengtu to Chungking, to say nothing of the work being done on the northern extension of the railway running from Burma to the Yunnan border. Construction had speeded up since the war. There was no sign of weariness, and thousands of refugees were being given work. Even that bloody section of rail between the conquered cities of Canton and Hankow was still humming with activity.

As Mr. Hung spoke, I watched him closely for signs of boasting. But he seemed unconscious of the extravagance of his story.

A few days later I remembered my skepticism with shame. There was a minor raid that afternoon which spent itself upon the railroad station just outside the city. It came late in the day, long after the usual raiding hour. Down at the station, the men had just finished unloading several carloads of 75-millimeter shells from a munitions train, lining them up on either side of the track to await removal by truck. The train meanwhile had moved away. At three-thirty all was serene. At three-forty-five the *ching pao* began its scream. There was no time to move that long line of shells. And at the end of the row, on a parallel track and only a foot or so from the last shell in line, were parked seventeen box-cars loaded with dynamite — most of the TNT in South China. The only engine near enough to pull those cars out of danger was several miles up the track. Mr. Hung and his men tried frantically to push the cars, but the load was too heavy. There was nothing to be done. So the men crouched low on their stomachs and listened to the drone of the planes grow louder. Fortunately for all of us, the bombs missed the dynamite cars. But one of the first to fall set off the long line of shells. They began exploding on either side of the track, not all at once but one at a time as the concussions set them off. They were exploding above ground, leaving the rails intact but filling the air with shrapnel. Each explosion was a little nearer to the seventeen cars of TNT. In a matter of minutes the shells would catch up to them. When that happened, the city of Kweilin would be blown off the map.

The seconds passed and at last the engine arrived from up the line. But it came in on the same track as had the munitions train before it, and the switch was on the far side of the station. In order to switch over onto the other track and pull the TNT cars out of danger, the engine would have to run the gantlet of those bursting shells. There was not much time. Mr. Hung called for volunteers, and two young American-trained engineers, quickly climbed into the cab. There was no time to back up the engine, no time to gather steam. With one man at the throttle and the other firing, the engine went through that line of explosions slowly, like a great impatient animal. One shell went off ten feet in front of it and sieved it with shrapnel. Another burst just behind, wounded both men, and almost derailed the engine. How it survived that baptism of fire no one quite knows. But it plowed through, rocking and shuddering. And it switched onto the next track and pulled those dynamite cars out of danger.

It takes a special kind of spine to be a railroadman in China.

A few days later, I began to see again. It was a delirious moment, and Skipper and I celebrated by raiding the icebox of every foreign missionary in town and systematically demolishing their stored-away delicacies in an all-night feed.

There followed several days of champing while we tried to find some way of getting out of the city and on to Chungking. The only fast method was by plane, and planes were few. They arrived every two weeks or so in great secrecy, and it was as much as our lives were worth to reserve seats for ourselves. The day finally dawned when we were herded out to the landing field, to

stand for five cold and dreary hours until the big green Junkers
en route from Hongkong to Chungking spiraled down to pick us
up. We rose up from the cup between the strange mountains
with a Chinese pilot at the controls, and headed into the northwest toward Chungking. I was sorry to leave behind the little
crowded, gutted city of Kweilin.

The plane droned with solemn monotony. Watching the thick
white clouds spread out below us, I tried to gather together my
impressions of the last month into some sort of whole. At first
they were hopelessly entangled in the small impedimenta of
everyday life and talk. But certain facts stood out. I had not
yet heard one word of complaint or bitterness or despair from
the people of Free China. That raid on Kweilin only seemed
to make them stand straighter and work harder. Queer, too, that
women should be taking so much part in this war. A good many
times I had seen girls in army uniform; propagandists, they said
they were, and relief organizers. A few of them were straight
soldiers. Ordinarily I loathe women in uniform. They look
merely unattractive and sensational. My own khaki officer's
uniform, which I was forced to wear whenever I was near the
front where Japanese planes were overhead, filled me with horror.
It was the object of much mirth. But these girls did not act the
rôle of self-conscious heroism. They tightened their belts, rolled
up their trousers, and worked hard. At the front they were sober
and matter-of-fact. Quite often they died.

The guerrillas, too, seemed remarkably well trained and organized. There had been no talk of peace with Japan amongst
them. Then I realized with a start that there had been no visible
hatred of Japan. Perhaps I was wrong here. I must find out
about this. The officials were a surprise. Replacing the mandarin-
coated oily individuals of not so long ago were wise and sensitive
young patriots, with Spartan tastes and a stubborn faith in
themselves and in their jobs.

Apparently the provinces so far visited were in no immediate danger of financial collapse. They were spending millions in direct relief on their refugees. And the building of roads and railways and whole cities was like a hurricane in the land! Trust the Chinese to start a vast reconstruction movement at just the time when they were supposed to be defeated by Japan! Mass education, Industrial Co-operatives, rural credit societies, new colleges and libraries, new young blood in officialdom — it just didn't make sense.

I leaned across the isle toward Robert Brown.

'Skipper!' I bellowed. 'Am I crazy, or are they using this war as a good old cathartic? Sort of cleaning out the corruption of several centuries!'

He looked at me blankly for a moment. Then he grinned.

'Of course,' he said. 'It's perfectly simple. The Old China falls bit by bit. So they go and put up a New China to take her place.'

BOOM DAYS IN CHUNGKING

THE Junkers circled slowly down through dense fog, a fog which for eight months of the year shrouds the great rock fastness of Chungking. As the city materialized below us, I saw that it was built upon a soaring cliff-bound promontory which thrust out a high tongue between two rivers. To the north the Kialing, to the south the wide Yangtze, forked at the promontory's point, separated, circled close again to form the narrow neck of the city, then once more turned apart and took their individual ways toward some Tibetan source. Round green mountains bordered the banks of both rivers, rising range upon range, each higher than the one before. The city itself blotted out the gaunt foundation which held it. Sweeping in closeknit blocks over the crest of the promontory and clinging on stilts to the steep cliff-sides were the homes of two hundred and fifty thousand people, now swelled to three times that number. Other settlements dotted the facing riverbanks, and the crowded city spread onto the mainland far out on either side of the bottleneck. Both rivers below us were flecked with small craft, sampans, patchy junks, and lumbering steam ferries. Only as the plane settled down to land light as dust upon a sandbar did I realize the height of the barbaric city that thrust itself upward out of the river mist. Moored junks and sampans spread fanwise along the perpendicular base of the citadel

where it entered the swift water. From there stone steps, carved
into the rock, zigzagged laboriously to the higher levels, winding
among small barnacle shacks that encrusted the tall cliffs. Life
swarmed upon the steps and the clustered junks, as insect streams
of humanity toiled from crest to river and from river to crest.

The sampan that carried us from the sandbar to the base of the
promontory was swept sideways for several hundred yards in the
current. For the Yangtze, here above the gorges, was full and
sleek. It was a terrible and insatiable river, filled with deep whorls
and suctions and voluptuous coils. No legend need tell of the men
who every day and every hour felt the embrace of its fat waters.
According to our boatman, scarcely any living creature had been
rescued from this half-mile width of pale river. Sampans and
junks, he said, capsized often enough; even the big, unwieldy
ferries contributed their share of dead to the hungry current. Our
boatman did not exaggerate. Months later I was to learn, to my
sorrow, the truth of his words. Now I looked down at the streaked
waters and hated them with all my heart. Like this piled-up city,
they were treacherous and savage. Here was nothing civilized in
this mountain stronghold; only man and nature existing in primitive and too precarious relationship.

At the landing steps we crawled into sedan chairs and began a
dragging, measured climb up the stone stairway, borne on the
shoulders of two chair coolies, feet literally higher than our heads.
There were over a hundred steps. Our chairs creaked and groaned
beneath us. It seemed impossible that the chairmen should not
fall. The brown sweat-gleaming muscles of their shoulders swelled
and their feet smacked the stone steps hard as they commented in
grunts upon our queer clothes, our big noses, and the possible
state of our budget.

Upon the upper levels of the city was the luxury of a few
paved roads that wound through the heart of the business and
shopping districts. The newer buildings, three or four stories

high, were surprisingly streamlined, almost modernistic. Only a close glance betrayed their flimsy construction. Fashioned of wood and cardboard and paper-thin plaster, they gave a curious impression as of exposition buildings or a theater set. But for a few sturdier bank buildings, the city might have been made of papier-mâché — the one small fact which was to mean her death.

The older shops, like those in Wenchow, opened onto the street; but here in Chungking their upper stories had been painted in baroque grays and silvers, whites and even pale blues. Windows were latticed, but in modernistic squares, strictly *comme il faut*. Neon lights glowed at night, incongruous in their ancient setting. Moving-picture houses brushed elbows with shops selling dog-headed seals of ivory and soapstone and white jade. Ageless blacksmith and drug shops stood side by side with undigested chromium and glass-plated imports from the New World. The color of the city was rather gray, in winter drab but under the summer sun quite beautiful. Signs and banners, laden with characters, hung out into the streets. Connecting the two or three paved roads were many hundreds of narrow stone stairways that wound up and down, almost invisible between the high houses. They were the traditional thoroughfares of the city, my ricksha coolie explained to me cheerfully as he wheeled me up the avenue. Until a few years ago there had been no *ch'eh tze* — no wheeled vehicle — in all this miserable city. Even the 'horse streets' would scarcely allow two cars to pass.

Stranger even than the gray avenues was the tidal wave of people they contained. Before the war, Chungking had been the great commercial center of the West, a backward old city without roads or modern touch, but roaring with life and activity, the river port whence goods were carried by junk to the lower Yangtze cities of Ichang, Hankow, and Nanking. With the recent completion of two highways, one running westward to Chengtu, another southwest to Kweiyang and Kunming, the city's trade ex-

panded. Now, as the new capital of Free China, its old walls
ranged with sudden chaos. For months refugees and government
officials from the lower Yangtze had been pouring into the close-
confined promontory that housed the ancient metropolis, swelling
the population to over seven hundred thousand souls, and jamming the narrow confines of the city with several times the
number of people they were meant to hold.

I sometimes dream that I am back in those frantic streets,
trying to force my way through the crowd. But even in real life,
it was useless to hurry. To move through that limbo was to
thrust and shove as through a nightmare. 'Downriver' sophisti-
cates in modish dress jostled shoulders with local blue-gowned
merchants. Rattletrap rickshas, transported upriver from Hankow, plunged through the feverish press, bearing black-haired
matrons of Nanking, aglow with permanent waves and exquisite
silk gowns, to their fashionable rendezvous. Adding to the confusion was the occasional official car or dog-eared bus, its passengers
erupting from every door and window, that roared past, horn
shouting, as the people surged and pushed to make way for them.
Never had Chungking's restaurants and stores known such prosperity. Never had her ricksha coolies pocketed such high and
wonderful fees. There was little wealth here, but many people to
buy. The boom had spread to housing and government buildings,
which for want of room were sprouting amid the suburbs. Here
in the new capital were nearly all the great names of China, the
intellectuals and scholars, the musicians and poets and westernized young officials who just now would give their lives for China.
Here too were some old left-over war lords, living in ancient
splendor, who could not be dismissed because of 'face' and who
would under no circumstances give their lives for China. Conversation in this modern Babel was a confusing medley of dialects;
the nine-toned sing-song of Canton, the guttural Mandarin of
Peking, the speech of Ningpo and Foochow, and the soft accents

of Shanghai struggled with one another in exasperated and half-understood debate.

Chungking was the crowned, the chosen city. No rival capital in all the world could boast such congestion. Even at midnight the people filled her streets in a bawling press, and her neon lights shone out well. For Chungking had not yet tasted the bitterness of war. Her time was soon to come.

Because the hostels for visiting reporters were not yet completed, I found a room in the Methodist Mission on the little alley called Dai Chia Hang. Missionaries were embarrassingly cordial to me. As for the Chinese officialdom, it almost annihilated me with kindness. Ever since our arrival at Wenchow over a month before, we had been treated as of royalty on tour. Banquets, complimentary travel on the railroads, speeches, fanfare, and general hullabaloo had been the order rather than the exception. There was no mention of America's lucrative trade with Japan, first in bombs and munitions, now in scrap iron and airplane gas, whereby Americans were growing rich by making possible the conquest of China. Apparently, whether we deserved it or not, we Americans were heroes to the Chinese; and the reason for it, ironically, lay in the dribble of funds we were sending and the spectacular work of our missionaries. So they cheered and fêted us; and their queer gratitude humbled us in our own eyes.

On the day after our arrival in Chungking, for instance, both Skipper and I were invited out to dine by a solemn-faced young member of the Executive Yuan, who proceeded to spend some twenty dollars upon our entertainment. Afterward he inquired conventionally and shyly if we would like to take tea with him and with his wife and with his three unworthy children in their home. Probably to his dismay, we accepted. His 'home' turned out to be a single room above a noisy restaurant. The room contained one wooden bed, a table, and two stools. Skipper and I sat down to tea by a candle's light while he and his family stood

about us in a smiling circle. I realized suddenly that they, like
most of the people of Chungking, were refugees. Nanking, he
told us, was their home. But they quite liked it here in the new
capital. If it were not for the one bed.

'Would you care to hear my first-born sing?' he asked suddenly.

At once a nine-year-old boy with a thin face and wide grinning
mouth sprang to the center of the room, stood at quivering attention, and burst into the national anthem of Free China.

'San min chu i ...'

His two sisters endured it as long as possible, then joined him in
off-key chorus. The song shook the frail walls. Others followed:
the patriotic songs of Free China known to every street urchin and
soldier and dignified matron of the West. Meanwhile the young
official who had just spent a week's budget upon our dinner stood
by, watching his son's face, and beamed and beamed.

In the days that followed, Chungking's hospitality called for innumerable feasts that left me in a state of perpetual indigestion.
The tradition of the Chinese feast is a mighty one. The guests
meet in late afternoon, generally in a restaurant, and perch themselves upon stools about an enormous round table. The first hour
is taken up with conversation and the delicate crunching of dried
melon seeds. Four cold dishes of sliced chicken, duck liver, 'ancient' eggs, and other specialties are then placed in the center of
the table, and the guests, after frankly polishing their chopsticks
and spoons, reach daintily across and help themselves time and
again out of the communal platters — a process which repeats itself throughout the meal. Next follow course after course of hot
spiced foods. In the middle of the meal come the sweet dishes:
hot orange soup with pigeons' eggs, perhaps, or *pa pao fan* (eight
precious foods), a sticky rice concoction filled with eight choice
and fabulous sweetmeats. Hard on their heels comes another
succession of spiced conglomerates, climaxed, oddly, by individual
bowls of plain boiled rice. Hot golden rice wine, mellow as mulled

sherry and far more delicate, is served throughout the meal in cups not much larger than thimbles. Toast follows toast until virtually every guest and a goodly portion of the Chinese nation have been duly honored.

I literally basked in the glow of these feasts. To begin with, the food was so perfect as to be indescribable. Moreover, there was an air of insouciance about them, of supreme *laissez-faire* that I found nowhere else but in China. Under most circumstances, I should object heartily to dipping into a communal dish side by side with eight or ten other guests. But here in the East the act was touched with a certain camaraderie and restful abandon. Especially did I welcome the customary joyous disposal of chicken bones and other débris in little carefree piles about our plates. What fun to toss one's too-cool tea upon the floor!

By this time I could handle my chopsticks with a certain amount of finesse. During the first month of struggle with these implements of torture, I continually beamed under the compliments of the Chinese at the table, who proclaimed that no foreigner had ever before used his chopsticks with such grace. Only after I had blushed charmingly upon several of these occasions did Skipper warn me that the Chinese will compliment most generously in order to relieve their guest of embarrassment at his own clumsiness.

One feasting custom bothered me. If there is an art which the Chinese enjoy more than that of eating, it is the art of talking. At the feast table, it erupts into speech-making. Half the guests will be called upon to speak before the four- or five-hour affair is over. Most of the speeches were overwhelmingly dramatic, though quite impromptu. It took almost no effort for any and all of these gentlemen to arise from their seats and speak, apparently without drawing breath, for a good twenty minutes, replete with gestures and parlor stories. They seemed born with a national *furor loquendi.* Unfortunately I am not so gifted along these

lines. One evening, when I unwisely spoke my bit in Chinese, the
utter solemnity and earnestness of my audience told me that I had
said some pretty funny things. Skipper, at my elbow, choking in
audible hysterics, did nothing to relieve the situation.

Feasts bothered my conscience for some time. It seemed as if
Chungking spent her money rather lavishly for the capital of a
nation engaged in fighting for its existence. Skipper, as always,
sprang to her defense.

'They're not exactly luxuriating,' he said. 'Feasts are a part of
China's life. They're a part of her morale. At home, even the rich
eat pretty humble food. At feasts they let themselves go. You
take away these feasts and you take away the whole social life of
the people. And you'd probably lower their morale just at the
time they needed it most.'

But it seemed to me then as if nothing could lower the morale of
Chungking. The city was on fire with something that was more
than patriotism. The almost simultaneous fall of Nanking and
Canton had depressed the people for a week or so; no more. The
challenge they sensed now was deeper than a call to victory.
Down to the last small boy on the streets, they felt the sudden
new birth of their country that had come like a miracle in the
West. The uplift made them give away their money by the millions of dollars, do volunteer work in relief organizations and
orphanages, dream of a regenerated nation. The drives for relief
money brought in overwhelming returns, and a good portion of
those returns came from the long-saved coppers of newsboys and
coolies. For the first time in China's long strange history, sacrifice
had become a national craze. A queer new exhilaration was
sweeping through the streets of the old city: the same combination
of jubilance and practical hard work that we found in Kinhua and
Changsha and Kweilin.

Even the hard-headed officials were affected. Stout, bespec-
tacled Doctor H. H. Kung, brother-in-law of Madame Chiang

and at this time Premier of China, who fed me excellent teas on more than one occasion, was as close to idealism as that worthy gentleman could hope to be. The astute banker had just endowed the budding Industrial Co-operatives with a five-million-dollar fund. Doctor F. C. Yen, the slim, soft-spoken director of China's National Health Administration, was furiously at work on a new health program for the nation, intricate, up-to-date, which might have taken years to organize without the sudden prick of war. The New Life Movement, now branching out into war relief as well as national health and education, had become a vast organization, with complicated work in almost every field of reconstruction; its director, Colonel Huang (actually a major-general but clinging to his old title of colonel), an enormous moon-faced giant of a man, for many years close friend and co-worker of Madame Chiang, led the social life and campaigning of the city with a laughing, roaring energy that should have stripped pounds from his generous person but somehow never did. Most of Chungking's officials I found to be enthusiastic and surprisingly direct, almost blunt in their adherence to the unsugared truth. At press conferences, they were quick to acknowledge Japan's gains.

Even more surprising was their stern loyalty to the Central Government, as the Kuomintang or Government of Free China was usually called. They did not glorify their Generalissimo — he would not have stood for it — but they gave him their complete and unquestioning trust. There were certain mutterings of dissent in the Communist quarters and among the coterie of Wang Ching-wei. The rest of the Central Government seemed molded out of steel.

I wondered at this until I saw the Generalissimo, and then I understood. One morning I met him while riding my Tibetan pony through the near mountains. He merely passed me by with a polite greeting, not in the least a spectacular meeting. But his presence struck me like a blow and I felt curiously abashed. Up to this moment, my young brain had decided that Chiang Kai-shek was without doubt a good deal overrated; that he had made some bad blunders in the past when dealing with the Communists; and that he was probably reaping the benefit of his wife's superior ability. Now my cherished theories collapsed in ruin. I remembered the bald statements of his closest friends and bitterest enemies that the Generalissimo in the past few years had built himself up from a clever soldier and scholar into a great man.

But things like that happen in romantic biographies, not in unromantic life. Yet if I had seen only his back, without knowing his identity, I should have thought:

'Who *is* that man!'

He passed me by, dressed in the uniform of the Sun Yat-Sen Republic, without insignia, and accompanied by some of his guards and associates. But he carried with him an electric and almost chilling presence, as of a personality tempered to bright steel. In no human being have I sensed such concentration of power. Or should I call it power of concentration; his inhuman and now famous ability to focus upon the problem of the moment and let all unused corners of mind and body rest? Here, two months after the near collapse of his nation, still faced with a job which no man could envy him, he looked lithe and jubilant as if the challenge made him strong. An inner resilience and vision seemed to carry him along. According to his friends — some of them non-Christian — his new-found asceticism and power were the result, at least in part, of his conversion to his wife's Christianity, which he adopted, according to his nature, thoroughly and without compromise, applying its force to every act of his daily life, and making prayer and meditation an indispensable routine. Whatever the reason for it, in some way he had grown into a man of stature. He was always pitiless in his demands. But his enemies were the first to concede that Chiang Kai-shek was wholly selfless; that his *raison d'être* was China.

They said the same of his wife. It did not take me long to learn the reason. A few days after I arrived in Chungking, I called on Madame Chiang for an hour and a half of tea and quiet talk in her home. Colonel Huang drove me to the door. It was a small foreign-style house in a row of identical homes; one of several residences where the Generalissimo and his wife are forced to live. In a sense they are without a home; for Japanese agents are quick to spot any given house, and their bombers are waiting. So these two must constantly move about, deprived of peace and settled existence. Even the little reception room into which I was ushered, though modern in design, was bare of a single intimate touch.

Madame Chiang herself surprised me by her beauty. Photographs in the press show her to be attractive, but they lose the force of her coloring, the sleek black hair and perfect skin. She was carefully groomed, and exquisitely dressed in a simple Chinese style gown of delicate silk. Her make-up was immaculate. She might have been a girl in her late twenties. Thoroughly American in her gestures, she spoke without accent of any kind, sitting with knees crossed on the edge of her chair, back taut and face overintent. Everything about her was strained close to breaking. Without her husband's inner serenity, his queer ability to focus energy upon one thing at a time, she was spending her vitality upon a dozen jobs at once, each of them a full-time enterprise. By now, she was living on her nerve.

The talk ranged back and forth, at first about her work. Just as her husband was leading the political and economic affairs of the nation, she, with the help of Colonel Huang, was leading the movement which was known throughout the West as 'Spiritual Mobilization.' It meant the unromantic hard work of organizing orphanages for the twenty thousand 'worphans' in her care, the opening up of work relief for war widows and starving women, the training of classes of girls, like the young Singapore girl in the

Changsha hospital, for war work and education. It meant the mobilization of the entire country along sacrificial lines. Overconscientious by nature, she gave the impression of a brilliant, feminine but capable woman with human limitations suddenly forced to become the leader of heart-broken millions, straining her mind and emotions beyond the point of endurance.

Once she spoke of her own recent experiences, and I began to understand the strain she was under. Only a few months ago in Hankow, for instance, she and the Generalissimo were writing letters in their private headquarters across the river at Wuchang, when the air-raid alarm sounded. They paid no attention at first. Raids were common and must not interfere with daily routine. All at once bombs began to burst on their own compound. In a shower of débris they ran to the little earthen dugout near the house. On the instant that they stepped inside, bombs rained about the entrance. Their home was pulverized. Fifty of their personal staff were killed. The soldier standing guard at the door of their dugout was so blown to bits that little trace of him was found.

A few weeks later, when the Japanese pounded at the gates of Hankow, the Government was evacuated upriver to Chungking. As always, Madame Chiang and her husband were among the last to leave. Before the dawn of the occupation, they took off after dark in their own plane. Halfway to Chungking, their radio suddenly gave out. There was no possibility of finding the fog-bound old city at night. At the advice of their pilot, they did the only thing left to them: they turned back to Hankow. It was not a pleasant situation. Provided that they could find Hankow in the dark without a radio, they had no way of knowing whether or not the city had already fallen to the Japanese. The air field was mined and was to be blown up at the first signs of the incoming enemy. Perhaps it had already been destroyed. Perhaps the force of their landing would touch off the blast. But they had to chance it. So they circled back through the night hours. They found the lights of the city. They landed on the field a few moments before it was to be destroyed. And they took off once more in another plane and swung back into the dark toward Chungking.

These were stories that had not been told before. I had known the constant danger of Madame Chiang's life; the fact that every town and city she or the Generalissimo must visit would become the target for bombs. I had heard of her visits to the front, side by side with her husband, and of their incredible escapes together. A believer in miracles might wonder a little.

One statement she made stuck in my mind. 'I know,' were the words, 'that nothing can happen either to my husband or to me until our work is done.'

I wonder how many of her friends in this country know what Mayling Soong of Wellesley College is going through.

Madame Chiang was only one of many hundreds of American-ized Chinese living and working in Chungking. They were easy to make into friends. Many of them had lost the ancient stylized dignity of their race. They received me with a casual informality that was amusingly American.

One night I slipped into my bed at the Methodist Mission and lay there in the dark listening to the voices of a group of Chinese guests assembled in the living-room. I recognized Colonel Huang's booming American slang. After a while, the crowd began to sing. Barber-shop quartet numbers, English folk songs, and 'Auld Lang Syne' floated through the walls, replete with Chinese accent. But one voice soared above the others. It was high and clear, one of the purest and most exquisite tenor voices it has been my privilege to hear. If Roland Hayes had joined a small-town sing it would have sounded no more startling. All at once the singer began a solo, and it was a song called 'Uncle Rome' and composed by my father. I held my breath in the darkness. When the applause had died down, he sang again, this time Father's

setting of Stevenson's 'Requiem.' In desperation, I jumped out of
bed, climbed into a voluminous bathrobe, and shuffled into the
next room. I was received with good-humored laughter; but I
could only stare at the singer like a girl possessed.

He was a smooth-faced Chinese of forty, slightly paunched,
with a bland, grinning face. His name was Teddy Tu. He was
assistant director of the New Life Movement and China's
greatest singer. He was also the composer of most of the new
patriotic songs which we had heard only a few days before in the
one-room home of the young official.

I told him, 'You've just been singing my father's songs.'

He stared for a moment. Then he began pumping my hand and
laughing like a young boy.

'You are Homer's daughter! This is too good! This is too good!
You must know that I have taken tea in your home. Yes, and
your mother sang for me once. That is true. Yes, in America I
have given Homer concerts. Completely Homer concerts! Every
one of his songs by heart. Yes!'

For the rest of the evening we alternately reminisced, slapped
each other's backs, and sang Dad's songs, until the crowd in
the room was thoroughly sick of us. It was the beginning of
a queer little friendship that was to last a month and end in
tragedy.

The following morning ushered in a fateful day for Chungking.
Since our arrival, there had been *ching paos* and a few small raids.
Several times, great fleets of Japanese bombers had crossed directly over the city without knowing it, blindly hunting us in the
fog. Several times they had dropped a few experimental bombs,
which luckily fell outside the crowded confines of the main city.
The thought of a bomb exploding within this seething place was
not a nice one. Always optimistic, the people thought that probably they would be spared, either because of the two or three
hundred 'foreigners' in the city or because no nation would have

the cruelty to drop a bomb inside such a slaughterhouse. Now on the afternoon of January 15, they had their answer.

Skipper and I were standing on the Methodist Mission porch, which almost overhung the high cliffs above the little Kialing River. On the far side of the river was a sandbar, occupied only by a few mat sheds. As before, we heard the deep roar of planes overhead without many qualms, thinking they would not find us. But in that moment a new noise was in the air — the far-off purr of machine-gun fire somewhere above us. A dog-fight was taking place up there in the deep mist. Almost at once there was one sharp explosion a few blocks away, and then the air filled with the familiar panic scream of falling bombs.

They burst on the sandbar about two hundred yards in front of us. They were five-hundred-pounders, and they cracked our ears and left us half-deaf. A few fell in the river, throwing up clear blue geysers, white-topped, into the air. Behind us in the mission-house windows splintered and plaster slithered down. Then a piece of tile flew up at my elbow. Belatedly we realized that shrapnel was hitting all about our ears. We lost no time in crouching down behind the river wall, peering over the edge in a very furtive fashion. Batch after batch of bombs struck the sandbar and dissolved upward into bulbous clouds. Glancing to the left, I was just in time to see a crowded city hill, farther along the promontory, heave itself into the air and disappear in smoke. The machine-gunning above us grew sharper.

Then someone near us yelled:

'Look! Look up!'

High above the river, a wisp of smoke was trailing down the sky. It lengthened to a pale rainbow streak. Very dimly through the fog we saw it fall and fade away behind the mountains. Somewhere over there a crew of scared young Japanese boys who thought they had done right were learning what it was like to burn.

The storm died away and left the city in stunned quiet. It was

Chungking's first taste of battle. The slaughter was high, well
into the hundreds; by all accounts a most successful raid. But
fifteen minutes later the people of Chungking were streaming out
across the sandbar in fascinated thousands to see their first bomb
hole. They poured out as ants upon a honey trail. A moment
later, each bomb crater became darkly outlined by a ring of
absorbed mankind happily straining its combined neck to stare.

'*Reductio ad absurdum*,' murmured Skipper at my elbow.

I joined the nurses of the Methodist Hospital in doing rescue
work. Several sections of the city had been hard hit. One bomb
had struck a poor men's teahouse, and we found not one living
among the thirty who had been quietly sipping their tea inside.
The wounded did not cry out. The children lay quite silent,
jerking a little and holding their wounds. We did what we could
for them and turned them over to the stretcher-bearers.

Near-by on a stretcher lay a young woman, her leg almost sev-
ered at the knee. We had applied tourniquets, but the blood still
fell in a small stream from the stretcher canvas. Just before she
was carried away to the hospital, I glanced over and saw that she
was grasping something and muttering a queer old whispered
song. I went to investigate. The thing she held in her arms was
her own very red, very healthy, homely baby, and she was nursing
him at her breast.

If Chungking had wondered whether or not she would be
spared, she now had her answer. From that day forward, every
coolie and priest and housewife and street urchin knew what was
in wait for them. All of us, foreigners and Chinese alike, began to
suffer from acute claustrophobia. The next time there would be
incendiary bombs. Only one main road led out of the city. The
streets were narrow, some of them a yard wide. The buildings
were high and tindery. The congestion was a terrifying thing.
Chungking would be a pretty toy for fire, a bright human pyre.
And on the day when the fog should lift, Chungking would burn.

So we waited. Every pale glimmer of sun would tighten our hearts. Would it come today? The streets were full of rumors.

'Tomorrow will be the day. The People's Political Council is to meet, and the Japanese know.'

'Have you heard? The planes have already left Hankow. Ninety of them!'

'They're coming this morning! They're coming up the river now! Wanhsien just telegraphed.'

One day when the sky was clear a fleet of sixty bombers actually did leave Hankow, bound for Chungking, but the fog closed in before they could reach us and turned them back. The authorities ordered evacuation of the city, but the people would not leave. They had no place to go. So they stayed and watched the skies. The rest of us tried to go about our work and pretend that we were not in a state of suspense; that we would not gladly run and run until we had left bottlenecked Chungking a hundred miles behind. Our ears strained all day long for the call of the *ching pao*. More and more I hated this dangerous old city, feeling her doom closing over me in high menacing houses and clotted streets.

Like rats we waited in our trap while the time drew nearer.

DOWN-YANGTZE

ON THE afternoon of January 21, two weeks after our arrival in Chungking, Skipper and I boarded a flat little river boat bound east four hundred miles through the Yangtze gorges to Ichang and the Hupeh front. It was partly the fault of our friend Teddy Tu. The emotional Teddy was to fly to Ichang later in the week on a promotion trip for the New Life Movement; and his grumbling protests, his mention of the raids, the imminent fall of the city, the lack of doctors, and the hordes of stranded refugees served to whet our appetites. There was work to be done down the Yangtze. Besides, it would be no hardship to leave Chungking.

Our shallow-draft steamer cut neatly through the current. As she thundered downstream, the shore cliffs flung by with startling abandon. We were moving fast. Just to improve matters, the American captain of the boat, a lean, thin-lipped individual of twenty years' experience on the Upper Yangtze, who thought himself extremely tough and sour, plied us for hours in the wheelhouse with remarks about the river calculated to make my hair stand on end.

'Worst river to navigate in the world — this upper stretch.'

'Worst?'

'Boats have to be specially built. It's low water now, exactly zero. That means we'll probably pile up this side of Wanhsien.

This side of the gorges. Plenty of boats lost on the river. Plenty of steamers. Just like this one.'

'Uh-huh.'

'There you are. Feel that!' The boat's hull shuddered in a series of heavy thumps. 'Scraping the bottom. God damn! Every god-damn boat I take down this river rips her belly out. And the junks ——'

'Junks?'

'Fool junks. Capsized three of them last trip.'

'Capsized! Did the people drown?'

'Yes, lady, the people drowned.'

'Couldn't you pick them up? Couldn't you ——'

'No, lady,' he said wearily, 'we couldn't pick them up. We can't stop on this river, understand? Only two anchorages between here and Wanhsien. Another three below that in the gorges. We just capsize them, see? Damn-fool junks.'

'You use the anchorages at night?'

'That's right. You're coming right along! And if we don't reach an anchorage before dark we don't reach it at all. Pile up in pieces somewhere. There's a devil in this river. My God, yes! Like to bust his teeth in.'

His voice droned on in happy pessimism. I looked out at the bleak twilight, at the windy gray river winding down and down between shelved rocks and the low dark mountains of eastern Szechwan. Spray flung over the snubbed bow, flicking the windows in front of the helmsman. Every few minutes the whistle whooped and echoed down the cold river basin. Devil in this river. Yes! Even here in this sheltered deck I could hear his lisps and his suckings beneath our bow.

The next afternoon we dropped anchor beside the big old town of Wanhsien. In all of China there is probably no dirtier, more picturesque, isolated, medieval, and altogether wretched city. 'The most awful outpost of civilization' was Skipper's irreverent comment. No roads led to or from the place. A population of some two hundred thousand Chinese, now swelled with unnumbered refugees, went its way without hospitals or universities, without sense of time or progress except that which washed in and out with the river traffic. It is safe to say that Wanhsien, on the day we walked her streets, was living quite comfortably somewhere about the Yuan Dynasty.

It annoyed me that the pulsing, volatile cities of West China should own such a weak sister.

'Why,' I grumbled, 'does every clean-cut situation have to have such glaring exceptions? You get all excited about the way the Chinese are tearing ahead in the world, and then you come to cities like this that are still living back in the Dark Ages.'

'Not even the Chinese are perfect,' said Skipper piously. I could see that the statement was, for him, quite a concession.

'It's so easy,' I rambled on, 'to grow sentimental over the Chinese; and then suddenly discover their faults — their inefficiency and carelessness, their childish optimism — and start right in to scorn them. Illogically. Not even give them credit for their virtues. Thank heavens their faults are pretty happy-go-lucky ones on the whole. Obvious, exasperating faults, but not vicious. Even Wanhsien is forgivable. Like a potty but cheerful old retainer. Sort of like a governess I had once.'

The city was a throwback, a sample of what all these big western strongholds must have been like in the days before the Japanese advance poured a migratory horde of universities, hospitals, Kuomintang officials, and intelligentsia into their old-walled interiors. Until the past year, the impact of Britain and America had scarcely touched China's populous West. Wanhsien, it is true, could boast a mission and its accompanying schools; probably it contained one or more middle schools; but Chungking University and the West China Union University in Chengtu were the only higher institutions of any standing in the West, un-

til the war brought the great eastern universities to join them.
Wanhsien had no civilian hospitals, no qualified doctors. American goods were rare here. There was not an automobile in the
city. Few Chinese wore European clothes, and even fewer spoke
English. European food was unknown. Typhoid, dysentery,
tuberculosis infested the city, and hygienic conditions were not
pleasant. And all because Wanhsien happened to be a stopping-
off place rather than a permanent station for the influx of refugee
culture from the coast.

It was certainly a spectacular place. The city clung as might
some warty fungus to the hillside which rose abruptly from the
river. Pyramidal stone stairways fifty feet wide, and precariously
steep, cut up through the rabbit-warren of tiled roofs. They made
broad ribbons of white, leading as though to temples. The mountains were high about. Cupped in the overhanging cliffs above
the city were a shrine or two, a monastery, a pagoda made visible
by the bright tile and stone that gleamed through the river mist.

We toiled wetly up the endless steps. The crowd that flowed
past on either side had about it a curious air of apathy and disease. These people were close to exhaustion and not very far
from death. Refugees, Skipper said, haunting the river steps and
the shipping offices in the forlorn hope of finding passage to
Chungking.

'They can't get out,' he explained. 'Wanhsien and Ichang,
they're both bottlenecks. When Hankow fell last October, nearly
everybody found passage upriver. Some reached Chungking.
Others got as far as Ichang, or here, and then they stuck. Not
enough boats can get up this river. A few days from now the
water will be too low for anything but the junks, which take a
month to the trip. Look at that family there — the well-dressed
ones. See how ragged they are around the edges? They've run
out of money and things to sell. And the local government isn't
bright enough or rich enough to do much about it.'

'What if Ichang is captured?' I asked, remembering the
Japanese drive beyond Hankow which was even then pushing
toward Shasi, less than a hundred miles below Ichang. 'How will
the people get out?'

'They won't,' said Skipper.

'But — can't ——?'

'No.'

Here and there we passed some tangled ruins that looked ugly
and quite fresh. Two days before, a flight of Japanese bombers,
unable to reach Chungking, had dumped their load upon the
heart of Wanhsien. I was poking idly through a shattered building when a coolie standing by said: 'That was a school for the
children of troubled people. For the very poor.'

I winced.

'In it were seventy-five small children,' he went on soberly.
'Their teacher made seventy-six. I helped to pull them out after
the eggs had burst. We pulled out seventy-six and they were
dead.'

I stared at the twisted rubble, feeling a little sick. The worst
had been cleared away. I saw no sign of death. Except — well
— just one. And that was only a child's embroidered shoe.

An hour later, Skipper and I stood upon the riverbank and
watched our boat steam off downstream without us. There was
good reason to jump ship. Conditions in this backwater of a city
were not pleasant. And correspondents had not yet been down
this river since the war.

'No doctors,' Skipper muttered to himself at specific intervals.
'Not a doctor in the place, except the quacks at the army hospitals.'

We visited these hospitals on our second afternoon in Wanhsien. It is only fair to say that they were notorious as among
the worst medical institutions of West China. Lying upon bare
boards or the dirt floor were rows upon rows of gray-faced young

soldiers. The single *pukais* that covered them were stiff with
filth and dried stains. Most of the men had no clothes. Nearly
all of them were encrusted — face, arms, body — with the red
rash of scabies, changed by weeks of scratching into open sores.

The officer who showed us through was bitter.

'It is not enough that they are wounded. This scratching is
worse. Would you think it possible for a man to die of scabies?
Oh, yes, they die. Though more of them go mad.'

Skipper exploded into indignant Mandarin.

'But scabies should be nothing! One sulphur bath and it is
cured.'

The officer said: 'The authorities, they do not know. They are
fools,' and walked away stiffly.

In the next ward, the ward for 'heavy wounded,' we moved
from bed to bed. The men grinned at us. Some had snapshots of
girls or parents tacked to the wall above their heads. One of them
said: 'Sit down, Hsien-sheng, sit down, little sister, and dine
with us a moment. See, I have excellent food!' And he carefully
turned back the edge of his *pukai*, uncovering three mandarin
oranges and a dozen peanuts.

We perched on the edge of the board bed, for there was nowhere
else to sit, and gravely accepted one peanut apiece. To have refused would have been a serious insult.

Near-by a boy lay upon his back and worked hard for breath.
Because his eyes were closed I noticed how long were his lashes,
as long as a girl's. The black hair that curled up stiff with dried
sweat and the fever-sharp bones of his face were not good signs.
Obviously the dirty bandage around his chest was too tight.
Skipper loosened it expertly, tried to examine the wound, and
finding the cloth firmly stuck replaced the bandage more comfortably. While this was going on, the boy looked up and smiled
a little in relief. I saw the wide black eyes follow every move of
Skipper's hands and every line of his face. I could almost see the

confused brain working, studying, trying to place this foreigner
who was curing the pain in his chest. Finally he got it.

'I know' — very pleased with himself — 'You are that "Jesus" person!'

Skipper's face flushed and he turned away, biting his lip, and
strode out into the yard.

That afternoon, the newspapers of the city blazed forth with
the news that at the instigation of the Central Government in
Chungking, expensive machinery, tools, and materials of every
kind were to be issued free of charge to all refugee artisans and
craftsmen in Wanhsien. The refugee camps were jubilant. There
was a certain straightening of backs on the city streets. For most
of China's refugees could do something with their hands; and
even the material to make a few dozen straw shoes would be
enough to set a man up in business. Because of the Japanese
blockade the demand for every commodity was so great that the
humblest object brought its price on the booming market. If
this medical situation could be cleaned up, there might be some
hope after all for the city.

The next morning we called upon the hospital authorities.

'I hear said,' announced Skipper jovially, bowing low, 'that
you are soon to install a most excellent sulphur bath with which
to cure your wounded soldiers of scabies. I wish to congratulate
you! There is no better and simpler cure in the country. Our
wounded are lucky beyond measure to be under your expert
care.'

The authorities were overwhelmed. They were unworthy.
The foreign doctor was too good, too kind. He must be the first
to advise them about the details of this sulphur bath which they
were indeed about to erect!

The long conference over, we went our way, very smug and
filled with the best tea. For an hour we wandered in the terraced
fields above the city and beneath the highest cliffs. Here the

river mist was streaked with sun. War and hunger seemed of some other age, no part of these drowsy hillsides.

Skipper pointed upward. 'Can you see the temple?' he said. 'There, near the top of the cliff? It's a Buddhist temple, dedicated to Li Po.'

'Let's go up.'

We joined the stream of climbers on the stone stairway that wound its way up the overhanging ledge. Now on the upper levels we could hear the long, measured voice of the temple gong, muted and deep as though it were an echo from some lost dynasty. Our fellow climbers — rich men, refugees, matrons, beggars, bug-eyed children — heard it too, and chattered in low tones about the famous temple.

We found it housed in a windowed grotto, sheltered beneath the arms of the cliff. An outer pavilion clung precariously to the in-sloping rock, the tiled roof supported by slim bright pillars. Within the cave rooms, squat bronze Buddhas stared pop-eyed and impassive through the curling smoke of incense.

A young Chinese divinity student, staggering under enormous spectacles and speaking excellent English, was glad to enlighten me.

'It is a most fine Buddhist temple. You must know that Li Po once came here for inspiration.'

'Are these visitors Buddhists?' I asked.

'Oh, no. Few are Buddhists.'

'That's right. I've heard that Taoists are more numerous.'

'But indeed no. Few are Taoists.' He was obviously amazed at my ignorance.

'Then perhaps — well — I suppose — Confucianists?' I muttered feebly.

'No, no! Almost no Confucianists.'

There was a painful silence while I inwardly cursed the Chinese race.

'All right,' I said finally. 'I give in. What are they?'

The student peered at me in owlish triumph. 'Some are Christians like ourselves. More than half the educated people of my country are Christians,' he explained carefully, as though aware of my limited brain. 'But most of these are what you call "tourists." They are almost without religion. So many of their superstitionings have now exist not.'

I pondered this foggy statement. 'But they do sometimes burn candles and worship kitchen gods, don't they?'

'A little, yes. In the country above most. But it is — what you say? — automatically.'

'And what about the devils that chase after them? I hear they get rid of them by crossing in front of boats and cars and letting the devil at their heels get run over.'

'No, no! Only few believe.'

'But quite a few burn paper money for their dead relatives. I've seen them do it. That's to bribe the magistrates of the underworld, isn't it?'

'That is corrects.' The young man sighed. 'Our underworld has always been patterned upon our life world. It is most unfortunate. What is to happen to us if the magistrates of the dead become as reformed as the magistrates of West China? The paper money will not bribe. Such catastrophe!'

I looked at him sharply. No flicker of amusement showed behind those enormous spectacles. But as I turned away, I watched a smirk tug gently at the corners of his mouth.

On the following morning we rode in sedan chairs many *li* through the hills to visit a Christian home for war orphans. The care of these twenty thousand-odd 'worphans' had in recent months grown from a benevolent enterprise into an experimental nursery of heroic proportions, designed to give even the most altruistic nation something of a headache. But China, it seems, was a conscientious parent. Not enough to feed and clothe the children for the duration of the war; oh, no! Most of them were orphans for life, their families killed by bombs or by disease. Therefore they must be given a good home and education until at least eighteen years old; they must also be taught a trade or profession. Madame Chiang, who inaugurated their removal from war zones to orphanages in the West, was now determined to raise the whole lot of them into the cream of China's future youth. Two of her orphanages had already been turned into laboratories where doctors and educators could work out a standardized diet for the other institutions, standardized schooling, professional training and recreation. The fifteen-year experiment, with enough funds to last it six months, was running at full blast. It is still doing so today.

The first 'receiving station' for war orphans was set up a year before in Hankow. Here the children poured in from all parts of the war zone like an invading army, until some fifteen thousand of them had passed through. A crew of volunteers, principally college graduates and teachers who could have found good paying jobs elsewhere, worked quite literally day and night on a seven-day week to find first temporary, then permanent, shelter for the orphans. At the receiving station they were first of all cleaned up and given medical attention. They needed both. Some were so ragged and filthy that even the *amahs* refused to touch them. The staff in many cases had to fall to and help the servants out. A good percentage of the children were sick and dying. Malaria, tuberculosis, typhoid, old shrapnel wounds, rickets, malnutrition and all its ugly complications, to say nothing of every children's disease known to science — it must have seemed more like a nightmare than an emergency.

Temporary homes were set up in missions, temples, private homes, until orphanages could be prepared in the safer reaches of the West. In some cases, the parents of the children were still living but too poor to feed or clothe them; and for their benefit, as well as that of the Government, which must keep track of the orphans, each boy and girl was registered and his past and future residence kept on file. In those early days the office workers were close to madness; it is known that they personally answered every letter of inquiry from thousands of worried parents the country over concerning the health and whereabouts of their children.

In fact, one of the strongest facts borne out by this whole vast experiment was the emotion involved. All that I had ever read of the Chinese had given me the impression that they were fatalistic about their children; that the death rate was at all times so high as to make of a dying child a pretty casual affair. Mourning was the rule, I supposed, but not deep and lasting sorrow; not the kind of love and terrible loss that we Westerners feel for our children. It was a comfortable theory. How unfortunate that it was not also true! Refugees consistently starved themselves to death in the effort to feed their children; the cases on record were too numerous to laugh off. The poorest peasant would dress his son — and daughter too — in red jackets of the richest silk and bonnets and embroidered shoes.

There had been that scene, for instance, during the late Chungking bombing. Far beneath a heap of boards and rubble we had found the body of a six- or seven-year-old girl. Her left arm had been blown off at the shoulder and she had bled to death. Beyond that, there was scarcely a mark upon her. After we had placed her on a stretcher, I could not help but notice the child's uneasy beauty. Long, tangled dark hair and a thin, perfect face gave her the story-book appearance of Snow White or a sleeping princess. Just then her mother found her. Not weeping or making any sound at first, she took the child into her arms and hid herself in the ruins. But after a moment, while we worked there over the wounded, we could hear the dry heaving that came from her. And I think I have never heard such sound of agony from any woman.

A week latei, during a visit to the orphan receiving station at

Chungking, a young soldier had turned up at the door so ragged and uncertain on his feet that we forced him to lie down at once. He was shaking with excitement. He had been given leave of absence from the army, he said, to come and visit his son. We finally dragged it out of him that he had walked from the Hupeh front, west of Hankow, to Chungking, across five hundred miles of almost impassable mountains. Then we had to tell him that his son had been shipped off exactly two days before to an orphanage in distant Yunnan.

The soldier shrugged and thanked us with indifference. He handed us a picture of himself.

'Please mail this to my son.'

After that he turned toward the door fast, walked blindly into the wall, and collapsed on the sill in a fit of uncontrolled weeping.

That receiving station at Chungking had left a bad taste in my mouth. A group of some two hundred boys, brought in from the streets only a few days before, had lined up in the yard to welcome me. In their gray long-trousered suits, their heads shaven for sanitary reasons, their faces stern with the dignity of the occasion, they looked, most of them, like tired old men. As children, they had about forgotten how to play. Their recent brush with violence had turned them into wary, bitter little adults. As I stepped into the yard, they snapped stiffly to attention and sang a queer off-key Oriental song about the war and their homes which had been destroyed and their parents who had been killed or made poor. Not one of them smiled.

But the orphans of Wanhsien seemed of another race. They had lived and studied together for almost a year; a year of good food and dry beds, a year of basketball and tag, a year of something a little like peace. They gathered round us in a grinning swarm. They roared when I took their pictures. They helped me change the film in a welter of repartee and frantic questions and talk of exposures and shutter stops that left me dazed.

Three-year-olds crawled onto my lap and drooled down their fronts.

Somehow in their months together they had built up a group spirit amounting almost to blood-brotherhood. In their small, vivid minds they were a unit, a force. Here in the shaded temple grounds where the orphanage was housed, these children had worked out a pint-sized Utopia of their own. Duty had turned into coveted responsibility. All day long in hourly shifts, small orphan sentinels stood at pleased attention on either side of the temple door, almost overcome by their importance. They fought for the privilege of working in the kitchen and sweeping the classroom floors. On sunny days, school met out-of-doors on the top of enormous boulders, some of them a hundred feet long, that separated the temple from the cliff edge. While we watched from a hidden vantage point, fifty or more children, in black padded uniforms, haunched like a flock of small fat crows on the gray rock and sang their bits with all the fervor of enlightened scholarhood.

The orphans would speak quite matter-of-factly about their past. They were neither proud nor ashamed of their suffering. They did not know it by that name. Tragedy was no different from any other phase of life.

A boy of nine told us impersonally about the time he was separated from his mother and father during an air raid, as they were fleeing before the Japanese advance. What did he do then? Why, he went on by himself to Hankow. Of course he had walked. Why should he not have walked? Not so far, he thought; perhaps four hundred miles. No, he did not expect to find his parents again, China being a pretty big place.

There was one little girl of ten or eleven who would not answer a word. According to the records she had been pried from the burning ruins of her home during a raid on Hankow — the only member of the family left alive. Since that day she had, for some

private reason of her own, refused to speak. She would not tell
her name. Solemn and wordless, she kept to herself.

For some months after their arrival, Wanhsien had been a
peaceful home for the war orphans. Now that the serious bombings had begun, their fate hung fire. The temple was not far
from a group of military hospitals. Meanwhile the children, veterans of a good many raids, behaved with proud precision while
a bombing was in progress. Small and stern in their black suits,
they would line up in organized units and march stiffly to the
fields. Here they would crouch down out of sight beneath the
boulders and never budge.

'And they'll pray!' one of the teachers remarked. 'Coming
from Christian families, they'll cuddle down there and they'll
pray.'

Two days later we steamed puffily out of Wanhsien toward
the mouth of the gorges, bound downstream to Ichang. Because
all foreign steamship companies had suspended service until the
Yangtze rose above the 'zero' mark, we consulted a Chinese firm,
to which a water level is merely a challenge. Their steamer
turned out to be both a tramp and a launch. But we were in no
mood for protest. The fact that there were no empty cabins on
the boat depressed us for a while; but two cabin boys, hearing
about it, firmly installed us in their own lower berths and cheerfully moved into the uppers with their patient friends. The four
of them spent the night climbing in and out of bed with infinite
noise, and a great deal of apologetic laughter when they ac-
cidentally stepped upon us.

Soon after we raised anchor, we swung into the gorges. Running through my mind were the eulogies to be found in my school
geography book: 'The Yangtze Gorges — natural wonders of the
world,' it had blithered: 'such wild grandeur has no equal on this
vast earth.' I smiled at the memory, but not for long. Pretty

soon I could only squat, cold and wind-blown, upon the forward
hatch and stare in frozen wonder.

The river, where it entered the gorges, narrowed abruptly and
swept forward as into a flume. Suddenly now in the shadow of the
first great canyon it swelled and grew black as tar. It swept us
along like flotsam in a dark millstream. The walls of the gorge
leaned above us for a thousand feet. Ahead, the mountains lifted
higher, much higher, and put their brown heads close together
above the racing river. Only a belt of winter sky was over us.
The water curled and twisted on in fat black coils, its current
streaked as though with heavy oil. It sucked our launch from
side to side, ponderously.

All that day and the next the cliffs were upreared above us.
It was easy to understand how impossible would be a Japanese
drive on Chungking from Hankow; this almost unnavigable river
and the unbroken mountains were as effective a barrier as the
widest ocean. Here on the right of the Windbox Gorge I could
just make out a series of nicks cut into the bare rock from base
to pinnacle of the giant precipice. According to history, a warring
general of some past dynasty had been surrounded by his enemies
and trapped in this gorge with all his troops. With a sort of horrible *sang-froid*, he sent his men up the sheer rock-face, ordering
them to chop out hand and foot holes as they went. The job was
done by force of numbers; every time a man fell, another took his
place. It is said that for every hewn nick in the rock a man died.
But those troops that survived the climb were able to ford the
river above the gorges, circle around behind their gloating enemies, and neatly finish them off.

Several times on that two-day journey we passed through the
'low-water rapids,' stretches of white water, each of them, to
my jaundiced eye, the entrance to some particular hell. We could
hear the murmur of the rapids far upstream. Finally we would
sweep around a bend and bear down upon a wide swath of some-

thing a little like whipped cream churning. Into this welter of foam and black rock our miserable launch then plunged her head. The water swept over the stubby bow and crashed into the well of the foredeck, while she bucked and twisted like — well — like a top-heavy launch in a stretch of rapids. Often enough the keel scraped against unseen obstacles. When this happened, the Chinese crew smiled in almost gentle reproof. Once we passed a British passenger steamer solemnly perched upon a wide rock ledge about eighty feet above the river. Last spring it had been caught in a whirlpool at high water, spun about, and neatly deposited upon the shallow ledge. Whereupon the waters fell and left it sitting there, a sur-realist boat upon a hillside.

Even here in the sunless canyons, we passed several straw villages clinging to the cliff-sides close above the high-water mark, where farmers lived a life without foothold and terraced the upper mountain slopes. Sampans and Ichang junks with patched sails straining sped down the current and wobbled precariously in our wake. Junks bound downstream were manned on the foredeck with six or eight or a dozen oarsmen, who stood, each to his oar, poling forward into the fast water and singing in unison the minor wordless river chant of the sacred Yangtze. Now and then, the helmsman would *yuloh* in high-pitched scream as he called forth the wind.

Close to the shore came the junks headed upstream on the long month's voyage to Chungking. They were hauled by a hundred, sometimes two hundred, coolie 'trackers,' who manned the tow-rope in a mile-long crawling, chanting line. Their paths were ledges hewed into the cliffs, so narrow that each day that passed saw at least one man drowned. Occasionally the bamboo tow-ropes, as thick as a tracker's thigh, would fray, strand by strand, upon the sharp rocks, then snap without warning and loose the doomed junk out of control into the waiting current. The mute wrecks swung along beside us, keel to sky.

So the days passed, and the wind flayed the skin of this dark river, beautiful and greedy, in his underworld.

Late on the second day we swung out of the last gorge and dropped anchor beside the sweeping foreshore and tumultuous *bund* of Ichang, treaty port of the Upper Yangtze. Half-wild mountains, heaped range upon range, cupped the little city in a sheltering palm. Even here in midstream, a never-ending drone of massed voices gave hint of the congestion within the town. Like Wanhsien, Ichang depended for westward transport upon the river, her one road leading east toward the active Hupeh front. Not all the boats on all the Yangtze were sufficient to move more than a fraction of her refugees upstream. They were properly stuck, and they knew it. Almost daily raids and threat of a Japanese drive on the city did not improve matters. Ichang was, to everyone concerned, a thundering headache.

My impressions of the city were for the most part second-hand, for I saw little of Ichang. At Hengyang, a mosquito had shot me full of malignant malaria, and ever since Kweilin the chills had been cropping up with monotonous punctuality. My parasites were crazy about me. Quinine had so far only stimulated them to greater efforts. Here at Ichang, with a fever of 105°, I had just strength enough to wobble along on Skipper's elbow to the residence house of the Canadian Hospital and collapse once and for all upon the guest-room bed. The next few days were taken up with more chills and a series of heart attacks which kept everyone, including myself, quite busy. The hospital was already jammed to overflowing with air-raid wounded. I was, to put it briefly, a horrible nuisance.

At length my bugs retired to brood in remote corners of the blood stream and I began once again to notice things. The young Canadian couple who had been helping Skipper feed me digitalis and brandy at all hours of the day and night turned out to be Gordon Jones and his wife, both doctors, both attractive, somewhat brilliant, and able to enjoy themselves under the grimmest possible circumstances. Understaffed, half-exhausted, they went their casual way in a matter-of-fact atmosphere of repartee and cynical good humor.

Most matter-of-fact members of the community were their children, Joan and Barbara, aged seven and three respectively. Air raids were as casual affairs to them as their morning milk. As my convalescence grew apace, Joan and I exchanged long and terrible stories of cats named Blackie and Chinese fairies named Heaven knows what.

One afternoon, because the day was so queerly bright, I was moved, bed and all, onto an upstairs porch, there to bask in the first hot sun of the winter months. Young Joan was keeping me company. In the midst of an earnest conversation, the alarm sounded. Joan paid no attention beyond remarking, 'There goes the *ching pao*,' in an uninterested tone of voice.

'Aren't you going into the dugout?' I asked.

'Oh, no, not yet. We play in the garden until we hear the planes, and *then* we go into the dugout. The bombs make a big noise, don't they?' she inquired politely.

'Yes, don't they?' I said. 'How about your mother and father? Where do they go?'

'Oh, they just keep on doing what they're doing,' said their offspring.

A moment later the urgent alarm began its hectic scream. The planes were near. Joan slid carefully down off the foot of my bed.

'Excuse me, please,' she said. 'I've got to go look after Barbara and the *amah*.'

Soon I heard their shrill voices below me in the garden. They were playing tag.

It was a queer little moment for me. All the foreign population were away at a meeting outside the city; the servants had forgotten about me altogether. There was no place in the town more

exposed than this upstairs porch, and I was too weak even yet to
lift my head from the pillow. I should have been nervous. Anything but a courageous female, I had been consistently terrified
since the day I entered Wenchow harbor. But this afternoon in
Ichang was not like the others. For once there was no agonizing
thought process — 'Shall I watch the raid from the garden or
the ditch by the road, and will the spot I'm in now be hit by a
bomb, or if I move shall I walk right into one?' Today there
were no decisions to make. Everything was all right because there
was not a thing I could do. Besides, the sun was out, and hot.
It was the first sun since that day on the Kinhua train. It lay
against my face like a warm compress. The world drowsed and
drowsed. No wind moved the branches of the willow tree at my
porch side. There was no war; the pillow was too comfortable
It swooped down from back of my left ear and curled up beneath
my chin.

Far away beyond the visible sky a familiar low drone rose and
fell. But I did not hear it, because I was asleep.

My favorite servant in the household was the antique gentleman who fixed the fire in my room and puttered at odd jobs
around the place. He was a Taoist scholar from Hopeh, the prolific sire of several daughters and innumerable grandchildren. He
had, it seemed, turned up a few weeks before at the mission gates
with his enormous family in tow, all of them close to death from
starvation and the long trek south and west from Peking. The
Browns, helpless in the face of such mass malnutrition, had taken
them in and installed them in the compound. After a lengthy
fattening up, the grandfather began to worry about his self-
respect. The time had come for him to go to work. The mission
wrung its hands. Could he perhaps be the official time-regulator
of Ichang's foreign population, and go from door to door each
Sunday morning with a clock so that the foreigners would be on

time for church? The old scholar was charmed. He set forth the next Sunday, shortly after our arrival, armed with an enormous alarm clock and a great deal of enthusiasm. But at church that day, nearly everyone was late. The entire congregation trickled in a few minutes apart right up to the end of the ceremony. Eventually the truth was out. When the Taoist gentleman started on his appointed rounds and reached his first doorway, the time was exactly ten minutes past nine. When he reached the next house, it read nine-fifteen, obviously a mistake, since the proper time was ten minutes past nine. With the horrible logic of the Orient, he carefully set the clock back to its proper time and continued to do so at each home that he called upon. The next day, he was hastily put to making fires and sweeping floors.

One afternoon Teddy Tu came to call. With a queer little sigh he sank into the easy chair beside my bed. I was shocked at his appearance. His bland face was pouched and yellow.

'Teddy, you're sick!'

'I am sick as a dog,' he agreed cheerfully. 'Something about my kidneys. Such a nice pair of invalids, you and I.'

There was an uncomfortable silence.

'By the way,' he said suddenly, 'you will of course write a book about the New China, will you not?'

'Lord, no!' I muttered disdainfully. 'I'm not one of these women who go whipping around through a country and then dash home and write books about the place. Not me!' I said.

'But you must! You will see so much, yes. You will have to inform America that Free China is not just a mixture of guerrillas and air raids.' He gurgled in unexplained amusement, the sound flowing out of him like molasses from a jug. Teddy's laugh always punctuated his speech like a comma; it made anyone who heard it faintly hysterical. 'Guerrillas and air raids,' he went on happily. 'Do not leave them out, naturally. They are so spectacular! But write of the other things, too. Yes, the hard work. The what-you-call morale. The stupidity! Are we not very stupid, we Chinese? The way in which we smash up our trucks and blow up our steamboats!'

'You understate the case,' I growled.

'It will be a very young book,' he went on happily, 'because you are so young and enthusiastic and — pardon me — female. See to it that you tell the truth!' he glowered in quick change of mood.

'Teddy,' I almost shouted, 'for the last time, I am *not* going to write a book!' All of which indicates how much I overestimated myself.

Just before he left, Teddy did a queer thing. He started to sing, very softly, my father's setting of Stevenson's 'Requiem,' the same song he had sung that night at the house on little Dai Chia Hang.

> Under the wide and starry sky
> Dig the grave and let me lie....

He sang it with his back turned, and for some reason I shivered a little. When he finished I realized — without surprise, for I was used to Teddy's free-flying emotions — that he was weeping. Before I could tease him out of it, he turned to me looking moist and childish and began to laugh, not hysterically but in real amusement.

'What is that very frightful song we used to sing? Something about — yes. "Oh, dry those tears."' He sang it in cynical glee, his clear young tenor voice making the blatant phrases almost beautiful.

'So why should I weep,' he cried then, 'because I sing Homer's "Requiem" for the last time?'

There was a moment's silence.

'Oh, stop it!' I snapped at him, exasperated with his melodrama. 'You're acting like a prima donna. You're ———' I broke off, for he was laughing at me again.

Then for the first time I could not laugh with him.

'Teddy!' I whispered. *'Teddy!'*

A week later I was considered in shape for a return flight to Chungking. Rickshas carried us along the *bund* beside the city wall, whose stone surface was almost blotted out with scrawled characters — names and addresses, most of them, scratched there by passing refugees, in the forlorn small hope that by leaving their destination along the trail, their lost families might some day pass this way and read and once again be united. We rattled through the devastated streets, past soldiers' barracks, down the crowded foreshore to the landing pier. There we were joined by Teddy Tu, who was returning on the same plane.

As the ancient Commodore flying boat, in from Chungking, swept down onto the swift water, the crowds that had collected along the bank suddenly set up a cheer. A moment later a Chinese officer in simple uniform without insignia stepped from the cabin door onto the landing float. He was the great Kwangsi general, Li Tsung-jen, returning from Chungking to his command of the Hupeh front. He bowed low. We bowed even lower. Everyone beamed and said 'Hah hah hah ...' in that colloquial series of open-mouthed grunts by which the Chinese signify their wordless pleasure at meeting one another. The last we saw of the famous little general, he was striding fast and straight-backed up the riverbank toward the waiting crowd.

The ceiling was low. Several times during the return flight, our pilot had to fly actually inside the gorges, a few hundred feet above the river. It was a heady sensation. It brought out the feeling of great speed and power that the upper levels of flight do not convey. From my seat it looked absurdly as if the wing tips would at any moment brush against the cliff-sides, here where we circled and swooped through the narrow canyons like a bird of prey. Flying low over Wanhsien, we could see the big white patches in the heart of the city, where within the past week new raids had burned and plundered.

'No doctor!' Skipper was muttering to himself angrily. 'Not a qualified doctor in the place.'

Teddy, beside me, was deathly sick in the bumpy air. Once I felt his pulse. It was erratic, bad. He grinned at me wryly and I forced myself to smile back. By the time the plane had sprayed into the current by Chungking's booming waterfront and come to rest at last beside its moorings, he was as shaky as I. While Skipper attended to our baggage, we wobbled arm in arm in search of a sedan chair; and there was some question as to which of us supported the other.

When we parted that afternoon, Teddy as usual had the last word. Face imperturbable as a moon, for all its pallor, he leaned from the window of his little car as it started up.

'Your book,' he called back, 'it will be quite terrible and filled with split infinitives.'

'Blast your eyes, Teddy! *Tsai huei!* See you again!'

I did not see him again, of course, because in a short time he was dead.

TREK OF THE COLLEGES

TUCKED away in the back of my disreputable notebook was a list
of names, written there many months before under the title 'Key
Cities.' Some of them were old friends: Nanchang, Changsha,
Hengyang, Kweilin, Chungking, Ichang — key cities in the
defense of China. Others I was destined not to see: Kweiyang,
for instance, capital of Kweichow, roaring with life and refugee
industry; Kunming in the Southwest, ancient capital of Yunnan
and northern terminus of the Burma Road, where new universities, hospitals, ammunition factories, and a thousand small
enterprises were taking root; and Lanchow in distant Kansu,
where the Silk Road from Russia emptied its truck and camel
caravans loaded with Soviet munitions, and where a reform
provincial government was hard at work pumping new energy
into one of China's darkest provinces. But there were others on
the list that set my mind on fire. Chengtu to the west, home of
the refugee colleges; Chengchow, that front-line city on the
Yellow River, bombed and battered and still free; Yenan, headquarters of the Communist armies; Sian, metropolis of the
Northwest, once the seat of the Middle Kingdom, legendary
stronghold of the oldest dynasties.

Sian! All right, why not? News correspondents had stopped
going there since Hankow and Kaifeng had fallen and the railway

to Sian had been cut. Fares by plane were too high for my budget. But there was a road — the only motor road into the Northwest — twelve hundred miles of it, that wound westward to Chengtu, north to Hanchung and Paochi, and eastward again to Sian. Not much traveled, this road, they said. Nowhere near as good as the Burma Road, and almost twice as long. Mail trucks and a few supply trucks, specially constructed, could make the grades, could get through. All right, then, find a truck!

Six weeks passed before the chance came: a week in the hospital, then five weeks of interviews and feasts, of struggle with the cold keys of my typewriter; five weeks of marking time in that tense, listening city, where the fog had not yet lifted; five weeks of search for a truck to Sian. Meanwhile Skipper received an urgent SOS from the Sian hospitals and booked passage on the next plane. Our plans for a mere three months' trip had long since fallen beside some path of this enchanted land.

Of late we could talk about nothing but our respective *affaires du coeur*. All of China could not compete with the engrossing subject. Mrs. Brown, better known as 'Brownie,' had arrived in Chungking after long and agonizing delays, and Skipper trod upon air. I was not so lucky. While still in Ichang a cable had reached me from Bill, announcing that he had quite a few doubloons, an offer from *Newsweek*, and would I mind if he arrived at Chungking in about a month? With a lump of lead in my chest, I had had to tell him that it would not work. My employers in New York might recall me at any time (they had not known that I would trot about China like this), and we two should probably cross paths on the ocean.

I mourned. So, I imagine, did Bill. He had retired from his editorial work in New York to accept a graduate scholarship at Harvard; and a return, after six years of freedom, to the student life of theses and Milton 'writtens,' of Cambridge and 3 A.M. coffee and the dusty solitude of the stacks, is not the cure for a man with natural wings on his heels and a girl in China.

My own Slough of Despond might have lasted indefinitely had it not been for the ambulance supply truck belonging to the Christian Service Council for Wounded Soldiers in Transit. The truck was destined for Sian with medical supplies for the northern fronts. But only one of the passengers could drive. Did I not wish to go to Sian? Could I not be the organization's temporary chauffeur?

Could I not! We left three days later on the long road into the Northwest. The trip which was to have taken us a week took three. Partly responsible for this was our truck, Eva. She was a Burmese bus. She was, God help her, built in Rangoon of Burmese teakwood, with the figure of an overgrown station wagon and the temperament of an ingénue. Her namesake was a missionary named Eva who accompanied the truck up the Burma Road on her trial run. Dodge Brothers were supposed to have contributed her engine; but no Dodge salesman could have conjured up anything quite like her unless he were in his cups. For there was something unreal about Eva, something of little green snakes and pink elephants. She was to be our faithless friend for the better part of four months. She was a perfectly *horrible* truck.

The loading of her took an entire morning and drew a large crowd of happy spectators. Into her interior of one-and-a-half-ton capacity we had to stow three tons of medical supplies and five human souls. The supplies overflowed onto her fenders and spare tire. A five-hundred-pound bale of cotton was strapped to her roof, causing her to look, and act, a little drunk.

Four gentlemen and I set out that morning upon what was to be rather more of a trek than we had bargained for. My fellow chauffeur was Andy Roy, young American professor from Nanking University — espoused, bechildrened, and altogether fond of life. He was six feet four and the picture of clean-Ameri-

can-youth. Leader of the party was Philosophy Professor Bill
Djang, the director of the 'Wounded Soldier Outfit,' as our organization was usually called. He was tall for a Chinese, be-
spectacled, cadaverous, educated in America, England, Canada,
almost everywhere. I was a little scared of Bill. For sheer in-
tellect he inevitably laid me low. He was curiously attractive.
His eyes were set deep, his brown skin drawn tight and smooth,
and his face all bones; but they were exquisite bones. Very different but equally talented was Bishop Chen, the Episcopal
member of the party, a red-cheeked, brown-bearded, and intensely sophisticated cleric who could write poetry and paint
with the touch of a master. Finally there was our mechanic, Mr.
Li, whose good-looking angular face resolved itself into a thousand
wrinkles when he smiled; and he smiled whenever one caught his
eye.

Just how we managed to fit into that truck shall always remain
a mystery. It took considerable planning. Three of us would
wedge ourselves into the hard wooden front seat, a performance
which took several perspiring minutes. It was typical of Eva
that she had no doors of any kind, and the careful manipulation
of knees and elbows became almost a ritual. Conversely, it took
us quite a while to remove ourselves from the front seat. Since
Japanese planes patrolled and machine-gunned the Northwest
Road, this fact caused us little joy. The remaining members of
the party would insert themselves into the two-foot-high space
above the rear load, lying out flat as corpses. With every major
bump, they hit the roof. Obviously the driver's seat had been
designed for children or Burmese; the wheel caught us exactly at
the midriff; Andy Roy's expanse of legs was an even worse
problem.

At noon on March 18, now 1939, we were sent lurching on our
way by the joyous crowd that had collected during the past four
hours. Eva swayed through Chungking's streets looking very

distraite, horn shouting, legs, arms, and medical supplies over-flowing from her interior, and Andy wedged at the wheel with the air of a large man pedaling a tricycle. Now that we were on our way I felt a queer sudden sadness, for I had grown to love as well as fear this city. The familiar streets rolled by, little Dai Chia Hang, the barber shop near the corner where I used to go for quite modern finger waves, next to it the tailor who had mended my long-suffering clothes and then refused to take my money because I was 'serving his country,' around the corner the crowded little restaurant where I and my friends had wasted so many good hours over almond milk and green scented tea and yellow rice wine. I craned my neck to look back with a sense of finality I could not quite explain.

During that two days' drive to Chengtu, I fell in love with Szechwan. It is the 'garden province,' the largest in the land, where ninety million people live and thrive off the hot, lush soil. The saying is that the food and produce of this one province could maintain all of China. The mountains here were not so high as those that flanked the Yangtze to the east. They were graceful hills, terraced into hanging gardens, alternately layered white with the watered paddies, green with young corn, yellow with the early flowering rape. Spring had set in, even now. Within the valleys and edging each small, manicured field were plum trees in blossom, white and dark pink. From above, the blossoms appeared as a heavy snowfall upon each valley's floor. From here, too, the terraced hills took on the patterns of granite. Caught in a nest of willows, long-haired bamboo, and these thick flowers, the squat farmhouses of clay and thatch were scarcely visible.

There were many clustered towns, each with its gray wall and spreading memorial archways, medieval gatehouse, and near-by pagoda. Refugees, laden coolies, and marching recruits crowded the highway. Caravans of trucks passed us by. The much traveled Chengtu Road was in excellent condition. During the weeks that followed we looked back almost wistfully to those first dreamy, perfect days.

The comfortable, bucolic atmosphere of the region was misleading. Just as the Central Government offices were concealed in farmhouses and inconspicuous buildings within a radius of twenty miles or so from Chungking, so were the industries that filled the province and the towns along this road well camouflaged as industries. Some of the smaller enterprises carried on their work in mat sheds and rickety shacks. Larger factories were spread out in many buildings, decentralized to make things difficult for Japanese bombers. Actually the apparently rural countryside and innocuous towns were alive with large- and small-scale production. A good proportion of Free China's thousand-odd munition factories were located here in Szechwan, turning out small arms, machine guns, and light artillery. Industrial plants of every size and shape, rolling mills, steel foundries, dotted the province. The Industrial Co-operatives formed a scarcely noticeable but important undercurrent to the feverish activities.

A few hours after dark we put up for the night in a crowded, booming little city half-way to Chengtu. Since it was too big a job to unload the truck and unwise to leave her unguarded all night, Mr. Li, our mechanic, was cheerfully prepared to sleep inside her. But our innkeeper solved the problem more simply. He merely took down the removable wooden front of his inn and, after moving the tables out of the little room, drove the truck into his restaurant. Here we lunched in peace and candlelight on Eva's running-board and consumed meat-filled pancakes, bean sprouts with black mushrooms, and delicately scented soup.

The next day's drive took us through more blossoming valleys, across a dark range of hills, and down onto the wide plain of the river Min, that stretches westward toward the 'white mountains' of Tibet. On clear days, one could see the great range of the

Minya Gonka edging the Szechwan plain in high, unbroken snows. In this plain lay Chengtu, capital of the province, a city of temples and traditions, of canals cloistered in bamboo, of slim river boats and gardens, of porcelain and Burmese jade, of charm and an ivoried culture. The dwellers of western Szechwan were not all of them Chinese; various Miao tribes, smaller, darker than their fellows, inhabited the hills and mountains of China from Szechwan to Burma. Their language and customs are entirely their own; their origin is the subject of much wordy debate. Occasionally one would see a Tibetan visitor from the near-by province of Hsik'ang (once part of Tibet) striding down the Chengtu streets with haughty step, ornate in heavy robes and with an unfortunate tendency to smell. Odd pieces of Tibetan art were common enough in the little *hutung* of curio shops.

Far more serene than the rowdy commercial and politically minded Chungking, Chengtu had for many years been smug in the knowledge that she was the cultural center of the West. Her local Y.M.C.A. glittered with gymnasiums and intellectual programs. The great West China Union University lay sprawled over several square miles of graceful campus outside of her South Gate. Her attitude toward the war was almost dreamlike. Later she was to become more militant along with her first serious air raid; but on the day that we reached the city, an occasional raid on the airport, five miles outside the walls, had been her only brush with violence. Though I was struck with the beauty of Chengtu, I was a little annoyed at her complacency. Apparently it took a certain amount of fireworks and slaughter to stir in the Chinese a fitting degree of patriotism. The crux was not indifference or even selfishness, but only their inherent optimism, their tendency to sit wondering if the teapot will fall off the table until it has actually crashed upon the floor, their subconscious feeling that the war was raging upon some other and less comfortable planet.

The only warlike institution in Chengtu was the school of aviation where Free China's pilots were trained for pursuit fighting. Their planes, most of them imported from France and America, were pitifully few in number, and the half-trained students were not permitted to defend the airport from attacking Japanese bombers. Traditionally the Chinese made excellent pilots, if they took the time to learn. They had a certain chip on their shoulder, a feeling that after one solo flight they could challenge the Japanese air force single-handed; they sometimes knew better than their instructors. Consequently they demolished an unfortunate number of their own planes. But they made up for it in a typical reckless courage and a good instinct for flying. Their initiative often gave them the edge on their more studious and less imaginative Japanese opponents, who became paralyzed if faced with a situation that was not written down in their rule books.

In a raid upon the airport a day or so before our arrival, two Chinese student pilots had tackled a fleet of twenty-seven Japanese bombers. They had taken off from the field, along with the rest of the squadron, in their single-seaters, with instructions to fly straight west and at all costs save their planes. The two were the last to take off. Each in his individual ship sighted the oncoming bombers, fought an inward battle with himself, and turned rebel. They barged into the three formations of Japanese, broke up at least one of them, and so rattled the rest of the flyers that they dumped their bombs on open land and fled eastward. The pair also to their vast surprise brought down a heavy bomber. A few moments later, when they swooped heroically to a landing, one of the boys discovered that he had been wounded slightly in the ankle. The shock was too much for him. He fainted dead away.

Today Chengtu's greatest claim to fame is the stream of refugee colleges and universities that have settled there for the duration of the war. Statistics show that some seventy-seven universities have moved to the West. The story of these colleges and their strange trek has become legend. The facts are difficult to believe. Some of the students walked fifteen hundred and two thousand miles. Others more lucky struggled along by cart or boat (usually so crowded that they could not sit down for several days at a time) or wheelbarrow. Some went in a body, setting up their colleges again in empty temples or mud huts. Others were on their own. They knew only where their college had planned to settle, and they made for that place. Sometimes it took them a good many months; sometimes they had to beg food on the way. And these were nearly all the sons and daughters of wealthy families, accustomed to more luxury and fewer chores than the student of America. In certain cases they took their professors with them on the road, and when they grew tired of walking would sit down by the roadside and hold classes. Quite a few did not arrive, for the roads and waterways were under machine-gun fire, boats had a way of sinking and trains of being bombed. Others died more simply, from sickness and lack of food.

My first experience with refugee colleges had occurred in Kweilin, whither the Christian college of Hua Chung, bombed out of Wuchang, had fled in search of peace. The choice of a new home was unfortunate. Hua Chung came in for its full share of bombing. A few days after the American hospital was burned we moved in with members of the college faculty, Americans and Chinese. They had rented a small house and were hard at work fixing it up with new furniture, good plumbing (miracle of miracles), curtains, flowers, and a magnificent new stove. The stove was installed in the living-room with no small ceremony. It was a momentous affair, that stove. It was the only scrap of warmth in the house, and Kweilin winters are only a little worse than New England's. Every morning at seven-thirty, Skipper, I, and eight or nine congealed teachers would emerge from our bedrooms and make for the stove, huddling about it in an attitude of prayer. We called it our morning fire worship.

On Christmas Eve, shortly before our arrival, a raid had wiped out the two boys' dormitories. That night the boys built themselves a mat shed and moved in with mocking ritual. They had no bedding. The few articles of clothing they had salvaged from the fire were piled in one glorious heap on the mat shed floor and redistributed on a communal basis. When, after Christmas, the English class met once more, their American teacher gave them as a title for their weekly theme, 'Christmas in Kweilin.' Afterward, she told me, she was scared to death; they were wealthy boys, most of them, and she was not at all sure of their ability to absorb punishment. Later, she gave me the themes to glance over. One boy had written his theme in the form of a sardonic letter.

Dear Locia [it ran]:

Merry Christmas! As you promised to present me a very delicious gift of Christmas by post, I have not received yet. I hoped your gift would arrive beside my pillow suddenly when I just opened my eyes after a very sweet yawn; but I was hopeless, however. I hoped the Christmas Saint would carry your gift to me in Christmas morn. Don't you think I am stupid to make such day dreams?

I am very glad to tell you that I am still alive, because yesterday I was in a very dangerous condition. At noon when I was eating my tiffin the siren blew, but I was still eating continuously. The urgent alarm broke out after about ten minutes, but I was waiting for your gift; therefore I still remained at the table in our dining room, although many schoolmates ran away from our hotel. About a quarter passes one, there came nine Japanese planes up in the sky; meanwhile I went to our dugout. I stood at the entrance of the dugout and looked at the nine iron-birds. I thought that the

nine planes were nine post-planes, and in them there were
many Christmas gifts from every cities of China, and perhaps your gift was one of them. Bom! I knew a bomb fired
at the back of our dugout; therefore I was going to hide me
in the cave, but at the meantime, I jumped into it and was
fainted by another bomb which bombed in front of the dugout. When I awaked, I was all right but covered with dirt.
Oh, I received such a wonderful gift from our enemy instead
of yours! Good heaven, I was still alive!

Ever yours,
LEWIS

A young realist wrote:

As the chilling winter wind began to blow, it usually reminded one's thought back to the happy Christmas season
that had happened a year ago. But in Kweilin, Christmas
seemed no longer familiar to us. Everywhere showed no
sign of the season. The shop windows had nothing of Christmas color and taste to put on. There were no holidays for
schools. Christmas was a forgotten Christmas.... Luckily
a Christmas dinner was held in the college. We sang at the
highest of our voice. We ate as much as we could. It was
very funny and interesting. Both faculties and students were
present and the dinner was escorted with lovely decoration
and music and made us recalled the happiness of Christmas
in the past and forgot the terrible air raid that had happened
the day before and we were refugees....

A third wrote:

We came back from the dugout. Our room was partly
gone. Over our head was the sky, and beneath our feet was
the crumbled stiles, stone and mud. It was the Santa-Claus
of evil, surely, who gave us such a gift on the afternoon of

Christmas Eve.... The next day I woke in a shed. The day was dawning up to be a fine one. Everybody in the room was still resting. 'Christmas' was the word in my mind. But that was too much with a blank wall in front of you. 'Merry Christmas!' someone called. My clouds of despair disappeared when I called back. Why not be merry? On the street I met schoolmates yelling, 'Merry Christmas!' all the way. Really, I was merry!

The day before we left for Chungking it was decided that Hua Chung must move once more, this time to a village near Tali, west of the Burma Road in far-off Yunnan. It would be one more agonizing trek for the big college. Here in the teachers' home there was considerable wisecracking about the proposed move. We hauled out a copy of Cressy's *Geographic Foundations of China* and looked up 'Tali.' 'In Tali,' we read, 'there is a fine climate all the year around.' Whee! 'Good fruits may be obtained and many fine vegetables.' Cheers! Only one thing made them brood a little. They would have to leave the new stove behind.

Meanwhile in Chengtu, nine refugee colleges were carrying on their classes, 'writtens,' morning chapels, hockey games, evening concerts, semester papers, Saturday-night parties, and mid-years. While Eva was having a broken spring attended to, I passed the days with the family of an American professor of gynecology from the Medical College connected with West China Union University. On the university's big shady campus were four academic refugees: Cheeloo, for instance, from far Shantung; Ginling, fugitive from Nanking; and the large University of Nanking. All of them were so devastatingly like my own alma mater (Smith College) that I had to force down a hopeless tendency to giggle. The same lectures from visiting celebrities, the same kind of talk — of exams the next day and a set of tennis that afternoon, and whether there would be time to visit Mount

Omei during Easter vacation, and the price of the new Zoo text-book. Apparently colleges on the earth, even refugee colleges under bombardment in West China, rejoiced in a terrible and wonderful sameness. All except living conditions. The campus was, quite naturally, crowded to the point of chaos. Classrooms were not large enough. Library books were hopelessly in demand. The laboratories were used day and night, in relays. Ginling girls were virtually camping out on wooden beds, several to a room. Only a certain amount of equipment had arrived safely from the eastern campuses, and there were never enough textbooks and implements to go around. But it struck me rather hard at the time that the inconveniences (some of them serious hardships) were accepted by the student body almost hilariously as un-dignified and amusing subjects for repartee.

The combined American faculties of the colleges gave me an inferiority complex which has lasted to this day. Feverishly alive to the trends of the outside world, they managed to be inhumanly creative. Only coincidence could account for the fact that the leading professor of dentistry was a spectacular baritone and the lady English teacher an experienced concert pianist and the gynecologist's wife a painter of some note. The choir that sang in the college chapel might have descended from the cream of Fifth Avenue choirs. Even as far back as our visit to Wanhsien, I had heard on the radio the faculty's performance of a Gilbert and Sullivan opera so perfect that I took it to be a recording from some professional company. A more talented and intellectually sophisticated crowd I have yet to find congregated in one city. In fact, all the university life of Chengtu was extraordinarily civilized, its social affairs gay and well dressed, its faculty *au courant*, and its tennis courts smooth. Its atmosphere failed, somehow, to blend with the antique remoteness of Chengtu. It was an atmosphere one might expect to find in an American college town that prided itself upon being very *distingué*.

The students too had a certain sophistication that startled me now and then. The girls often wore casual and all too familiar sweaters and skirts. Both girls and men worked hard and played hard. Their new sense of danger and responsibility was unfamiliar to them, and it set well upon their shoulders. Fortunately they were not aware of gallantry.

Even their tolerance was instinctive. Only the other day, in reading over the summary of a Christmas play to be given by the students of Ginling, I had to stop and marvel. The play was an allegory. Its main characters were a group of four refugee women — a Chinese, a Japanese, a Finnish woman, and a German. Early in the play, each woman states the case for her nation. The Japanese woman, declares the summary, '... says that Japan is a small country with a large population and that they must have a place in which to expand, and that China was not fair to them and was always having anti-Japanese movements, and they had to fight.' The play was written by a Chinese student.

To the west of Chengtu, near the Tibetan borders, were many villages and towns which had changed little since the days of the Mongol invaders. They were typical of certain isolated districts which had not yet felt the touch of Western culture. Their whole scale of life was primitive. Nearly all of their money was used for food, none at all for education. A few of the country people did not yet know that China was at war. Promptly the business of teaching them, of educating them in national affairs and personal hygiene was taken on by the Chengtu students. Nearly all the students in West China are hard at work on this very special kind of propagandizing. They are pretty clever about it. They go by groups into the worst districts, visit every house, make inventories and draw up charts as part of their classwork in Sociology, set up schools and clinics, organize Industrial Co-operatives and women's clubs, and just plain get out on the street corners and shout. According to one freshman's diary on her adventures, their technique was as follows:

> This morning I went out with the propaganda group to tell the people about the present conditions in China. First we went to the public park, but we found that there were only a few people there, so we returned and stopped on a very big wooden bridge. We then started to sing; people all gathered around us with their wondering eyes gazing at us. The leader of our group then stood up and told them where we came from and what was the purpose of this propaganda. He also told them that we could help them cure some of their diseases. Having heard this many people came forward and asked us for medicine, and then the medical students treated some of them. The rest of us began to speak to small groups about the present Sino-Japanese War. Before we had started, we had dressed one of our students in the clothes of a farmer. So as we talked he stood among the people and asked us many questions about the war; in answering him we gave much information to the people about the war.
>
> At seven o'clock we arrived in Chienyang. Just then the big drops of rain came down. We walked through the rain toward the Local Government Headquarters — the place where we were to sleep. On the way we sang songs loudly, in order to show the spirit of our Service Group. Sometimes when we opened our mouths widely to sing, rain came into our mouths. People on the street gazed at us in surprise. When we arrived at the Local Government Headquarters, we fixed our bedding, and each took two tablets of aspirin.

During my week in Chengtu I discovered a treasure hunt in full swing. The story was so fantastic that quite a few American papers turned it down as highly improbable. One can hardly blame them. The entire affair conducted itself in an atmosphere of Xanadu or the Arabian Nights.

Up to a certain point, the tale is proven fact. In the eighteenth century, a war lord by the name of Chang Hsien-feng, setting out from his Shensi stronghold with a hired army, took it upon himself to invade Szechwan, lay waste the province, and, according to accurate statistics, put quite a few million people to the sword. And he seized as personal booty his favorite metal — silver. A large part of the silver coins and objects in Szechwan were gathered up by his conquering soldiers and laid at his feet. According to the lowest estimate I was able to obtain, the treasure is valued in modern Chinese currency at $80,000,000; guesswork, perhaps, but an interesting sum. At the height of Chang's success, a defending army was sent against him, and he suffered one defeat after another. At last it became clear that his days as a conqueror were numbered. Besieged at Chengtu and facing certain death, the war lord decided to bury his booty where it would not be unearthed and enjoyed by his enemies.

So much is history. Archaeologists have long been aware that Chang's silver cache is buried near one of the streams that flow in and around Chengtu. Then one March day in the year 1939, a scholar presented himself to the Szechwan provincial authorities bearing certain documents. His tale was fantasy, perhaps, and it went like this. When Chang buried his treasure in the river bed, he sealed the tongues of his workmen by the simple (and traditional) expedient of having them killed. But one laborer survived for a few hours, and when his son found him, he still lived. Before his death, he passed on to the boy the location of the cache, ordering him to write down the site in code and hand the secret down through the family, from eldest son to eldest son, until the day should come when China faced danger and crisis. Only then was the treasure to be presented as a gift to the nation.

His orders had been obeyed. Now the eldest son considered the

hour had come to turn over the hoarded books to his government. But by this time, the eighteenth-century style of characters was difficult to decipher. Several possible sites were indicated. After a good deal of sober and unromantic investigation, the Provincial Government decided that the chances of finding the silver were high enough to warrant a fifty-thousand-dollar excavation project. Since the difficulties were many, it might take anywhere from a week to two or three years to unearth the treasure. Perhaps it would never be found. No one knew. Only one thing was certain: the cache was large enough to be a sizable support for China in her war. Today the search still goes on.

There was an awful fascination in watching the diggers at work. I spent a long, lazy day with them on a sandbar in the middle of a small river just outside the city wall. The news had spread, and already crowds blackened the riverbanks. Deep in the pit, I shuffled happily around, eyes glued on the sand. Excitement almost overcame us all when a few old bones were dug up, some of them human, and rock slabs carved with the style of characters typical of Chang's century. Darkness finally sent us home. But the day marked a certain milestone in my life — the first and last time that I shall ever take part in a search for eighty million dollars' worth of silver.

A long week later, Eva was pronounced fit to go on. Her broken springs were healing, and the bale of cotton strapped to her roof had been removed. It was a rejuvenated Eva who bore us proudly through the Chengtu streets. As we drove by the crowded campus for the last time, I noticed a herd of cows grazing calmly in a hockey field.

'They are Madame Chiang's experimental cows,' Bill Djang told me. 'They were brought up here from Nanking because they're too valuable to lose. As a matter of fact, they only arrived here the other day. It must have been quite a journey for a herd of cows.'

I did not answer him, for I was staring at a strange caravan coming toward us through the North Gate of the city. Borne on the shoulders of a long line of chanting coolies were a series of dazzling objects: great hunks of heavy machinery, cotton looms, and, last but by no means least, eight shiny new bathtubs — all, we were told, arriving this day after an eighteen months' trek from Nanking.

Just a little way outside the city we passed a group of marching students, outward bound to do propaganda and medical work in the surrounding villages. Both girls and men were in the group. They held their heads up high like children on parade, and they sang as they marched. Behind them, four straining, chanting coolies carried a piece of massive machinery on four stout poles. The poles were laid upon their shoulders in the form of a cross.

(6)

THE GREAT NORTH ROAD

Eva swayed across the Chengtu plain, headed north between fields of young grain. The sandy road swarmed with travelers. Donkey carts and wheelbarrows trickled dust across the fertile land. We opened our shirt-collars to the hot sun. We waved to every other coolie and farmer on the road and laughed uproariously at our own remarks.

The passers-by stared at us and at our truck with unconcealed amusement and a touch of disbelief. If Eva herself was a truly wonderful sight, the foreigners and Chinese wedged inside were better yet. They stared at Bill Djang's long legs clad in knickers and tennis shoes that dangled from the rear of the truck. These Chinese from the East were indeed taken up with the strange ways and remarkable clothing of the big-nosed foreigners! Even the children in the Szechwan schools were wearing American shoes, and army officers brushed their teeth twice a day.

'Andy,' I muttered to the long figure tangled up in the gears beside me. 'What *do* they think of us, anyway? The Chinese, I mean.'

'That depends on the Chinese you have in mind,' was his careful answer. 'The most prominent emotion is a pure and wonderful curiosity. Those who have seen a good deal of foreigners either like us or dislike us quite normally — generally the former, Lord knows why. But they don't scorn us the way they used to. They appreciate our mechanical inventions. They think our science is great stuff.'

'What about the Chinese who have seen only a few foreigners in their lives?'

'Well, it's a funny thing. They look upon us pretty much as the people back home look upon the Chinese: a likable race with plenty of culture and not too inferior on the whole.'

'They're almost patronizing, aren't they? I've had a lot of country people treat me as if they were my old nanny. Awfully fond of me, and determined that I should not do anything stupid just because I was a foreigner who naturally didn't know any better.'

'They're a complacent race,' Andy said. 'And so are we. Of course you've noticed that our stock out here has skyrocketed since the war.'

'Noticed! I've been fêted and feasted until my health is permanently shot.'

'All because of missionaries and relief funds,' he went on in a small voice. 'They know about our little export trade with Japan too.'

'But they prefer to be naïve and like us.'

Andy nodded shortly. Just then Bishop Chen's rosy bearded face appeared above our heads like a vision, as he leaned forward from his lofty bed in the rear of the truck.

'That noise,' he inquired mildly, 'is it not the sound of an aeroplane?'

I braked the car with undignified haste. In the sudden stillness we strained our ears. The sound was most certainly an approaching aeroplane. But even as the fact sank in, Mr. Li, our mechanic, was chortling.

'It is a Douglas!' he explained in Chinese, stumbling over the foreign word. 'Your American plane that is used by the passenger

service. But would it not be amusing if it were an enemy bomber'
— he shook with laughter — 'and we could not remove our legs
from this truck? Wonderful!'

At ten o'clock that night we had reached a point twenty miles
beyond Hanchow, hoping to make the next city by midnight.
Whereupon Eva broke down. She gave a lurch and an almost
human grunt and deposited us in the ditch. Something was very
wrong with the steering mechanism. Investigation proved that
the large bolt which connected the right wheel to its shaft had
broken in two, and half of it was missing. Without the missing
half, no blacksmith in the province could weld a new one. Thereupon the next cold night hour was spent in combing the last mile
of road and ditch by headlight glare in search of half a bolt.

We found it. Then began the long ride back to Hanchow with
Eva, driven at a snail's pace, stubbornly nosing off the road every
hundred yards or so while the rest of us eyed the chilly darkness
with increasing gloom. Even though bandits had grown scarce
since the spread of war, this was 'bandit country' and we were
easy prey.

Three hours later we drew up before the vast iron gates of
Hanchow. They were closed and barred. The wall was forty feet
high. Like many of the 'old school' cities of the West, Hanchow
was locked up at midnight and no one could leave or enter the
city until dawn. We sat in a silence loud with mental blasphemy,
until Mr. Li clambered creakily out of the truck.

'I will persuade the sentry to open the gates,' he announced
in his polite, cheerful voice. A moment later he was pounding on
the mighty portal. '*K'ai men!*' he howled. 'Open the gate!'

From within came the startled Chinese equivalent of 'Who
goes there?'

Mr. Li thought fast, apparently of Bishop Chen.

'We are the Episcopal Church,' he snapped right back.

There was an impressed silence on the other side of the wall.

The Episcopal Church, whatever it was, had an elegant title. Still, one had to be careful. The gates swung outward and a head peered furtively through the widening gap. Taking a stand beside the open gates, the sentry motioned us through, with rifle trained suspiciously upon us.

'Enter, Episcopal Church!'

We entered. Bishop Chen suggested that a local Chinese seminary in Hanchow might be able to put us up. Again the valuable Mr. Li paved the way by pounding on the compound door.

'We are two foreigners, three Chinese, and one car,' he announced simply.

A few minutes later we were perched upon stools about a table while in the breaking dawn the larder was systematically looted and every edible dish in the establishment placed before us.

In America, a broken bolt would have caused serious delay while the part was replaced from a factory. Here in a remote corner of China, an exact duplicate was welded by a local blacksmith. In less than two days we were once more on the road. A night spent at Mienyang, and again we toiled from dawn to night across the endless plain.

My driving that day was very undistinguished; in the first hour I knocked down a house and a man. The villagers had an unfortunate habit of building straw canopies out over the road to protect themselves and their market produce from the hot sun. One of these canopies was a little low for Eva's high-flung roof. There was a rending crash as we went through. I slowed down and peered back at the scene of devastation; but the Chinese owners were virtually doubled up with laughter.

An hour later, I knocked down the man. He was an ancient farmer in stately dark blue robe. He lurched across the road directly in front of us, and in spite of our fifteen-mile-per-hour speed, before I could place my foot upon the brake I had hit him a good round smack and knocked him twenty feet away. A terrible crunching noise accompanied the sound of the impact, and my heart stood still. He lay sprawled in the dirt while a great red pool spread itself around him. We piled out and gathered about in a terrified circle while coolies and donkey riders and farmers peered over our shoulders.

It seemed we had broken his wine bottle. Seldom had I seen an old man quite so furious and quite so drunk. Too comfortable to get up, he thundered curses at us from where he lay. His vocabulary was idiomatic and wonderful, and overjoyed the appreciative crowd. After relieving his outraged bosom, he pocketed our substantial gift of ready cash and wobbled off down the road.

That night was spent in the home of a Christian pastor who welcomed us with a joy so great that it was close to tears. His beds were made of wooden boards, but the breakfast which he served us at dawn was a feast.

The road that day led through the sunrise into the tumbled mountains that crusted the plain, first of the great barriers which divided Central China from the dust-driven Northwest. The land here was not so kind. There were fewer villages, and the streaming wayside life had almost disappeared. The mountains were unterraced and coarse; they bristled with dwarfish evergreens. They rose each range a little higher and darker, a little more savage. At first the road followed the wanderings of a nameless river that slipped through the land in deep coils at the bottom of its gorge. Sometimes the ledge of road, blasted into the mountain-side, lay wholly under the arms of its overtowering cliff, and our fantastic truck would brush fenders with the ugly rock while her far wheels upon the crumbling lip sent a scruff of pebble and sand cascading into the gorge. Andy and I alternately clung to the wheel in a cold sweat.

Late in the morning, the road left the river and began to climb these dark ranges, sweeping up in impossible serpent curves at times so sharp that we had to back and hedge forward in order to round them. Eva boiled and snored and frequently died on the steep grades. Our only fellow travelers were long trains of loaded carts drawn by soft-eyed mules that trailed across the mountain passes in slow, patient file. There were few places on the road where we could pass them, and we ate their dust cursingly. Twice we overtook great caravans of camels bound into the North with their double humps loaded high. The deep-toned camel bell proclaimed their coming far across the ranges. The big animals were boogery. They stamped wild-eyed and nervous as we edged past, and their drivers fought to keep them in line.

I realized suddenly that on all the long ride from Chengtu we had passed only one fleet of trucks. The traffic on the road was strangely slight. A reason for this was the road itself, which would not permit the passage of the vast truck caravans that were now moving over the more improved Burma Road. Most of the military supplies coming in over the Central Asia road from Russia were being used in its terminal Kansu city, Lanchow, where many of the Soviet pilots were in training. But there was a definite need for an exchange of cotton and medical supplies between Central China and the Northwest. This road should have been swarming with animal carts. Later, in Sian, I learned that the blame was shared by a dearth of automobile tires necessary to preserve the surface of the road, and a petty quarrel between Kuomintang and provincial transport commissions that tied up efficient reorganization. It was one of the few instances of non-co-operation that I found in all Free China, but it infuriated me. I cursed too the carelessness of Chinese drivers who had small reverence for delicate machinery and who left their broken-down trucks strewn along the highways of the West.

Fortunately the red marks on the ledger were more than balanced by the almost superhuman way in which goods were transported through the free provinces — by donkey, camel, mule cart, oxcart, truck, and coolie — and communications kept open under circumstances that would have caused most nations to knuckle under in despair. Roads and railroads running a few miles from the Japanese lines were heavy with a traffic that was under constant fire. The highway from Indo-China to Nanning and the West, until the day the Japanese moved into Nanning, roared with truck fleets, manned by Chinese 'hell drivers' who braved daily air attacks. Mail continued to get through by over-land muleback. The 'seepage' of goods into Free China from the blockaded ports of Chekiang, Fukien, and Kwangtung was a hair-raising business, and the death rate among the junk-owners who ran the blockade must have been high. The tale of transportation here in the West would form a small history of heroism and patient tenacity all its own. And because the outcome of the war rests heavily upon China's ability to keep her goods moving and her internal communications open, the history is a vital one.

That night at Hanchung, after fourteen hours of driving, we gazed upon the plain wooden beds in our Chinese inn as if they were made of down. The American missionaries with whom we had planned to stay were in no condition to take us in. Only the day before, their doctor, superintendent of the hospital, had been killed. He was returning with his wife and two children from furlough in America. The mail truck in which they traveled had left the road shortly outside of Hanchung and plunged upside down into a muddy swamp. The wife and youngest child in the driver's cab had not been injured; in the rear of the truck, the doctor, his eldest daughter in his arms, had been pinned under the swamp water. But in falling, he had foreseen the outcome and had thrown his blankets and coat around his daughter's head, keeping out the filtering mud long enough to save her life.

The dawn revealed Eva with a flat tire. While the men were down in the dust repairing the damage, I wandered about this

big old city of South Shensi. Quite a few industries and colleges had taken refuge in Hanchung; the town reacted to its
blood transfusion and thundered with new life. The crowd in
the streets, as in the streets of nearly all Free China cities today,
was fifty per cent in uniform. A few were soldiers in training.
Others were in civilian uniform, the olive-drab, high-collared
khaki worn from the earliest days of Sun Yat-Sen's republic.
Civil officials, female relief workers, student organizers, and
government employees wore the uniform; and since a good part
of each city's population belongs in these categories, and since
the civilian uniform is also worn by army officers who seldom
bother to don their insignia, the street crowds are apt to resemble
a marching horde.

On an impulse I asked the shopkeeper who had just sold me some
cigarettes the same question that I had asked many times before:

'How do you like the soldiers, Hsien-sheng?'

His answer was much like every answer I had received.

'They are not so bad. After all, they are defending our country
from the invaders, and my father who is connected with the army
tells me that they are very brave. They are not to be feared as
they once were, is it not true?'

I nodded sympathetically, remembering tales of the old civil
war days when soldiers were hired mercenaries, little more than
bandits and hated and feared by every peaceful citizen of the
land. In those not very far-off times, soldiers supported themselves by systematic looting. Socially they were far lower than
coolies. Even the wounded soldiers, left behind by their armies,
carried on their own reign of terror in hospitals and throughout
the countryside.

Now. for the first time in China's long history, her armies were
fighting side by side with her people. The soldier, no longer the
gangster, was the defender of the nation. These boys passing me
on the street, with their incongruous straw sandals and ragged

puttees, their baggy faded uniforms and too tight belts and the cotton visored caps set straight and stern upon their shaven heads — they were no bought renegades; they were the farmer's son, the merchant and the craftsman, the tough, smiling young coolie, the citizens of China. Most of these would die yet for their country.

But would they become the new, the latest heroes? Was China to follow the wondrous example of more civilized nations who put their soldiers and sailors upon pedestals and every few years send them out to slay each other in the cause of righteousness or Fascism or Democracy? China's civil wars had not troubled to whitewash themselves with a single ideal; they were frankly contests between acquisitive war lords for personal power and fat fortunes. The people cared little who won. They hated the whole miserable business. The concept of a war with ideals attached was something very new. And what if China won her war? The possibility was there. Would she then, in her glory, become a military race? Old China — the one truly pacifistic nation left in her world?

'They are not so bad,' the young merchant had said of his country's soldiers. That, in brief, is the answer that Free China gave me: a grudging admiration for the army, an admiration that lagged behind the people's own willingness to sacrifice and work for their united government. Not yet were the people conscious of heroism or of glory. Not yet! They still fought only to be left alone. And the war was two years old. China's love of peace was instinctive and would die hard. Perhaps she could, alone of the nations, weather a victory without becoming a World Power. Perhaps she could set a strange example to the Christian peoples of the West.

Once more we set forth with Eva on the long road. This morning the highway approached the higher peaks, crawling and twisting always upward until the air grew bitter cold. At noon we reached a village that clustered beneath evergreens on the wooded slope of a sacred mountain. We dined that high noon in a courtyard of the famous little temple that knelt there, low and graceful, within its grove. Its roofs, encircling the court above white pavilions, spread upcurled arms to the sky and to the twisted pines. The painted tiles were feathered with growing weeds that thrust proud shoots at the sun and tickled the nose of the nearest gargoyle. Bordering the flagstone paths were white blossoming plum trees, chaste and pure in the cold air. The temple's inner walls were delicately latticed. An iron phoenix, a thin poised crane, a lioness clutching her cub, stood upright upon pedestals before the carved doors that led to dimmer sanctuaries. We perched here upon stools before the lacquered table with bunched white blossoms nodding at our shoulders and dipped ivory chopsticks very carefully into the scented foods. Beyond the outer courts a villager played upon his flute.

Bill Djang said with a grin: 'Today I could forget that I am a Christian. I could snap my fingers and slip back two or three centuries. What would you say if I burned a candle before the Goddess of Mercy? Would you be shocked?'

Bishop Chen smiled. 'We are creatures of conflict,' he said, turning to me. 'You may consider us modern and almost American because we speak good English and tell good parlor stories. Watch out that you do not burn your fingers on us some day. For we are very Chinese. Our present is a mixture of oil and water. This temple and this war. They do not blend well. You must watch out for us because today we cannot always tell you how we shall feel about this or that. Our past has deserted us; it was not good enough. We have only our day-to-day, our present. This, you will admit, we make the most of and enjoy while we may. But sometimes our present deserts us too.'

I thought back over my contacts with westernized Chinese,

my constant and hopeless blunderings with them. The Bishop
was very right. 'Creatures of conflict': it was a good phrase.
No matter how American were the dress and speech of my
friends, their reactions were wholly and confusingly Chinese.
Like hypersensitive children, they were unable to tolerate
criticism from anyone except themselves. Reading these words,
they will be offended. Likewise, they cannot criticize. To make
another lose face is an unforgivable sin. It is impossible to tell
what these smiling gracious people hold in their mind, what
thoughts they have of me. They would let me commit disastrous
mistakes for as long as I am capable of committing them, and
nothing would persuade them to warn me. Our American frankness and abruptness are a constant shock to them. A few of the
most modern among them have adopted our directness of speech
and dealing; but very few. The rest continue to shield, to smile,
to excuse, to procrastinate.

Call them foolishly proud and unnecessarily courteous if you
like. But there is something behind all this super-graciousness
which must be preserved. It stems from pure humanism. Probably no race on earth has as much respect and love for human
personality as the Chinese. Their instinct to shield man from
any loss of stature, no matter how slight, extends itself to coolies
and farmers and rich men, and is very strong. They have infinite
pity, for death or physical suffering, yes — but still more for
human weakness and the tendency of all men to fall from the
high place where he belongs. To them, it is the greatest tragedy
of all. Years spent in America and England cannot often take
their pride away.

'Bishop Chen,' I said, fumbling for the words. 'There will
some day be a blend. Good Chinese way of life and good foreign
— they should not be so hard to mix. Right now the things of the
West are too new and the East too old. But let them age together
a little. After the war, you watch! You'll find that you can take

the good things we have to offer and let the rest alone. And your own culture will be preserved. There will be a way. I know it!'

We were so seldom serious that I blushed over the intensity of my words. I blessed him now for not smiling at me.

'Of course,' he said simply, 'it is what we believe in — our future.'

He wiped his fingers upon a steaming towel and with a half-bow poured tea ceremoniously into my cup. Sudden wind shook down a snow of plum blossoms and scattered dried melon seeds upon the ground.

A few moments later as I wandered down through the village street between houses of mud and thatch, I saw a crowd gathered laughing around some small object in their midst. The object I found to be a Himalayan black bear cub. The mother had just been shot by a local villager, and the fate of the cub was under discussion. Would they or would they not have enough food in the village to feed him? Chinese have virtually no sentiment toward animals; but there was something comic and wholly valiant about this small bear that set him apart. He was the nearest thing to a Teddy bear that I have yet seen, standing about a foot tall on his hind legs, with thick black fur, shoe-button brown eyes, a white patch on his chest and another impudent tuft of white upon his chin. Everyone who picked him up was his lost mother, and he hugged us impartially with both arms and muttered deep in his throat. At once I settled his fate by unwisely buying him outright for the wonderful price of a few dollars.

From that moment Edward Bear became the mascot of the expedition. He traveled in a comfortable sack with only his nose exposed. Just once during our acquaintance did he weep. Not all of Eva's wild-horse tactics could disturb him. At night he slept wrapped up in my padded Chinese bedding somewhere around my feet. He was the most adaptable bear! Mankind was his boon companion and source of all food; he would cuddle in my arms for hours like any sentimental lapdog. He also ruined my last pair of silk stockings. Eating was his one great problem; he finally learned to take his cereal and milk out of a dish, but the effort was an ordeal. His only system was to plunge his head into the food over his ears, suck and swallow noisily for as long as his breath held out, then emerge in a horrible condition to be wiped off and comforted and sent back for another try. Most spectacular of all was Edward's temper. If asked to stop scratching the furniture or go outdoors when he preferred to stay inside, he simply lost it like a spoiled boy. Whereupon this minute bear would rear upon his hind legs and uttering great animal roars charge us with forepaws flying. It was necessary only to pick him up by the scruff of the neck and administer two or three excellent spanks. He would become silent and painfully respectful. Apparently spanking was a familiar experience out of his less civilized past. On the whole, Edward was quite a bear.

That afternoon the sky darkened and a thick sleet began to fall. Rapidly the narrow ledge that was our road became a ribbon of mud and ice. Andy and I took turns in fighting to keep the truck from slipping off the canyon rims. Every hairpin curve became a skirmish that left us tense, as the wheels beneath us lurched and slithered from side to side in the crusty slime. Above us, the dirt cliffs grew soft. They began to dissolve finally into small landslides that threatened to block the road. Twice within a single minute I had to brake to a panicky halt while a boulder large enough to carry us off the road thundered past in front of us.

Once we rounded a curve on a stretch of ledge cut into the cliffside and came upon a mountain sitting in the middle of the road! The overhanging hill had split in half and slid downward as far as the projecting highway, where it stuck. There it sat, perfectly intact and covered with trees, looking very out of place. At the moment of our arrival, it was almost blotted out by a swarm of workmen, two or three hundred of them, covering it like ants. They were hacking calmly and deliberately at the soil. I strolled over to watch them. They in turn watched me with open curiosity. The nearest coolie put down his pick and wiped his face and neck with a piece of rag that was tied about his waist. In spite of the cold, his loose high-necked jacket was open down the front. All of his skin was burned a red brown by the sun. His ribs protruded, but the muscles of his body were long and taut. It is said that the Chinese coolie, underfed and tubercular, is the strongest and most enduring laborer on this earth.

Now he wiped the sweat from his shaven head and turning to me called out, 'Are you Swiss?'

I said no, I was American; wondering where he could have met a Swiss in this remote land.

'American!' he grinned. 'Did you know that there is an American hospital near here? They take in our poor and do not charge them a single *mao*. They make us feel very safe. Yes,' he said in a matter-of-fact voice, 'even we country people know what the Americans are doing for us.'

I remembered with sudden shame that here was a specimen of what we in America would call the 'smiling, anonymous coolie.' He has borne the brunt of our patronizing attitude long enough. The Chinese, more instinctively democratic than ourselves, call him a 'horse person' or a 'carrying person' or a 'big fellow person' (a cook), depending upon his trade. There is no sharp division between a coolie and his fellow citizens, in his own mind or in the mind of anyone else, except in his ability and inability to do things. Certainly the 'coolie class' exists only in the minds of the foreigners. Farmers, coolies, merchants — they are in no way anonymous. On the contrary, they are very much individuals.

Coolies, I discovered, nearly all come from farming families. They move to the cities to make a better living, and sometimes they succeed. More often they are poor. The average coolie will rent a room for himself and his family, perhaps with one or two other families. The crowd will sleep on wooden beds, rolled up in padded *pukais*. The rest of their furniture will consist of a square wooden table and stools. Their possessions are few: chopsticks, rice bowls, a kettle and cooking-pan, a washbasin. Those who live near a river or lake will probably wash from head to foot at least once a day. The myth of voluntary uncleanliness is born from the fact that in some cities and towns water is a limited commodity and must be sparingly used. On the whole, I found the Chinese poor somewhat more inclined to wash themselves and their clothing than the slum-dwellers I had once known well (and loved well) in London. In even the humblest families drinking water is always boiled and served hot. The coolie will eat three times a day if business is good. His meal will be rice or millet bread and a little salt vegetable, very occasionally meat. He owns probably two or three cotton summer suits of trousers and coat and one padded winter suit. Once a year at the least he will visit his family in the country. He has a good learned name and a fund of stories from the lore and legend of past dynasties and traditional classics. Perhaps he can read characters, perhaps not. He takes his orders from no one but himself. If he feels like obeying your request, he will do so. Being Chinese, he cannot help but enjoy himself at least part of the time. Down in the dust and too sick to pull his ricksha — wholly doomed — he can still watch a street fight near-by in undiluted glee. He lives in the present because it is so absorbing. His conversation with his family and fellow workmen might be a mixture of money matters, family matters, Confucian ideals of filial piety, the present war, and an intricate and wonderful repartee. The amount of word play and teasing wit in the coolie's conversation is almost nerve-racking.

The farmer has more use for his intelligence. Though not yet up-to-date in his tools and methods, he is considered a brilliant and tireless agriculturist. The fund of information he must know and the things he must do are appalling. That much-abused term 'peasant' would look worse than foolish if applied to the Chinese countryman. Its implication of the Simple Life would drown in the welter of technical detail that forms his world. The farmer absorbs a lifetime of training and needs all of it in order to keep alive. He must know everything about cattle, everything about seed and fertilizer, everything about irrigation. Usually his fields are small and his problems enormous. Every young rice plant must be transplanted by hand, every road combed for precious manure. His conversation will cover a thundering amount of detail — of soil and weather, produce, tools, animals, and prices. The women will be wrapped in the affairs of all women of all races: children, household matters, cooking, and religion — for they are far more spiritual and inclined toward superstition than their worldly husbands. Especially amongst the old people one can hear lengthy philosophical arguments, sprinkled with classical references and stories of ancient times that are handed down through the humblest families in the land.

The farmer, the coolie, the merchant, even the beggar, have one thing very much in common. They are aware of their stature as men and as individuals. They feel inferior to no man. Their place in society is unmarked and undefined. Not a defiant sense of equality, this; just the curious fact that inequality has not yet occurred to them. Probably the phrase 'smiling, anonymous coolie' would strike the aforementioned coolie as very funny.

The workman near me who had just praised the American hospital now turned to me again.

'Do you know,' he said, 'you are the first foreigner I have yet seen. My father spoke to me once of your strange big noses. But he did not tell me that your faces were so red.'

With a friendly smile, he shouldered his pick and went back to work.

Twenty minutes later, the mountain had been removed from

the road. Things are done like that in China — appalling obstacles removed — by force of numbers. In the fall of 1940 I was to read Japan's assertions in our press that they were planning to cripple the Burma Road by bombings. I was to remember this road and the fifty cents' fee for the repair of bomb holes and the ferries that operated at important bridges in case the bridge should be damaged. Perhaps I had good reason to smile.

It was dusk when we sighted, far ahead, the Chung-nan Range, last and greatest mountain barrier between Szechwan and the valley of the Wei — between Central China and the ancient Northwest. The big range thrust up round-headed peaks, thirteen hundred feet high, still capped by deep spring snow. In the gathering twilight, the road was a dim coil that spiraled upwards toward the high pass and lost itself beyond the snows. Already we were above the timberline and the cold fondled us until we were stiff and drowsy. The sleet was snow now. Our truck was in a perpetual skid. There was no question of attempting the mountain pass ahead in the darkness and the storm. We were discussing the possibility of sleeping inside the truck when ahead of us we caught a glimmer of lights. It was all right. There was a village at the foot of the range.

Shelter in the little place, called Suan-hsi-p'u, was precarious. The mud-walled huts were already crowded with refugees from the storm. For an interminable time we scoured the village. Our heavy clothing, at first soaked through, was now freezing into crackling sheets; while Edward, as unhappy as the rest of us, wept for his dinner. At last, two young men came hurrying up and insisted upon giving us sleeping space in the little office of their industrial co-operative near-by. The office was without heat of any kind and not much drier than the street, but we could not refuse. Since my bedding was as wet as the rest of me, I slept in my ice-filled clothes that night on the mud floor of the dreary little hut.

The next morning we tottered to the door. Looking out, we caught our breath. The village of thatch and mud was made queerly beautiful by its frosting of snow, and the red morning sun set the snow on fire. Skyward to the north, leaning almost above us, the great range waited, serene and very high. A scaffold of white lay against its old sides. Strangely, the plum trees that lined the village street and all of this small valley were in blossom, not yet blighted by the cold. They gathered in round bouquets of dusty pink against the soft snow. A caravan of homely camels, just arrived in town, ambled solemnly down the street. Their matted coats wore a new sprinkling of tinsel from the long night's trek through the storm; and this morning the camel bells carried a persistent note of gladness, almost of comment upon so much beauty and so much sun. Edward, peering in rapt wonder from between my ankles, gave way to a sudden mysterious emotion and, loping forward with loud cries, dived into the nearest snowdrift.

'It is a Chinese scroll — a snow scene,' said Bill Djang at my elbow. 'Do you understand now why we cannot describe our country? Give me a thousand artists, each with a thousand moods — a painter of snows, a painter of camels and small bears, a painter of bamboo or rice paddies or the steep mountains of the South or the tigers of Shensi and Kansu — tell them to paint this nation and they would all go off and commit suicide!' He grinned and stretched. 'You must admit that our land is nothing if not spectacular.'

And then, because the sun and the snow had gone to his head, he leaned against the doorway and laughed.

A fleet of trucks bound for Lanchow had come in during the night, loaded with searchlights for defense against night bombers. The soldiers in charge were stamping about to keep warm and discussing the chances of going on in the heavy snow. As I took my place behind Eva's wheel, they crowded around me, enthralled at the sight of a female with a bear driving a truck. They were especially fond of Edward, who is a chummy bear and gave them flattering embraces.

'Where are you from?' I asked, absently leaving out the 'honorables' and other delicacies with which the sentence is usually flavored.

The nearest soldier grinned and bowed low. 'That is a very difficult question, madame,' he answered. 'I shall strive to answer it correctly. We were once told that we came from China.'

The others snickered audibly and watched to see if I would be offended. Fortunately I had learned from bitter experience that an air of injured dignity or exasperation, even when it is justified, will only bring down scorn and a terrible amusement from the Chinese upon the head of the offended one; and the surest way to make them into friends is to laugh. A sense of humor is an open sesame in China. If a coolie should bump into me on the street or refuse to do as I asked him, to curse him out would be paramount to butting my head against a bland stone wall. Probably, the coolie would enjoy my anger. But laugh with him or at him, and he will outdo himself in atonement. In fact, the instinctive effort of so many foreigners in China (and I was no exception) to hang on to their dignity in front of the Chinese has been an everlasting and ridiculous barrier between the two races.

So now I laughed at the soldier's teasing words, and at once I was *persona grata* with the crowd. They answered any question I could ask out of my limited vocabulary. Yes, the searchlights were bound for Lanchow. Heavy night raids had begun there lately. The Russians? Well, they kept pretty much to themselves, but there were plenty of them around, nearly all pilots in training and mechanics. Since the early months of the war, very little traffic was coming in over the road from Russia. Russian military aid was rumored to be scarcely more than a trickle; for the road was bad and very long, and trucks were useless after but a single trip. Most Russian shipments now came through from Burma. Neither foreigners nor Chinese who visited Lanchow were permitted to see and hear what went on among the Russians there. All was secretive and dark.

The information corroborated certain rumors in Chungking. I decided then and there that a trip to Lanchow would be a waste of time.

We bucked the mountain pass that morning in snow so heavy that it left us often enough bogged down on the steep grades. As luck would have it, there was a small stream of coolie pedestrians on the road. Their system was to help us tie ropes to Eva's wheels and pull her sideways out of her rut, thirty or more men on each rope, laughing, singing, and thoroughly enjoying themselves. Once a truck passed us heading south. It was literally sliding sideways down the precarious ledge, while the crowd of men and women in the back alternately giggled and cheered the strange descent. A curious bravado, these people have; part ignorance, part courage, part fatalism. But there is less fatalism than I had imagined, and less ignorance; and more of nervelessness and a plain enjoyment of danger that I had not associated with the Chinese.

The mountains gradually rounded out about us as we reached the higher levels. The road grew worse. A Japanese army would find it no easy task to cross the snow-bound range. Now it struck me with new force how important was China's topography — her plains and mountains and rivers — in determining the course of this war. Probably no subject is more abused. Nearly all the misstatements that I have read in the press have been the result of a natural haziness as to the physical details of the country and its supply routes — details that are uncomfortably important for a military understanding of China's war, past, present, and especially future.

Here in the Northwest, for instance, the Japanese had been

held up for many months on the east bank of the Huang Ho, or Yellow River, unable to cross that hearty current under the bitter fire of the defending Chinese on the opposite bank. Japan's northwest drive that had swept through Shansi earlier in the war had now stalled beside this river, while Shansi's mountains to the rear, though not high, had made the so-called 'occupied' province a safe beehive for guerrilla armies and a headache for Japan. But say, for instance, that Japan's northern armies were able to cross the Huang Ho (a feat which could be accomplished whenever the sacrifice of men demanded it) and drive forward sixty smoothgoing miles to Sian. Say that they were able to push even farther westward to Paochi. What would be the result? They could cut this motor road at Paochi and choke off the comparatively small traffic between Shensi and Szechwan. But the branch road to Lanchow lay within sight of our little town of Suanhsi-p'u, safely south of the Chung-nan Range, and could be defended with a minimum of troops. The mountain range would also serve to halt any attempted drive southward to Chengtu and Chungking. The northern route from Sian direct to Lanchow was mountainous, destroyable, and four hundred and fifty miles long. In any case, during a drive through Shensi, the Huang Ho would still be Japan's greatest enemy, a vulnerable spot where supplies could be choked off and her lines of communication cut; moreover, the drive would be a needle-sharp thrust into solid Chinese territory — an invitation to the guerrillas to clip the drawn-out attack into sections and swallow it piece by piece, as they were to do in the coming battle for Changsha.

Elsewhere, too, the course of war had reached a physical *impasse*. Japan's drive up the Yangtze was to reach Ichang and halt once and for all before the four hundred miles of trackless mountains that lay between Ichang and Chungking. In the summer of 1940 she was to force her way into Indo-China on the pretext of a projected drive into China's southwest; but a glance at the topography of that country, the almost impassable mountains of Yunnan and Tongking, should have revealed how flimsy was Japan's excuse for an occupation of this rich French colony; for that matter, an invasion of Yunnan would have been far easier over the mountainous but passable motor road from captured Nanning straight west through Kwangsi. Today, only in less mountainous Central China is there room for further conquest, or in the provinces of the southern coast; and here are no vital supply lines to be cut. Japan has before her only the joyless prospect of capturing more cities of no military importance and stringing out her already overburdened lines of occupation and attack. Thanks to China's formidable geography, as well as to her unexpected courage, she has a fighting chance.

With the noon sun white upon the snow, we crossed the high divide and began the slithering descent. When we nosed down the last grade, dry now and far below the snow line, I suppressed an awful impulse to lean forward and plant a kiss upon Eva's shiny steering wheel. The drive across the wide fertile plain felt like a ride in a kiddy car. We spent the rest of the day and night at Paochi, northwest headquarters of the Industrial Cooperatives. A tour from Co-op to Co-op convinced me that I must come back here for a longer visit and report in detail upon one of China's youngest and most energetic experiments.

Though we had been driving through North China for several days, the last day's ride from Paochi straight west to Sian gave me my first chance to unglue my eyes from the road and look about me. The difference between this land and the Szechwan Red Basin or the hot, moist South was startling. In fact, it did not seem quite possible. China's Northwest could be condensed into one small word — loess. The stuff is like clay, sometimes blown into light yellow dust. It sifts down from the deserts of Ninghsia and Outer Mongolia and falls as a blanket upon the North — upon Hopeh and Shansi, Shensi and Honan and Kansu.

There it has accumulated through the ages into a shifting layer, sometimes several hundred feet deep, of hard-packed ivory soil, so adhesive that it can be sliced like cheese. The outer layer blows free as a never ending dust that plagues the land. Deep caves can be tunneled into these loess hillsides in a matter of hours; there is no danger of collapse, for the walls are firm as plaster. Cave villages honeycombed the hills to the north of this province. Here in the plains, the villagers merely mixed loess with water and shaped it into the walls of their houses and their cities.

Above all, the loess is fertile. The tubular structure of the clay draws water to the surface by capillary attraction — the one reason why the North is inhabited today. Because watered rice paddies are impracticable here in this dry climate, wheat and millet and *kao liang* are the staple foods. Fields on either side of the road were solid green with the early spring wheat. In the South, the country people lived in scattered farms; but here the farmers, long oppressed by bandits, clustered into villages. Like small squat brown castles, the villages dotted the surface of the plain, surrounded by high crenellated loess walls, and crowded with mud houses and overspreading trees. Oxen replaced the water buffalo of the South. Yoked together in stolid partnership, they tilled the broad fields and hauled heavy carts in dust clouds across the flat land. The people too were different. They were taller than the Chinese I had known, and tougher. They faced a terrible constant labor in the dry North, where drought was a personal devil, where winter was too bitter to bear and summer a glare of sun on pale loess. The borderline between a good year and a famine year was quite thin here; and the people had become through the centuries of strain more taciturn and less emotional than their fiery fellows to the south.

Japanese bombers had dropped their appointed bombs upon Sian and were heading back to their bases when we came in sight of the city. From many miles away we saw her walls in the afternoon blaze of sun. They rose in square sheaths, as about some giant fortress. The gate house lifted well over a hundred feet.

The wide dusty streets of this northern metropolis were an unexpected relief from the overcrowded, overpopulated towns of the South. I saw little devastation, although defenseless Sian had been bombed indiscriminately, sometimes daily, sometimes weekly, for almost a year. Later I learned that ruined houses were rebuilt from wood and loess and tile within a few days after their destruction. In spite of the afternoon's raid, the busy crowds, the blue-canopied rickshas gave little sign of war. Even the temples of the city, among the oldest in the land, the drum tower and the bell tower, stood in grave serenity — firm and untroubled by the blast of modern bombs. Sian was still the stronghold of dead kingdoms, the ancient capital of her land. She bore her scars well.

A few moments later, with Edward Bear in tow, we strolled into the living-room of the English Hospital residence house. The entrance was unintentionally dramatic. A meeting of Sian's medical personnel had just ended and precious coffee was being served. The room was filled with doctors. Among the group was Robert Brown; and I remembered that he had of course been expecting our arrival some ten days ago. Now the roomful of men stared at us in wordless surprise. They had decided a week ago that something must have happened to us on the road. I did not blame them. Mentally I counted the days since we had left Chungking, and they were nineteen.

Only Skipper kept his eternal devastating calm in the frozen silence. He came forward casually with his hand outstretched and a grin on his face.

'Joy, it's good to see you. I was beginning to wonder when you'd turn up. Do you mind if your coffee's a little cold?'

Much later, when the excitement had died down and I had partly forgiven him, he turned to me again.

'You're just in time,' he said. 'I have to leave for the Yellow River front tomorrow morning. Think you're too tired?'

Every accumulated ache of the past three weeks magically left my bones. Before I could speak, Bill Djang answered for me.

'It is not that she is tired but that her face is dirty,' he remarked with exasperating truth. 'She'll go.'

That night, before I went to bed, I took Edward Bear upon my shoulder and went out into the city. A few blocks away, flames from a little burning shop that had been fired in the afternoon raid still flickered and glowed in the dark, busy street. Rickshas and bicycles wheeled past and few heads turned toward the smoldering ruins. From an upstairs restaurant across the way, music blared out in jangling nasal twang. Men and women strolled the sidewalk arm in arm, in the sophisticated manner of the foreigner. Here on the corner, a ricksha coolie lit a bunch of sacred paper money and crouched before the tiny flame in respectful supplication to his god.

I sensed a queer stubborn courage in Sian. It owned not one anti-aircraft gun, not one machine gun. The casualties here were in the thousands. But within a week this small burning shop would be replaced. Probably it would be given a gaudy false front, grander than before. The silver dragons that adorned the sides of every ricksha, winding their painted scales about the black chair-back and under the bright canopy — I noticed that they were kept spotless and very shiny. The sidewalks were swept clean. Workmen were busy washing down the streets, settling the dust. One of them chanted in rhythm to his swinging arms, singing the alien song in a high clear voice.

The sky was not yet altogether dark but rather a deep thick blue. I could still see the city wall against this sky. At the end of each wide straight street there was a gate and above it a gate house upon the wall, one hundred feet high and grave like a fat temple. This one to the west where the sky was still light — perhaps I imagined that it was larger than the rest, and older. It stood asleep, as old things will. Its upcurved roof spread wings in benediction over the city.

7

DOWN THE LUNGHAI BATTLE FRONT

A FEW days later I was perched sideways on the back of a donkey not much larger than myself, whose small hoofs kicked up explosions of dust along a far-off country road. The road ran parallel to the Lunghai Railroad and close to the banks of the great Huang Ho. During the centuries, the road had eaten its way into the soft loess until it lay coiled as a giant trench twenty feet beneath the surface of the fields. Behind me was Loyang, the provincial capital, ahead of me the battered, bloody little city of Chengchow. And between this sunken road and the river were the entrenched forces of the Honan guerrilla armies, and on the farther bank the forces of Japan.

At second intervals the ground shook under the roar of cannon, and rifle and machine-gun fire cracked and purred in the sunny air. As usual, peace and war went hand in hand. The day could not have been more beautiful. Lean wind-blown poplars growing along the lip of the loess banks made the road seem deeper still within the ground. Unseen locusts laid a blanket of rasping sound over the hot spring earth, a sullen undertone to the skirmish that was in progress beside us.

The road was almost crowded. War fronts mean little to the Chinese. Much more important than mere safety is the careful fertilizing and harvesting of their crops, the bearing of grain to market, or the sale of their black pigs for a good fat price. Brown-faced young farmers passed me, perched on the shafts of their ox-carts. Coolies padded by with heavy loads slung on bamboo poles across their shoulders. There were women with children in their arms riding upon donkeys, and refugees with their goods piled upon wheelbarrows. Nearly all these travelers smiled at me and chatted casually with each other. They paid no attention to the guns.

Skipper had gone ahead to make some business arrangements, and I was alone with my *ma fu* or 'horse person,' as a donkey's owner is called. When he suddenly decided to take a short cut across the fields, I was helpless to stop him. Orders mean little to the workingman of China, who has an inflexible mind of his own and does exactly as he pleases. So I obediently climbed out of the sheltering road. As we crossed the wide fields I strained my eyes for a sign of action. But like so many battlegrounds, the terrain appeared lifeless — a sound stage without actors. The machine-gunning may have been some distance off, though it sounded a stone's throw away. Nothing moved in the flat green land beside the river, while the unseen guns cracked and roared in the air about us.

Once there came the familiar whine of shells directly overhead. We flattened down in the young wheat. A moment later the shells burst near a deserted railroad bridge behind us. I silently cursed my companion.

'Honorable *ma fu*, I hope you encounter a very large stray bullet,' I muttered in dreadful Chinese, and he shook with laughter.

Only a few days had passed since we had left Sian in an effort to reach Chengchow. But already it felt like a few months. There was something a little too active about this front to suit my peace of mind. To put it briefly, I was scared. For over a year now the Japanese forces had been held up on the east bank of the Yellow

River, unable to force a crossing under the guns of the Chinese. The Lunghai Railroad, running sometimes within sight of the river, was, typically, still in cheerful operation. The thousands of shells flung at it by not very skillful Japanese artillery units across the water had occasionally damaged the rail-bed for a few hours, nothing more. From Sian, the famous Green Express, favorite of tourists in the strange old days before this war, carried us brazenly through Tungkwan, where even at night the Japanese were dropping one monotonous shell every sixty seconds into the city, and on to Loyang, which was promptly raided the moment we arrived. I almost kissed that Green Express. It was so nonchalant, even for a train. It ran sometimes half a mile from the Japanese lines across the river. Twice on the trip, when Japanese raiding planes appeared, it quickly deposited us in the surrounding fields to cower down amidst the wheat and pray that we would not be seen and machine-gunned, while it picked up and glided for the nearest gully, there to lie uncoupled, strung out for hundreds of yards along the track, virtually unbombable. Both it and we arrived untouched at the end of the two days' run.

At Loyang we interviewed famous old Wei Li-huang, commander of the Honan war zone, and one of China's best generals. He was a small busy man, reputedly a military genius, and he fed us an excellent lunch. We discussed Japan's chances of crossing the river. If she succeeded, declared the Marshal, she would find herself in a very unpleasant position with a very unprotected rear. Even her Shansi territory on the far shore was honeycombed with Chinese troops waiting to strike from behind.

'Just now,' he said, with what seemed to me unnecessary emphasis, 'all has been quiet. Peaceful as the reigns of Yao and Sun. But we expect some action soon.'

One more surprising fact came to light: the fact that Marshal Wei was using some Eighth Route Army, or Communist, troops in this area, which is far to the south of the Communist-controlled districts. They were co-operative too, he said. Good soldiers. Very good soldiers. He quite liked them.

Up till now our journey had been easy. But from a point beyond Loyang all the way to Chengchow, the railroad had been torn up to hold back the Japanese advance. So we took to the road. Today, as I lay stomach down in the green wheat, I thought of the ten miles already covered that morning and the thirty miles still ahead and felt a little gray. The donkey had reduced me to the point where it was kinder to myself to walk than to sit upon anything at all. So as soon as we reached the road once more, I paid off the *ma fu* and started out on foot.

Almost at once the firing died down and the world sank into a peaceful, drowsy coma. Those thirty miles slipped by as on a treadmill. Blisters went unnoticed. No longer jarred by the painfully modern sounds of war, the ancient ways of China stirred into life. So did my suppressed romanticism. We were wayfarers together, I and these farmers and ragged boys and wide-hatted country people. This is how man should travel — crawling across the earth's surface mile by leisurely slow mile, stopping to chat, stopping to sip golden tea in a village teahouse, staying the night only when the dark came. Why should it matter when I start or when I arrive? Why should I arrive at all? For in China there is no beginning and no end, no time and no destination. Tomorrow is as good as today. I can say: 'The journey will take me a week or a month. Does it matter?' Unhurry! That was the word. The sun was hot and the dust felt good underfoot. Forgotten for a moment were those thirty long miles ahead, while I, the wayfarer, the Marco Polo, stretched myself by the roadside with my dusty boots out straight and smoked a cigarette in the land of Han.

Chengchow was a near shambles. Frequent shellings, over thirty bombing raids on the open city, three thousand civilians already killed and many more wounded — that was her record to date. She was easy prey. The Japanese lines were less than ten miles away. When, almost a year before, the Japanese captured Kaifeng, fifty miles to the east, the fate of Chengchow hung in the balance. A queer thing saved her. When the Japanese had advanced to within a few miles of the city walls, the retreating Chinese dynamited the Yellow River's dikes, just above the city; the waters rushed in between the advancing enemy and the besieged town, carving out a new river bed. Today the great Huang Ho, that used to flow northward into the sea, flows eastward between Chengchow and Kaifeng, and on toward the coast until it empties into the Huai River. The Japanese have not yet been able to cross it. Chengchow is still a front-line city, her days numbered. But at the time of our visit and to this day her trade has been booming, her markets crowded, and her commercial life intact among the ruins.

The American mission hospital where we stayed was up to its neck in cholera, refugees, air-raid wounded, and bombs. It lay next door to a military headquarters which was a favorite target of the Japanese, who frequently miss their mark. To date, some twenty-nine bombs had fallen within the hospital compound. The missionaries were not a mass of nerves because they apparently had none.

They insisted that we go out to see the dynamited break in the river dike. We needed little urging. It was one of the most historic spots in all China, and except for the local missionaries, no foreigner had yet seen that famous break. Even before we came within sight of the river the trenches began. It was a well-defended sector. The Chinese troops looked well clothed, disciplined, and very bored. Things had been quite dull up here, they said. We commiserated with them and wandered on toward the river. There we could see it! A few inches of water still trickled in the old wide river bed, giving the appearance of two rivers forking.

The new course cut away from the old at right angles and flowed calmly through what had once been fields and villages. The opposite bank supposedly marked the beginning of Japanese territory, but we saw no sign of life. The river's edge where we now stood was honeycombed with dugouts and machine-gun emplacements, connected by winding trenches. At the moment the guerrillas were absorbed in millet soup, one of the humble but staple foods of North China. They grinned and made me sit down to eat with them, and when I choked over the tasteless gruel, they grinned all the more.

'It is splendid,' one of them told me. 'We have nothing to do but keep the Japanese from crossing the Huang Ho. And that is so very easy. We need only to toss a pebble at them. Perhaps we shall be here for the rest of our lives.'

'Now you are boasting.'

'Of course,' he laughed.

But so far he has been right.

Two days later this same front exploded into life. At a feast in the honor of the departing mission doctor and his wife, we asked the Chengchow garrison commander, General Shun, for permission to cross the river and pay a visit to Japanese-occupied Kaifeng. The procedure was not unusual; foreigners were frequently given passes by both the Chinese and Japanese to cross between the two cities. This day, the permission was refused us. Carefully General Shun explained that there was to be a major battle the following day. We listened, amused, to his remarkable statement, thinking it an excuse for refusing us the pass. On the following morning, the guerrillas that infested the region between the two cities stormed Kaifeng in one of the famous battles of the year. Three times they broke into the city. The local Chinese puppets were summarily put to the sword; there were high casualties among the Japanese garrison. Prudence and the knowledge that reinforcements would soon arrive for their beleaguered enemy prevented the Chinese from taking the city outright; the blow to Japan was merely loss of face. Perhaps it made her think twice before attempting to force a river crossing. But the three-day attack upon strongly garrisoned Kaifeng was the equivalent of a shot of rum to Wei Li-huang's guerrillas. Everyone in Chengchow beamed at everyone else these days.

One night after dark I attended a meeting in a small, half-ruined Chinese church near the hospital compound. It was a private meeting of the Chengchow directors of our 'Wounded Soldier' organization. We sat about a flickering vegetable-oil lamp in a dusty office and drank tea out of porcelain bowls. Maps were thumbed. Locations for mobile medical units were chosen. I learned that the organization had actually been started here, by the Chinese Christians of Chengchow. Many months ago when heavy fighting went on in the Yangtze Valley and Nanking was about to fall, trainload after trainload of wounded soldiers began to move through Chengchow. The soldiers were in transit to western hospitals; which meant in this case that they were in a quite horrible condition. Confusion ran the war in those days. The people of Chengchow, visiting the trains as they lay over in the station, found the wounded lying upon the bare boards without bedding. Some had had no water or food for too long a time. Their undressed wounds were already festering. In many cases, the December frost had molded the soldiers fast to the floor boards of the car, held there by their own frozen blood.

So Chengchow became very busy. Hundreds of volunteers were organized into relief units to board the trains, give the wounded tea and rice, dress their wounds, cover them with blankets, and save an impressive number of lives. Because the troop trains ran only at night, the hours between dark and dawn were interrupted with one emergency call after another. It became so difficult to round up the workers every hour or so that all volunteers decided to sleep on the floor of the church, where they could be ready and on call. They slept on that stone floor every night for a good many months, until the Japanese took Kaifeng and the railroad was torn up. But their little organization grew. It grew until it began to care for nearly all the transient wounded in China's war.

I looked about the office, at the dark heads of these pastors and church elders bowed over the map while the lamplight dimmed and flared; and I had a sudden feeling of repetition, as if this scene were an old and familiar one, re-enacted a hundred times; as if I knew it well. There had been so many others like it since my arrival in Free China. Staring hypnotically at the pencil flame upon the lamp wick, I dreamed them again — those candlelit moments. Many months ago in Hengyang, there had been a meeting like this of the 'Wounded Soldier' workers. The little meeting-room in the basement of the church had been decorated that evening with wreaths and a flurry of red ribbon in honor of Christmas. There had been the same dust, the same shaking lamplight, the same soft, intent voices talking plans and budgets and ending with a prayer. The young pastor who took us into his home for the night during the long journey to Sian — he had been like this, too. His industrial relief work in the city had made that place a haven for all refugees. Instead of a lamp, there had been a candle on the table when we sat down to dine with him in the gathering dawn, and he had placed bowls of hot delicacies before us, and bending his head in the yellow light had asked us to say grace.

Scene after scene — so many of them! I had not thought that the Chinese Christians would be like this. Along with a good many of my generation, I held in my mind, side by side with an honest belief in God and Christ, a dim sense of apology for my religion. Perhaps it was distrust of religious language which can be so embarrassingly sentimental and unintelligent; perhaps an adolescent fear of being thought pious. Age-old prejudices ran through my mind now and melted with the lamplight. 'The missionary has no business forcing Christianity upon another race.' — 'The Chinese are just as well off without our Christianity. Other religions are pretty good, too.' — 'What good does our religion do the Chinese anyway? Why don't we let them alone?' — 'these "rice bowl" Christians out in China. . . .'

Tonight I faced a plain fact which could no longer be explained away. The Chinese Christians were, with few exceptions, the strongest members of their race. They were leaders in the Government, leaders in education, especially leaders in relief and sacrifice; but always — leaders. A few Chinese, born into Christian families, accept their Christianity as we do, with a good deal of nonchalance — something to be turned on and off like a faucet. A few have probably adopted it for what they can gain by it. But most of them have taken on this new creed for better or for worse only after some strenuous thinking; and like their Generalissimo, they have a curious way of taking it literally. Always a practical people, they remold it from a creed into a way of living.

It is an astounding thing to see the potential strength in our religion suddenly come to life; to see what it can do when it is free of complacency and piety and borderline fanaticism and sentimentalism and the everlasting compromise with which we smother it. What now of this missionary business? The missionary's work as I saw it was largely medical or educational; but the making of new Christians was part of it, too. I had noticed with some relief that the missionary made no dogmatic claims that his religion was the only truth. Nevertheless, he did tell the story of Christ and the message he brought to anyone who cared to know. It could still be called 'conversion,' and that word usually made me snort in exasperated scorn.

Once a Chinese pastor had told me: 'Don't you think my people have a right to know about Christ? Don't you see what a comfort it can be for them? Yes, and power, too?' And I had thought, 'I've never looked at it just that way.'

The scene came back with a rush. The pastor had been addressing a large crowd on a village street outside of Hanchow, where we had visited the Christian seminary on the road to Sian. I had tagged along with him to watch him preach, and my tongue was still lodged firmly in my cheek. Now the audience was drifting gradually away; but a few still lingered. One woman began edging up to us, eager to speak but still hesitant. She was a country woman, rather old, dressed in shapeless blue trousers and jacket, her head bound around with a dusty cloth. Like so many Chinese, she had grown beautiful with age, brown skin drawn tight across her almond face and high round cheekbones, a thousand wrinkles at the corners of her eyes from too much laughter.

Very puzzled, she said to the pastor, 'Please may I ask, Hsiensheng, but did you not say that our sins may be forgiven?'

'Yes, old one, that is what I said.'

The woman protested. 'But how can that be true! I have borne my sins with me since I was in my green years, and always the weight has been heavy.'

'I am sorry, old mother. You need not have done that. Right now you have only to ask God to forgive your sins and help you to sin no more. He will hear you.'

It was good evangelist talk, and I grinned to myself. But the old woman stared at him. 'Did this Jesus person tell you?'

'This Jesus told me.'

'And I can get rid of my sins?'

'Yes, old mother.'

'And Jesus' God will help me to stop sinning?'

'If you ask him to.'

The last of her doubt went away, and I was not prepared for her emotion. I forgot that in this moment the most intimate and

useless burden of her life had been swept away. Now she cried
and laughed together. She squinted through a thousand smiles
and wiped dirt and tears noisily and happily upon the hem of her
jacket. She shuffled off down the road, finally, muttering 'Jesus'
God. Jesus' God,' to no one in particular . . .

The lamplight flickered and the scene closed.

The story of Chengchow is more or less the story of Jang Jin Ju.
I saw him first while I was dangling my feet over the edge of a
trench in the mission compound waiting for an air raid. The raid
had turned out a false alarm, and I was just folding up my moving-picture equipment and preparing to stand up, when I happened to glance around full into his face. Jang Jin smiled.
He was only a thin young coolie; but there was something immortal about his smile. It was a huge China-boy grin-from-ear-to-
ear, a mouth tilting in pure glee, a reeling blissful slitting of the
eyes, a hooligan smile, a Dopey Dwarf smile! It came on like
an electric torch.

Just then a group of refugee children who had been playing in a
bomb hole came over toward him. They clustered around the
older boy, who seemed to be their hero.

'Show us your arm, Jang Jin! Show us your arm!'

With a start, I noticed for the first time that his sleeve was
empty. He rolled it up now and proudly displayed the red stump
of his wrist to the admiring group. 'The doctors are always sticking needles in there,' he explained carelessly, 'just as if it did not
hurt at all!'

As I strolled back from the trenches with the American doctor's
wife, I heard someone stumping along at our heels. It was Jang
Jin; and with another start and a feeling almost of pain (for I felt
I knew him intimately), I saw that his leg was off above the knee.
But his wooden-legged hobble was suspiciously like a swagger, and
he grinned rapturously at our rears.

'That's our office-boy coolie,' explained the doctor's wife, a lady of ample bosom and Irish humor. 'His full name is Jang Jin Ju, but we call him Jang Jin. He may look awkward, but it amazes me how he gets around. He can run races on that leg of his. He follows me about like a faithful hound, perfectly happy. If I look at him, I think he stops breathing.

'Sometimes,' she chatted on, 'I forget about his hand and give him some hard job to do; but he usually gets it done somehow. You should see him file papers with his shoulder and chin. If I do anything for myself these days, the boy's insulted. He's helping with the out-patients just now, and I could swear he knows every patient in the hospital by name and ailment. The children too. He plays with them by the hour. In his queer way, he is almost an adopted parent to everything small on the compound.'

I felt a little skeptical about this. There seemed to me a gleam in Jang Jin's eye that was anything but paternal.

'Does he always stay with you during raids?' I asked.

'Jang Jin? He's a perfect rabbit about these raids. You should see him tremble all over and hold his nose and try to disappear into the earth. People who have been wounded once are apt to be like that. It's odd, he always brushes his teeth after a raid, the only time we can get him to brush them. To get the gunpowder out! He claims he does not care for anything Japanese in his mouth.'

'What's going to happen to him now?' I asked. 'Aren't you two going home on furlough this month?'

'Well, we were going to send him away to a camp with the other cripples,' answered the doctor's wife. 'He's not our servant really, you know — just a refugee boy in here for treatment. We gave him a little work to do and he's stuck to us like a burr ever since.'

Jang Jin, stumping along near us and perfectly aware that he was being talked about, was struggling with his facial expression in a terrible effort to appear nonchalant. Finally he gave it up and smirked.

'When the word got about,' went on his mistress, 'that the cripples on the compound were to be sent to a camp, Jang Jin came
to us by himself. In all my born days I've never seen a boy cry
like that. He literally flung himself at our feet and sobbed and
wept and clung to us until we had to promise he could stay on and
serve us when we get back. Mercy, he almost had me in tears!
My husband swears it was all an act, but I don't know...'

Her voice trailed off. I looked over at Jang Jin, caught one
more blast of that supreme and impudent smile, and silently
agreed with the husband.

Later in the morning I was being shown about the hospital by
an American Red Cross worker who lived on the Baptist compound. As we entered the out-patients' waiting-room where a
hundred or more refugee sick huddled on benches, a voice of
authority rang out from the front of the room, giving instructions
to the waiting crowd. I stared. It was Jang Jin, and he was
strutting it up and down before his respectful flock like a dictator
before his troops, herding the patients into the various examination rooms, and calling out names in exact imitation of the mission
doctor in charge. The doctor's inflection, the note of authority,
the manner of twitching the head — Jang Jin did it all without a
tremor. And apparently without a pang, for he caught our eye
and only smiled upon us like a saint.

'He's an actor,' I said, as we went outside.

'Have you ever heard him recite poetry?' asked the Red Cross
worker, with a sort of convulsive heave at the memory.

'Poetry!'

'Well, yes — I guess that's what it is. His own poetry! He
just makes it up as he goes along and reels it off for half an hour
without a break. Rather decent poetry, too. At least he thinks so.
Get him to make some up for you. He's not exactly shy about it,
anyway!'

It was the next morning that I ran into Jang Jin while out walking in the compound. He was sitting propped up against a mat shed in the center of the yard feeding a refugee baby from a milk bottle. Around him stood his usual contingent of admiring children. The sight was so startling that I stopped and watched. He held the small creature along the crotch of his mutilated left arm, as gently and firmly as it had ever been held before, while the right hand administered the milk. He seemed quite expert about it.

As I strolled up he smiled angelically at me and before I had time to say a word had inquired about my honorable name, health, and native home. He further offered the information that he was sixteen years old, and how old was I? There is nothing very bashful about Jang Jin. For a moment we exchanged polite formalities.

'How did you lose your leg, Jang Jin?' I asked. For he obviously felt nothing but pride in the matter.

'Bombed!' he said, and grinned in slitted rapture. 'I was at the station, just arrived, you understand, when suddenly airplanes came and dropped their bomb eggs.' Here his hand planed down through the air and he emitted through his nose such a perfect imitation of a power-dive that I involuntarily squeaked.

'Yes, I know,' I said hurriedly. 'I've heard them too. But what about your hand?'

'Oh, that came later,' he explained. 'First they took my leg away in the hospital here. It was very uncomfortable,' he added with what I thought to be unnecessary understatement. 'That was when I was robbed.'

'Robbed?'

'Of everything,' he said. 'Five dollars. So I obtained my wooden leg and went out and begged for three months.'

'Oh, Jang Jin, what a shame!' I said.

'A shame? But no. I was very good at it. I saved eight dollars and bought a new white suit for just a dollar fifty. That was before somebody took it,' he said sadly.

I digested this a moment.

'You mean you were robbed again?' I asked, feeling a little confused.

'Oh, no; I lent it to a man. He had no suit, you see, and he
promised to bring it back that night. But he never came.'

There was silence for a minute while we wordlessly mourned the
white suit.

'After that my hand grew sick and I came back to the hospital
to have it removed too. They are very kind to me here. I must
stay forever, I think, and look after them,' he finished with a sigh
of martyrdom.

'But what about your family, Jang Jin?' I asked. 'Do they
know where you are?'

'My family?' For a moment his air of Puckish vanity disappeared and he spoke with a trace of bitterness. 'The Japanese
have taken care of my family. We all left Peiping by train last
year, my father and mother and brother, and the train was
bombed. When I woke up beside the track, I had no family. The
Japanese took very good care of them by blowing them to pieces.'

I tried to think of something to say.

'What did you do then?' I asked lamely.

'I walked to Hankow,' he said, watching me slant-eyed to see if
I were impressed.

'But it's hundreds of miles!'

His smile came on again.

'Oh, yes. But very good exercise!'

'What do you do during raids?' I asked.

'Oh, I used to go outside the city where it is safe,' he told me
with perfect frankness. 'But I kept thinking about these people
here. The foreigners, you know. The doctor's wife is deaf in one
ear and I must be here to warn her.'

I remembered his terror of raids and smiled inwardly.

'The bombs always come here,' he added 'They fill your ears

with noise and your mouth with Japanese powder.' The thought caused him to spit accurately at a passing toad.

The baby, bored with so much conversation, began to weep bitterly and Jang Jin was all anxious parent again, rocking the thing with real tenderness and administering milk with the air of an *amah*. As I walked away I heard this paradoxical youth crooning to the child in a strange minor chant. And I began to see why nobody on the mission compound could fathom Jang Jin and why everyone on the compound loved him.

The following day of early April was a day of terror for Chengchow. Although the people of the city had had weekly bombings since the beginning of the war, nothing in all their experience could equal the vicious treatment that was dealt them on this day.

The first alarm wailed forth at noon. We hurried from the luncheon table to the trenches. There is no time in Chengchow for a dignified retreat. The Japanese are too near. Often the planes are overhead by the time the alarm rings out. And the mission compound is no place to be caught out of cover. We crouched in the trenches that stretched through an open space in back of the hospital mat shed where I had talked with Jang Jin the day before. For what seemed hours, the planes power-dived over the city, dropping their bombs with dainty and careful precision. No anti-aircraft to annoy them. No defense, no machine guns, nothing. We waited helplessly while the ground shook and the air beat to each explosive roar and the world went mad.

This time, our section of the city was unaccountably left alone. Five minutes after the planes had left, the hospital ambulance was clanging through the city to the bombed areas. And in the press of work to be done, we forgot that the 'all clear' signal had not sounded.

Then word came: a building in one of the hospital's refugee camps had been completely leveled; more than half of the four hundred refugee women and their children who had been inside, just sitting down to lunch, were dead, others wounded. Soon they began streaming in, by ambulance, by stretcher, women with wounded babies, husbands carrying their injured wives, children afoot holding on to their mutilated bodies and keeping back the tears as they had been taught to do. Shrapnel can make unbelievable wreckage of human flesh. Other wounded from all parts of the city were brought in until the compound was littered with them as with dying leaves. The hospital was long since overflowing. Now the serious cases were taken inside for immediate operation, while the overflow were laid, about a hundred of them, on the floor of the flimsy mat shed, where the doctor's wife and two other American nurses gave them first aid until there should be room for them elsewhere.

It was fully an hour after the raid, and still no one had thought of the 'all clear' signal. I was standing near the compound gate with the Red Cross worker when without warning we heard the low familiar drone of heavy bombers in the air. We hurried to the trenches, where already many people had taken shelter. There we stood while the drone grew into a roar and the planes were near. Suddenly the mission doctor's voice sounded above the waiting silence.

'Is my wife here somewhere?'

For a moment no one spoke.

'The mat shed!' Somebody yelled with a touch of hysteria. 'Three of them in there. Haven't come out yet!'

Realization struck us. The noise of the wounded and dying within the mat shed was more than enough to drown out any amount of bombers. The three women had had no warning. Overhead the planes dipped their noses down into the start of a screaming dive. Instinctively and foolishly we all started to climb out of the trenches at once. But someone was ahead of us. Someone who, even before the doctor spoke, had remembered his mistress's deaf ear.

It was Jang Jin. He materialized from behind us, stumping along at a dead run, cleared the trench in one clumsy, impossible, peg-legged leap, stumbled, caught himself, and flew on like an avenging spirit. Head back, arms flapping wildly, he streaked over the ground as if some invisible deity had him by the scruff of the neck. Then he disappeared into the mat shed and a moment later we saw the bombs start down, directly toward us, from the low-diving planes. We were in for it!

As we huddled back into the trench, the world about us erupted into thunder. This time, five bombs exploded on the compound. Two burst in the doctor's garden, one by the gate, one fifty feet from our trench and only thirty from the mat shed door, just where it would have caught anyone coming out. The last to fall seemed to make a direct hit on the mat shed itself. For long minutes we held our aching ears while dirt and débris rained about us, and we watched the great pall of smoke and dust and gunpowder that hid the flimsy shed from our sight. It was a heart-breaking moment. There seemed to be no hope for those within. Then the drone of the planes died away, the dust thinned out, and we gaped at a mat shed which apparently was not even damaged. Only an ugly crater lay alongside, its lip resting affectionately against the straw matting of the wall.

It was that close! Six feet from the wall — a good-sized bomb. It had cut down thirty trees in the garden around us. The force of the explosion had all been spent in the opposite direction, and the building was so flexible that it merely swayed back and forth and failed to collapse. But what of the occupants? We started in a concentrated rush for the door. Inside there was dead silence and smoke. The wounded lying about the floor were too shocked to speak or groan. Standing up in the center of the room were the two missionary ladies and the doctor's wife.

'Don't look so distressed. We're perfectly all right,' she said in a matter-of-fact voice.

'You couldn't be,' someone blithered foolishly. 'The bomb exploded against the wall.'

'Yes, and we're as deaf as posts, all of us,' she said with a snort. 'But not a soul in the place seems to be scratched. We were just starting out the door when Jang Jin blew in like a ghost and said the planes were overhead. So of course we crouched down where we were. I'll never get this gravel out of my hair!'

'You were starting out the door,' said her husband in a tight voice. 'You would have met the big one that burst about thirty feet outside.'

There was a queer silence.

'Where's Jang Jin?' I asked.

Nobody knew.

'I didn't see where he went,' said the doctor's wife with a sudden look of fear on her face. 'But he must be ...'

We all began looking for him at once in the murky dust; frantically at first, with our hearts in our throats. Not Jang Jin! Not after that crazy wild run of his under the diving planes. Not with his terror of bombs.

'Jang Jin!' yelled the doctor. 'Where are you?'

We waited in a gathering silence. At last a small fluttering sound came from across the room. We stared. There was a low bench near the door. And from beneath the bench protruded two skinny legs — one wooden, one sound — and a small, tightly clad rear that quivered and shook like an agitated jelly.

'Here, sir,' whispered Jang Jin ...

There was a full moon that night. It shone with cold benevolence upon the gaping ruins of the city. I stood for some time by my window listening to the night sounds that are pretty much the same the world over. No sound of suffering, no groans or sighs, though many people lay awake in agony and watched this same indifferent moon. Only the crickets' song and the wary rustle of a dark garden.

Then, as I listened, a discordant noise broke the near-silence. Down by the kitchen door a suppressed struggle was under way. It began with a low gurgle, grew from a gurgle to a rasp, from a rasp to a gargle, from a gargle to a perfect furor of spitting.

I looked down through the moonlight at a slim familiar form — one-handed, peg-legged. Jang Jin was brushing his teeth.

8

CO-OPERATIVES

It was mid-April when we arrived in Sian, the long strange road from Chengchow safely behind us. Skipper was as anxious as I to study the Industrial Co-operatives at their Paochi headquarters. On the morning after our arrival, before I had found time to draw more than half a dozen breaths and slip a batch of articles into the mail, he had shoved me aboard a westbound train.

The Chinese Industrial Co-operatives, now nicknamed 'Indusco,' were first outlined in detail early in the war by a Shanghai group of old China hands which included Rewi Alley, Edgar Snow, and a brilliant young Chinese, K. P. Liu, who told me the story over hot wine and *pao-tze* in a Chungking restaurant. In 1938, 'K. P.' received a telegram out of the blue ordering him to fly to Hankow and join in organizing Co-operatives in West China; Madame Chiang and H. H. Kung had agreed to sponsor the idea with a very practical loan of $5,000,000. The movement was under way.

Today there are two thousand Industrial Co-operatives in Free China. Before the end of the war, the leaders of the group hope to have thirty thousand in full swing. Loans from the Central Government and Chungking banks, and private gifts from China and from abroad, so far total close to $27,000,000 in Chinese currency. In spite of government backing, Indusco remains a private organization, with both foreigners and Chinese in charge; in close touch and co-operating with them are the missionaries. The commodities turned out by the Co-operatives include almost every necessity on record: soap, paper, cotton goods, shoes, stockings, towels, woollen blankets, medical supplies, glass, pottery, foodstuffs. There are mining Co-ops to produce raw materials, machine shop Co-ops to repair tools, transport Co-ops to distribute the finished products, and Co-operative Stores to sell them. There are Co-ops for tanning, dyeing, sugar-refining, contracting, carpentry, and printing. The complete list would make dizzy reading.

Each Co-operative is started by a technical engineer and a financial organizer who go out together as two apostles. They study an assigned region, decide what can be manufactured most profitably from the available materials and most easily sold, then gather the necessary craftsmen from among the local refugees who are ready to give the thing a try. If skilled workers are lacking in the district, refugee workers are imported from danger zones near the front and settled in the chosen spot with their new industry. Failing that, destitute refugees are brought together in classes and taught the craft. While the engineer orders the proper machinery and tools from the factories, the organizer arranges for a short- and a long-term loan, the first to cover running expenses for a year, the second to take care of overhead. Each loan is at very low interest rates. The workers then buy their shares, not less than three nor more than twenty shares a piece. Most of them pay in credit to be gradually worked off, in cash if they have such a thing. A committee of all the workers is set up to run the Co-operative. A man may have but one vote on this governing board, no matter how many shares he owns. Through the board, with the organizer acting as paternal advisor for the first few months, the workers decide their own hours, set their wages.

'Well,' the organizer will say at the preliminary conference of workers, 'how much would you like to pay yourselves?'

'Really! We pay ourselves?'

Immediately wages would skyrocket.

'Very well, now, how high will you price your article so that you can still make money?'

Down would come the wages.

Once under way, there was seldom chance for failure. The demand for every commodity in blockaded Free China was too great. As the profits began to flow, a certain percentage was set aside for interest and payment of loans. The remainder was divided in a multitude of ways: 15 per cent for bonus, 20 per cent reserve for emergencies, 10 per cent for expansion, 10 per cent for a mysterious item called the 'Common Good Fund,' and other incidentals. A good many Co-ops have already paid off their loans, some of them prematurely. Among the two thousand, there have been two or three failures and one case of dishonesty.

The Co-ops are units of free enterprise. They may exploit themselves by long hours and strict rules as much as they like. They can grow as rich as they please. But the allotment of a single vote to each worker, the rule against absentee ownership of shares, and the limitation on the share control supply the needed check against the old life of misery and exploitation these men had once known in the factories. Whatever they do within their own Co-operative is of their own choosing. It makes a difference.

So far I had seen only isolated Co-ops in various cities of the South and later on in Szechwan. In Paochi, I was to see them *en masse*. The little town at the end of the Lunghai Railroad, once a small and sleepy place, had grown overnight into a young metropolis. One more western boom town had come to China! Squatting on the railhead, a long way from the Japanese, it was the logical reservoir for the flood of refugees from the east. Paochi was the photographic replica of an American boom town. Her

streets were an uproar of feverish crowd and carnival. They became rivers of mud with every rain. The flimsy wooden stores
wore false fronts. The town had long since burst her walls. The
East Gate now lay close to the center of the business district.

There were thirty-five Co-ops in Paochi on the day we arrived
(now there are many times that number), and the place was beginning to be known as Co-op City. The executive staff, in charge
of all the Co-operatives in the Northwest, was housed in a lattice-
walled room which served as office and sleeping-quarters for three
Chinese district leaders and one visiting Englishman from the
Science Institute at Lanchow. The place was a glorious mess of
desks, cots, typewriters, and executives. I was astonished to find
that the room was part of the official quarters of the *hsien* magistrate, Mr. Wang, a thoroughly surprising gentleman. A long-time
Christian, this quiet little man ate, slept, and dreamed Co-operatives, preached at Sunday services, conducted wide administra-
tive and educational reforms in the county, and with the help of
nine college-graduate helpers ruled a model *hsien*. He welcomed
us as if we had been old comrades. Sleeping-space was at a
premium; therefore he put up a cot for me in his own office and
installed Skipper in his dining-room.

The richest gentleman in town called upon us the next morning
and promptly offered me the use of his blooded stallion. When he
produced the beast, I could hardly trust my eyes. Not yet in my
lifetime have I seen a more beautiful horse.

'He is the result,' said his owner, 'of many generations of
cross-breeding between Arabian and other Asiatic stock.'

The stallion was black as ebony lacquer, thick-haired, his mane
and tail brushed into midnight rain. Long inaction had left him
straining to run. He was rearing and half wild. Mounted, I set
forth with a guide to visit the Co-operatives some miles outside
the city; but I felt rather like an Arabian princess upon a royal
steed. The horse and I released a good deal of the aching energy

within us that day. We scattered dust, chickens, and laughing
country people like chaff in our wake.

The Co-operatives at work in the country about Paochi were
thriving little affairs, some lodged in mud-walled compounds,
some in caves. The tools were home-made but competent; the
workers lived in shacks and adjoining caves. Cotton-spinning
and towel-weaving Co-ops used the same type of wooden spinning-
wheels and looms once part of colonial life in America. In the
yard of a cave-dwelling soap Co-operative, workers were pounding
out the gleaming cakes in a stream of never-ending conversation.
Two young women, both nursing their babies, stood at their husbands' elbows and made admiring comments upon the weather,
the female foreigner, and the excellence of their soap. The group
wore such broad and unceasing smiles, I was afraid that they
would split their faces. One by one the babies were thrust into
my arms to be held until they wept. More were produced from
the cave interiors for my inspection.

'Is it really so good here?' I asked, inviting any complaints
that might be troubling them.

'Yes, it is good,' the smiling woman said. 'There is nothing of
badness here.'

'In Hankow,' added her friend, 'our husbands worked twelve
hours a day and received forty cents. Here they can work ten
and make three times as much.'

'Ah, but she is homesick!' her husband railed at her. 'These
women of ours, they think of nothing but visits with each other
and a wasting of time at the market. Here in the country they
will surely pine away. When we have won this war, we shall have
to return to Hankow and set up our Co-operative there in the
busiest street in town.'

'Yes, it is lonesome,' the woman agreed. 'But without this we
would have starved, I think.'

'And you have learned to run a Co-operative,' I added.

'That is the best of all,' she said simply.

Near-by a group of crippled soldiers were running a spinning Co-op; they were part of several thousand legless or armless men — awkward, half-helpless, wild with inaction, facing an apparently hopeless future — who had been taught to work in spite of handicaps, and were once more laboring for China and making themselves independent in the process. They fell all over themselves, showing me the glories of their small Co-op; they fought to give me information, interrupting themselves a hundred times; they were not going to move from this glorious spot for the rest of their unworthy lives.

The men in the carpentry Co-op were not so enthusiastic.

'It is very dull here,' one said. 'But we make good money. Of course the men are all anxious to get back to the city.'

'Will you continue your Co-operative?' I asked him.

'Naturally,' was the surprised answer. 'But not here. It is a good system, do you not agree? Of course you know that it is also doing much for our country. We will have to keep it going, for it gives us a chance to be patriots.'

He spoke the literal truth. The little guerrilla industries were doing quite a job for Free China. They were killing many birds with a single stone. They build up transport systems, put new life and energy into backward villages; they have so far provided work — in China it is the same as life — for at least three hundred and fifty thousand people; they are so mobile that they can operate at the edge of battle lines without fear of capture; they are too small to be easily bombed; they improve housing and living conditions and standardize products so that repair materials will be available. Take the blanket Co-ops for instance: wool had formerly been an export product; then the Co-op organizers, who dearly love to utilize local raw materials in combatting Japan's blockade, put a few thousand half-starved people to work making blankets out of the wool; the blankets, in turn, were bought up by the Central Government for distribution to other half-starved people. The system has a certain fascination. One can pick so few flaws. Natural resources are being used, goods produced, and people saved. In spite of the small number of these Co-operatives, experts insist that their produce has already done much to lighten Free China's needs. More and more cities are depending on the Co-operative Stores for their purchases. Co-ops have been organized in every province of China except Kiangsu. They are becoming a national institution.

'Queer beggars — these people,' the visiting Englishman remarked that night, as we huddled about the stove where the tea was brewing. 'Try to get them into Co-operatives and they won't do it because they're afraid they won't be able to pay back their loan. Especially the country women. Cautious as the devil. But tell them, "This work helps China," and they fall all over themselves wanting to begin.'

He told me something about the agricultural Co-operatives he had been organizing near Lanchow. These rural Co-operatives, sometimes called 'credit societies,' are more simply formed out of a single farming village or family; the eldest and most respected is chosen as its head and the group is given a loan with which to buy farming tools and seed. Whereupon the farms are under way. The rural Co-ops had been a feature of Chiang's government for the past ten years. In this spring of 1939, they were increasing literally at the rate of ten thousand a month.

According to the Englishman, the country people (95 per cent of China's citizens are farmers) scarcely know what dishonesty is. A loan to the Chinese is probably the safest loan conceivable. He had just called on a rural Co-op on the way to Paochi. He had had a hard time getting them started; they had no savings and were afraid of a loan. Finally he said, 'Buy chickens with loan, sell eggs, save money,' to the wife of each family. The system worked. When he visited them last week, they were making a four-hun-

dred-dollar yearly profit. In fact, the leader of the Co-operative
had gone in to Lanchow just the day before with enough money
to pay back the entire loan.

'You mean he carried it on his person?' the Englishman asked
them with his thoughts full of bandits.

'Oh, no!' they laughed at him. 'He took a big sack of
grain in to market. And in the middle of the grain was the
money.'

The next morning I wandered down the main street of Paochi
marveling at the number of little triangles that were painted upon
doorways and compound gates, triangles that were symbols of
Indusco. The busiest building in town was the local Y.M.C.A.,
built by the Co-op leaders (all of whom are Christian for the simple reason that nearly all educated people in China are Christians)
and now the community center for the whole crowded little city.
Non-Christians as well as Christians jammed its services and
social affairs. The Buddhists and Taoists in town were having
quite a good time learning hymns. In fact, the place was so popular it was all one could do to squeeze through the door when something was going on.

I began to realize that Indusco's biggest contribution was
perhaps outside the pale of finance altogether. Its leaders had
large-scale reconstruction on the brain. They did much more
than organize Co-operatives; they started new schools for children
and adults, classes in co-operative living for the workers, recreation clubs, Y.M.C.A's, women's clubs, new co-operative newspapers and magazines, libraries, dramatic societies, evening
meetings for group discussion on present conditions in China, and
community singing. They had already set up eight new schools
in Paochi for any and all refugee children, and sixty more were
scheduled to open within the next fortnight!

At the headquarters of the women's Northwest Co-operatives,
a certain Miss Chow told me with some pride that they had to

date started twenty adult-education classes for their women workers, with room for a thousand pupils. She was full of another enterprise that morning: a spinning and textile training class for destitute women who would later be formed into a weaving Co-op. I glanced at the curriculum of the class and almost giggled. It included Economics, Politics, Reading, Present Conditions in China, and Singing.

I was taken out by Miss Chow to visit a spinning Co-op near-by. The women sat spinning out-of-doors in the hot sun-filled courtyard. They nodded and smiled at me, and something in their mood caught me and made me want to sing.

One girl could not have been more than sixteen. Miss Chow saw the direction of my stare.

'That is Wu Chao-ti,' she explained to me in English, and the girl, hearing her name, looked away in embarrassment. 'She came here from Hankow with her parents. Her father sells eggs. Her mother was killed in a bombing here quite a while ago. Then a soldier who lived in the cave next to them fell in love with her. He was forty and very ugly, so they say. But the father had not enough to feed his daughter and so promised her to the soldier. She refused. But it could not be for long. Just in time we heard about her and invited her to join this Co-operative. Now she makes enough money for her father too. She is so happy we cannot look at her without a good feeling inside of us.'

While we stood in the courtyard, a small and ragged boy came up to us.

'Are you the head lady?' he asked Miss Chow with a worried frown.

She nodded.

'Then you must do something to help my mother,' he said with great firmness. 'She was to have joined the textile ladies here. But yesterday morning a girl baby was born to her. She says that now they will not want her, for she is too weak to work. She has been crying all yesterday and last night and today, T'ai T'ai, and she grows very sick.'

Miss Chow was indignant. We followed the boy into his cave home near-by. The woman lay upon her clay *k'ang* with a single covering over her. The baby was held in the arms of another woman. The mother was young and her face was swollen from constant weeping.

Miss Chow lost no time. 'It is all right,' she said, 'you are still coming to work with us. You will come in a month from now when you are well.'

The expression on the girl's face made me grin foolishly for minutes afterward. So much incredulous joy is good to remember. That day it spoke eloquently for the Industrial Co-operative.

The night before we left Paochi, the local school for organizers graduated its current class with some justifiable ceremony. Organizers of Co-operatives naturally did not grow upon trees. They had to be basically educated to begin with, and young — because the life was not an easy one. Since Indusco is a complex affair, they must also complete a long stiff course in Co-operative organization. Consequently, when they start out on the road to begin their work, they are worth their weight in precious stones.

The Commencement exercises had a solemn pace. The students and engineers gathered there were almost overcome with the feeling that they embarked tonight upon a new life. Many of them had given up highly paid jobs in the cities to come out and do this thing. Co-ops were in their blood. They sensed a chance to work for China in the broadest sense. In a curious way they were evangelists. The mood was catching. I felt idiotically happy. It was the same mood that infected the workers, the same mood that had spread through this brawling city like fire. The people had become aware of co-operation not only as a way of working but as a way of life. They buzzed around like bees, flocked to mass meetings, worked overtime, plastered their walls with slogans. They were suddenly patriots!

Curled up in a third-class compartment of the Sian-bound train, I purred comfortably and meditated Co-ops. They were so neatly designed to fit permanently into China's way of life; an industrial version of the family unit that is the backbone of the land. The over-powering conscientiousness of the Chinese will continue to make them good risks. Long after the war, banks will be eager to lend and as loans are paid off, the money can be used again and again as a perpetually revolving fund. The industrial and agricultural Co-op could become a good and strong means toward recovery. Certainly there was no sign among the workers that they would be ready to give up the experiment with the coming of peace. Even the humblest son of the humblest laborer suffered from a malignant case of Co-operative-on-the-brain. China was made for small industry. The concentration of populations in villages and country districts, the poor conditions in the cities, the familiarity of small units, all pointed towards Co-operatives. Some day, consumers' Co-ops might follow.

Just for fun, I took out my notebook and began to form a list. I had reached the bottom of the second page when Skipper peered over my shoulder. I read it to him:

'Co-ops,' it went, somewhat abbreviated. 'New relief units. New Life Movement. Very many new schools in every *hsien*, supported by the Government and charity of the villagers. New colleges and medical schools. The Science Institute in Lanchow cleaning up the province and doing experiments in improved livestock and planting — right in the middle of a war. Jimmy Yen down in Hunan heading up the Rural Reconstruction Something-or-other. Women all over the place fighting in battles, doing propaganda work and teaching behind the lines, nursing the wounded, forming a million and one committees, taking on all the dirty work, traveling with the armies as relief workers, dashing about doing God knows what, etc. . . .'

'Don't swear,' said Skipper, giggling.

'... As much mileage of roads and railroads built in Free China since the war as existed in all of China before the war. New libraries. New industries galore. Patriotic songs sung all over the streets. New decent young officials. New blood in the army. New orphanages...'

I began to run down.

Just then one of the other passengers in the compartment strode over to the window and looked out in vast excitement. He was a lean, serious young man who peered out behind large tortoise-shell glasses.

'Look!' he said to us, speaking in English. 'You can see there now. The river, do you not?'

We looked and agreed that we saw the river.

'And you see the dam, of course? I do not wish to boast, but it was I who built the dam. Now we are working on the canals, all throughout this valley. You can see them everywhere. They have made our valley fertile. It is, you understand, part of the Government's irrigation project. Already we have watered many thousands of square kilograms. So splendid, you think?'

'Well, well,' said Skipper in a choked voice.

It was the last straw.

═══(9)═══

GUEST OF THE GUERRILLAS

ON OUR return to Sian, we found Bill Djang and Andy Roy in wait for us and virtually watering at the mouth. An invitation had reached them from Marshal Yen Hsi-shan, Commander of the Shansi-Hopeh war zone, to visit his hidden headquarters in eastern Shensi, then cross the Yellow River into Shansi, and, with a guerrilla escort, make a survey of medical needs and set up mobile dressing stations behind the Japanese lines. The invitation included the honorable Doctor Brown and the but slightly less honorable Miss Homer.

We were flattered. Only one foreigner, an Englishman, had been permitted to glimpse that part of China since the beginning of the war, when even the missionaries were forced to leave. It was an active, isolated sector, clothed in secrecy and considered inaccessible. Marshal Yen we knew from hearsay. For the past twenty years he had been Governor of Shansi, which he first developed into China's 'model province' and then permitted to return to its former chaos while he concentrated upon the more enchanting development of his personal bank account. Since the war, his loyalties had once more transferred themselves from Marshal Yen to the welfare of China. Unfortunately his province of Shansi fell an early prey to the Japanese. But within the past few months, the wily old war lord had made a brilliant comeback.

From his provincial capital, now moved across the Huang Ho to
Shensi, he continued to direct the affairs of his province. His
command embraced all the Chinese armies that infested Japanese-
occupied Shansi and Hopeh, from the Yellow River to the sea,
including even the famous Eighth Route Army, a command which
he seldom exercised. Recently his troops had won several important victories in southwest Shansi. We suspected that possibly
the Marshal was beginning to resent the publicity bestowed upon
the Communist armies and had decided to be a little less secretive about himself.

Our guide was to be one of Yen's secretaries, a certain Colonel
Tien, who became in the end a kind of uncle — or perhaps aunt
— to the expedition. The Colonel, slim, brown-faced, peered
cheerfully at the world through horn-rimmed glasses and, for
all his perennial smile, took himself very seriously. Warfare and
danger did not disturb him; but the world bothered him a lot; he
fussed over its small details like the aforementioned aunt. He
carried a thermos bottle under his arm as if it were his first-born,
and when it broke he almost wept. He was terrified of running
out of gas, of falling off his horse. Metaphorically he tucked us in
bed every night. A graduate of an American university in the
twenties, he was in the embarrassing position of having forgotten
most of the English which his employers imagined he spoke flu-
ently; his laborious slang smacked of the jazz age. But before we
parted, a month later, we had grown unexpectedly fond of the
little man.

It was decided then that we would progress in Eva via the
road due north to Lochuan, head eastward in a four-gear army
truck over a mountain road (the mention of which caused a shudder to burst from Colonel Tien) to Yen's headquarters, cross the
Huang Ho into Japanese territory, and after a tour of no man's
land continue on north in Eva to Yenan and the Communist
areas.

The sun gleamed upon Eva's emerald roof as we sallied forth that morning in early May. There is something about Eva — she does not start forth, she inevitably sallies. Behind us in Sian the air-raid sirens sounded; here was one raid which would not disturb us. During that first day, we drove through the valley of the Wei, already green with young wheat. The valley had been used by some of the earliest emperors as a graveyard; their tombs were vast mounds of earth, some a hundred yards across, and a hundred, two hundred feet high — queer old pyramids of West China that lay like monstrous haystacks upon the valley floor. The river's tributaries confronted us, one after another. Many and devious were the methods of fording these streams, part of a book that should one day be written on 'Chinese Bridges.' If there was a bridge at all, it would be a curious structure built upon wooden stilts, rather like a row of marching storks and just about as reliable. For the wider rivers, ferries were used; actually they were small rafts, and the process of maneuvering a truck onto a small raft always left me wringing wet and nervous as a hound. By far the neatest arrangement was the concrete runway spread flat upon the river bed, which acted as an excellent bridge when the stream was dry and an equally efficient ford during flood. Occasionally Eva had to ford a river without any bridges, ferries, or runways, but absolutely on her own; in order not to stall in midstream, she took these waterways at top speed, gurgling, blowing, water above her fenders and a stupendous wake. They were very wet affairs.

Our first night was spent in a hayloft at Yowchow. It was the last soft bed we were to experience for two months, and it gave us fleas.

On the next day we covered exactly twenty disreputable miles. An all-night rain had transformed the narrow dirt road into a sea of mud. Mountains, cliffs, and steep grades added to our misery and to Eva's. We soon lost count of the number of times we left

the road altogether and squelched down soggily in a wheatfield.
As a last resort, we commandeered a brace of oxen to haul us
over the mountains. And thus did our truck arrive at the town
of Ichüen, towed behind the two impassive animals, half-ob-
literated in mud, with a cracked gasket and a broken spring.

The night was spent in nursing Eva through her latest illness.
By four in the morning her gasket was patched and her springs
upholstered with a wad of Chinese straw shoes. We were able to
reach Lochuan by noon. There we transferred to the rear of an
army truck, already jammed with supplies and a dozen guerrillas.
It was to take us east to Ichuan, from where on the next day we
could walk to Yen's headquarters.

This eastern Shensi was wild country. As we thundered and
bounced on our way, I noticed that scarcely any life moved
among the bare brown mountains. Here wolves ran in packs; we
could hear them bay as the dark came, and now and then catch a
glimpse of one. Wildcats were common enough. Once a small
tiger slunk across the road in front of us; I was startled, for I had
associated tigers only with Chinese paintings, not — somehow —
with China.

This last stretch of road constituted for all of us the worst experience that the Northwest had to offer. One of our companions
in the back of the truck, an engineer who had worked on the road,
confessed that some of the grades were well over forty per cent.
The statement meant little to me at the time; I only knew that
on certain hills where the truck stalled and we were forced to
walk, we unconsciously went up sideways, digging in the edges of
our boots for leverage.

'This road,' explained the engineer apologetically, 'it was ordered by Marshal Yen after he had established his headquarters
here in Shensi. The distance is one hundred miles and he gave us
but three days in which to build it. Since then it has been getting
worse.'

A moment later he added that only two trucks a week were sent over the road — big Dodge trucks with four gears; and the drivers received a day or so in bed after each trip.

Well, well!

It was generally a ledge, with a cliff rising straight up on one side and a yawning drop on the other. Unfortunately, when the truck stalled on the impossible grades — a frequent occurrence — the brakes and gear were not sufficient to keep it from sliding backward down the mountain and probably off the precipice. To forestall this, the mechanic would leap out and hastily jam a wooden wedge behind one of the rear wheels. It was typical of his race, that day, that the wedge was kept in the rear of the truck beneath the feet of several absent-minded guerrillas.

Once they lost it altogether. The truck had stalled on an outside curve with its snout high in the air and was sliding down not too slowly toward the brink of the canyon. For agonizing seconds we all fumbled for that wedge. When it was found and frantically lodged in place, there was less than one foot to spare between it and the road's lip. On the next grade the mechanic was so rattled that he dropped the wedge over the cliff. Instantly the truck was thundering backward down the narrow ledge. Most of us jumped. There was a scrambling of arms and legs along the road. Then the driver, who had kept his head, crashed the truck rear on into the face of the cliff, the only course of action which could have saved us.

By the time we reached the foot of the mountain range, it was dark and our driver was thoroughly, and frequently, sick to his stomach. And when, late that night, we crawled at last into the little terminal town of Ichuan, we were all of us in something of the same condition. I think the memory of that road and the knowledge that we must return over it again haunted us like a family ghost throughout the fortnight that lay ahead.

The next day's travel was on foot, to the 'secret' headquarters of Marshal Yen. Colonel Tien would use that term, although it made us feel ridiculously subterranean and spy-like. As it turned out, it was nothing if not secret, that headquarters. The ten miles of footpath, scarcely visible in the long grassy bottomland, followed the wandering of a river. It was a cold blue stream that ran between shelving rocks. Every mile or so we stopped to dangle our toes in the water, while occasional travelers and mule-drivers along the path gazed at us in silent laughter. It was a wonderful ten miles. It took us ten hours. When, near sundown, we arrived at the famous headquarters, we were so filled with the dusty dreams of that day, so cowishly contented and somnam-bulant, that the abode of Marshal Yen scarcely struck us as odd at all.

It was a wild, impossible place, this city of soldiers; exotic, per-haps, but intensely practical. In a gully between steep hills sharp as cliffs, the men had built themselves a cave city. The thick loess soil of the canyon-sides had been shaved down, as neatly as if it were yellow cement, into a series of terraces. Each story was connected with the next by loess stairways cut into the soil, that zigzagged like a fire-escape up the side of a skyscraper. Along every platform were spaced the cave doorways, hundreds of them, each covered by an attractive latticework. The floor of the canyon had in its turn been shaved as smooth as a tennis court; it was a wide yellow avenue stretched taut between the storied city. Only one building stood in the gully — the great assembly hall built entirely of loess without a trace of betraying color. Here in their city of caves, some four thousand young Chinese officers were in training, secure and hidden by the face-less yellow soil in which they lived. Japanese pilots, perfectly aware of the general location of the place, took their bombers constantly overhead, blindly looking for this valley in which there was no man-made thing to give itself away.

We were assigned to a second-story cave halfway up the valley.

It was exactly like the others, about forty feet deep, dark and cool. A table and three or four stools were the only furnishings. Along one side of the cave ran a solid loess platform or *k'ang*, of the consistency of concrete; this was our communal bed, built to sleep fifteen or twenty occupants. For the next six weeks we were to occupy nothing but *k'angs*, the traditional bed of North China. We would spread our bedding on the waist-high dais, side by side, head to wall, crawl between our *pukais*, and sleep like so many laid-out corpses. Frequently various members of the Chinese army would share our *k'ang* with us. As time went on, I thought nothing of going to bed with twelve or fifteen gentlemen at once; a fact which did not ruffle Bill in the least, even after I married him.

In the caves adjoining our own were a crowd of what I took to be students, including several quite lovely young girls. They were, we discovered, a traveling troupe of actors and actresses, sent out as patriot government workers to keep up the morale of the army. (Dozens of these volunteer troupes of professional players were touring the army camps, even to the front line.) They were as intrigued with us as we with them. Gathering in a semicircle about our doorway, they began to sing songs for us, difficult songs, some of them in parts. The party became hilarious, the audience enormous. Before the débâcle was over, the troupe had railroaded even me into singing for them, which was a horrible experience for everyone concerned. At the end, a young boy of twelve or thirteen, dressed in the faded blue uniform of the Eighth Route Army, sang us a few songs in a high, clear voice. He was the much spoiled mascot of the camp, this Communist soldier; and remembering constant reports of the strained relations between Yen's troops and the Communist armies, I filed away the information with some surprise.

The next morning we had our long-awaited interview with Yen. It lasted two hours and covered a good deal of technical ground.

Marshal Yen himself, far from being the pompous war lord we had half-expected to see, turned out to be a wily, dyspeptic old man. His face was ordinary enough, but the gleam in his pouched eyes betrayed his intelligence. It changed him from a pleasant old gentleman with chronic indigestion into a brilliant old rascal. Today there was an air of smugness about him. He had made a spectacular comeback, and he knew it.

The conversation covered many things, most of them vital to China.

'The success of my guerrillas?' He used his hands like a Frenchman. 'But you do not understand. My soldiers are not guerrillas in the usual sense of the term. They are organized for large-scale warfare. But they use ambush, surprise attack, desperate forays; like your General — what was his name? — Mad Anthony.'

Our eyes opened wider, as he meant them to do.

'My men here are trained here by the Communists of the North, who are very skillful,' he went on, and I stared even more. 'It is not to our advantage just yet to stage great offensives or retake cities, except to maintain morale. Our present objective is to draw the Japanese into the open away from the protection of their city walls. We attack the highways and railroads. We catch our enemies as they bring back supplies, which is, you must see, quite profitable. Only last week we mined a hillside on either side of a Japanese railroad. When a troop train passed, our little landslide saved us from wasting a single bullet.'

We nodded without skepticism. Chungking had already acknowledged the Marshal's claims.

'What about your losses, Marshal Yen?'

'So far about eighty thousand dead and ninety thousand wounded,' was the reply. It sounded plausible enough. 'At first,' he went on, 'our losses were over four to one in favor of Japan. Later they became about equal. Now, in my own terri-

tory at least, the losses are one to thirteen in our favor. Today
there is nothing worth while for the enemy to capture. The last
time that the Japanese attacked Chihsien, for instance, they lost
seven thousand men and took the empty town and three days
later were forced to give it up. From now on, Japan must face
all losses and no gains. Already this is telling upon the morale of
her soldiers.'

The Marshal was feeling pretty good that day. His own magistrates, he told us, were governing in all but one *hsien* of Shansi.

'What about your wounded?' I asked. 'How do you get them
to base hospitals on this side of the river?'

For a moment Yen looked a little tired. His answer was simple
enough. With the roads destroyed, it took over two weeks to
move a man from the front by stretcher to proper medical treatment in the rear. By that time it was generally too late, though
the villagers, organized into stretcher corps, were doing what
they could. Emergency hospitals hidden in the Shansi mountains
saved the light wounded. Supplies, too, were hard to transport.
Like the Eighth Route Army, his men were often dependent upon
what they could capture from the Japanese. Ammunition? It,
too, was for the most part captured booty, though the small
arms could be made in local blacksmith shops.

For two hours Yen talked on. Within a few days, we should
know how much truth existed in his words. Finally, as he rose to
go, I asked him a question which curiosity always forced me to
ask and which inevitably sounded foolish when I had asked it.
But he only grinned.

'Opinion of the Japanese?' His face became dead-pan, but
there was a glimmer of amusement in his eyes. 'Their people I
do not know. Probably I would like them. To their military I
do but two things: I hate them; and I thank them. For how many
centuries — you can name them — the private slogan of our government has been "Keep the people ignorant!" Always our

enemy has been the people of China; the people, that is, when they happen to discover what their government is up to. In their ignorance lay our safety and our stored-away fortunes. Now Japan, our enemy, has forced us to educate these people. Japan has forced us at last to unite. Japan has caused us to be clean and decent in our ruling and to take pride in our justice. It is a very good joke. Our land is no longer ignorant and helpless. Our Japanese friends have waked us up!'

His lips twitched. He turned around, drew in his slight paunch with both hands, and strode out into the sunlight.

There was an eclipse of the moon that night. The camp newspaper (it is typical of China now that a guerrilla band should have its own daily paper) had predicted the event for some time. Down on the floor of the valley the soldiers had gathered, several thousand of them, trim in their neat uniforms. According to their nightly tradition, they hunched before a great bonfire and sang their marching songs. The men knew them by heart and roared them out well. They were patterned on the calls of the coolies and trackers; strong and minor and a little savage. They echoed the pulse beats of the Huang Ho and the measured pace of camels and the wild lost dust of these loess hills.

While the men sang the moon rose free of the mountains. At first it was round and white. But half an hour later the shadow began its creeping march. The soldiers sang louder, feeling the drama of the moment, squatting on their heels with chins in air staring at that slow segment of black upon the moon's face. When the last white crescent was swallowed into the eclipse, a sigh went up from the men. Then a boy's voice broke into the soft minor chant of the Yangtze oarsmen: '*Ho hi-ee ho* ...' Others took it up, and the song swelled; swelled and swelled and then grew hideous. An enchantment came upon the valley. Our bonfire burned in Aladdin's city. The chant was a Tartar yell. This grotesque place of caves, the dark, and the singing and the unnatural moon all at once grew mad as a fairy tale. And in that moment New China seemed to die and the heart of dark old Asia came to life.

Then the moon crept forth. The singing died. The world swung back through time. Without speaking, we lit our candles and went about our business.

Soon after dawn we were sent on our way by a crowd of grinning generals and colonels. From now on we traveled on ponies. They were homely little beasts, imported from the Mongolian deserts, shaggy and tough and as unpredictable as mules. They crossed places I would have sworn no hoofed creature could have trod.

The footpath we followed that day ran at first along a ledge overhanging a river. Then it began abruptly cutting across those loess mountains, almost as if the mountains were not there. A good deal of the time we had to walk. The dusty little paths were so steep we could scarcely get a foothold on the soil. Climbing, we sidled up crabwise, digging in our boots for leverage. On the way down, horses, packmules, and the rest of us sat upon our respective backsides and slid.

Once we came to what looked to be an impasse. A thirty-foot section of the path, which at that moment was a dusty little two-foot ledge halfway up a cliff, had fallen away into loose dirt. Below us yawned a hundred-foot drop onto the floor of the gully. We stood silently gazing over the edge with mental goose-pimples standing out all over us. Finally Skipper, who knew these horses better than the rest of us, mounted without a word, backed a few feet, and started across at a fast trot. The loose dirt gave beneath every step of the pony's hoofs. If his full weight had once landed on the crumbling earth, it would have been all over. But his feet kept up a running balance along the ledgeless ledge. Four seconds later, he and Skipper were smugly laughing at us from the far side of the break. Dumbly we stared at each other.

Just as dumbly we mounted and sped across that thirty feet of void. From that moment, when the going was too difficult for our human extremities, we turned matters over to our superior ponies and left it up to them.

The day wore on with no food and not very much water. This land was a wasteland of yellow mountains, rock, and no trees, and I cursed it heartily. There had been no question of loading our already overloaded mules with special provisions. We had trusted to luck that there would be villages or teahouses along the way. Luck was not always with us. It was a wild and deserted region. We covered forty miles that day, neither fed nor watered. To my bilious eye, the endless mountains, the dust, the disagreeable little white paths winding up and down and up, developed into a nightmare.

All at once I became increasingly aware of a low murmur that had been in our ears most of the day. It was no longer a murmur. It was a far-off roar.

'What is it?' I called ahead.

Colonel Tien turned around and shouted two words:

'Huang Ho!'

We almost cheered. They had told us that we should probably reach the Huang Ho before dark. But we had forgotten the elusive monster. For the next hour the roaring grew in our ears. How could water thunder like that? There must be a falls. Then without warning we topped a mountain and the yell of the great river hit us like the blow of a fist. It lay there uncoiled a thousand feet below us, barely visible in the graying light.

There was a falls! The Yellow River Falls — why had we not heard of it? That ponderous mass of sulphur water flung off a sheer cliff into a canyon so narrow and so deep that an eighty-pound weight attached to one mile of rope had failed to find the bottom.

'That is greatest falls in Asia,' remarked Colonel Tien com·

placently. 'No one knows because no one come here ever.'

For a moment we stood in the barren twilight looking down into that wild, mist-filled canyon, and I think all of us felt a little scared. We climbed down the cliff-face, ledge by ledge, our incredible horses scrambling and slithering behind us. Every moment I expected them to descend upon the back of my neck.

Some two hundred feet above the water, the path became a ledge, cut parallel to the river along the cliff's face and overhanging the yellow flood. For a while the ledge was wide and safe. Skipper and I rode at a gallop, leaving the rest of the party some miles behind. Once a machine-gun emplacement, a round igloo of gray rock, loomed out of the half-dark ahead, and the crew yelled with delight as we thundered past.

This was all very well. But as the minutes wore on, the night came down over the gorge without a moon. The ledge gradually narrowed to a width of less than a yard. Our ponies' hoofs clicked on the extreme edge. We had to sit them sideways with our heels above the dark maelstrom, while the cliff-wall brushed their flanks. Somewhere below, the river thundered on unseen, its spray misting our faces. The indistinct outlines of the gorge had faded into total blackness. We had no flashlight with us. The tiny ledge was rough and boulder-filled.

In rising panic I yelled ahead: 'Skipper! How about waiting for the others?'

There was no answer. Perhaps he did not hear me over the roar of the water. I tried again.

'It's too dark!' I howled. 'The horses will fall. Oh, damn!'

Skipper, thinking I was close behind, had forged ahead into the night, and the only sound that answered me was the uproar far below and the pounding of my own heart. If there had been some convenient bedclothes at hand, I should have dived beneath them.

The next moment my horse lost his footing on the narrow ledge and fell. He fell forward in a complete somersault. I had just time to shove forward out from the stirrup and the ledge came up and hit me. The impetus rolled me over twice with my legs out above space. Behind me in the darkness, the pony floundered. How we managed to stage our acrobatics on that strip of rock I shall never quite understand. For the space of perhaps five seconds there was no sound or movement from either of us. Then I wakened to the fact that I was stomach down with my legs dangling. I drew them up gingerly and got to my knees. Feeling my way backward, I found the pony crouching with legs curled beneath him. I hauled his head up.

For a moment we stood trembling. Then we started on, because there was not much else to do. But this time, without a twinge of conscience, I sent my pony ahead of me and cheerfully clung to his tail.

Twenty long minutes later I saw lights ahead. Skipper's unrepentant voice hailed me from the darkness. Soon we were drinking millet soup in the village stables which were to be our lodgings for the night.

This little town, perched jauntily upon the river cliff, formed the western terminus of the ferry crossing that connected Shensi with her sister province Shansi, Chinese territory with the territory of Japan. Shortly before our arrival, a Japanese artillery unit had hauled a single cannon atop the Shansi mountain across the gorge and, obviously unable to ford that patch of white water, had hurled indignant shells at the village. The townspeople had watched from a safe distance.

'It was very good sport,' one of them told us, 'to perceive those expensive shells wasted upon our mud huts.'

Another remarked seriously: 'We cannot understand how the enemy managed to take their cannon up the mountain-side. There is no road for one hundred miles from here. They must be very clever, do you not agree?'

We agreed. Japanese troops sometimes have a way of accomplishing the impossible. Quick in admiration were their enemies the Chinese.

As long as I live I shall not forget the ferry crossing. Here was the one stretch of river for several hundred miles which could be crossed — and that only because there were three convenient backwaters, one just below our village, the other two along the farther bank at points about a quarter of a mile above and below us. Only a backwater would permit a boat to land without smashing itself to pieces against the shelving cliffs. The river was deep (according to the Chinese, an improbable one mile), and the current was a millstream, a torrent of bilious yellow water lipping back in high rapids as neat as a marcel wave.

Our homemade ferry was built along the general lines of a gigantic washtub. Without further ceremony, we were herded down the cliff and into its round interior. The horses were picked up bodily and deposited in our midst. Then with one man braced at the tiller and, in the bow, twelve half-naked oarsmen standing to the two massive oars, we pushed out into the current. For one wild minute we swept sideways down the white water, the boatmen half-yelling, half-singing to give beat to the oars, the helmsman shrieking directions above the roar of the river, horses milling and boogery, the old boat groaning and leaking in every humble seam.

A soldier bellowed cheerfully in my ear, 'If we miss the backwater we will terminate in Tungkwan in pieces.'

We did not miss the backwater. A moment later, the tumult and the shouting died and we stepped quietly out upon the shores of Shansi, the territory of Japan.

If anything, the land here seemed drier than ever. It looked very much like our Grand Canyon, but scabby and yellow. What seemed to be corrugated mountains and a maze of valleys were actually part of a vast loess tableland, crossed and criss-

crossed with deep gullies and crevasses that had been dug in the
soft soil by long-dead streams. It was strange to wind through
the unnatural gorges, to climb achingly to the top of a dusty
mountain and come out instead upon a high fertile plateau of
young grain. Something almost grotesque, deformed, about this
loess land.

Once occupied by the Japanese, it was now a kind of no man's
land, fought and refought over in the seesaw warfare for which
the province is famous. A town would be held one day by the
Chinese, the next by the Japanese, and a week later again by the
Chinese. Valleys were captured and recaptured, cities burned
and rebuilt. There was no specific front, no trenches or well-
defined lines. Here the Japanese held the major cities, while the
guerrillas, in front of them, in back of them, on all sides, harried
and worried their enemies, sometimes driving them out, sometimes fleeing before them in swift unseen retreat. It was a queer
land and a sudden land. It was also a devastated place. Burned
villages, little ruined teahouses by the path, gave mute evidence
of the not too pretty war that was being waged in these secret
valleys.

Today, from seven in the morning until sundown, the pale dust
curled with studied insolence around our ponies' hoofs. We clung
to our saddles when we thought no one was looking; we stared
over the hot vista of hills upon furrowed hills, all apparently
for us to climb; we felt very pale. By this time we were used to
the scarcity of food. But today there was no water. Eight hours
of travel and blazing sun found us seriously thirsty. At mid-
afternoon we sighted a cave village halfway down a cliff-side and
we felt better. No food, perhaps, but certainly water. Laboriously, with our tongues hanging out, we climbed down the
ledge.

On the platform before the cave mouths, a single mule, bony
and raw with open sores, was harnessed like Samson to a mill-

stone, shuffling around his ordained circle. The mule was blind. Beside him stood a brown-faced woman in ragged trousers and blouse. Trash was collected in fly-covered heaps upon the loess ledge. The place had an unexplained air of misery and decay. Something was wrong.

Skipper wandered into the nearest cave while the rest of us negotiated with the woman for water. A moment later I heard his voice: 'Joy, come here a moment.'

I blinked my eyes in the dimness of the cave. Stretched along the *k'ang* I could just make out a number of forms lying upon their bedding. The eyes of the nearest man glittered unnaturally in the darkness.

'Typhoid,' said Skipper briefly. 'Everyone in the village is down with it except the woman outside.'

We did what we could for them, but there was not very much to do. The water we boiled and drank gratefully, too thankful to worry about pollution. There was a lump of dirty brown sugar left in my bedding roll and I idly offered it to the blind mule. At my unseen touch he drew back shuddering. I nuzzled the sugar into his mouth. For a moment he licked and mumbled it. Then suddenly he thrust himself forward, squealing, not like a mule, blindly, crazily hunting my hand for more.

When we left, the woman scarcely glanced in our direction. The blind mule once more paced in unbroken rhythm about his millstone. The heaps of trash and human excrement crusted beneath the sun. In the mouth of the first cave the flies were thick, but no sound came forth. Here in China does tragedy seldom retain her grace, but only her detail, shuddering and dirty, and without pathos.

The events of that day gave us no hint of the queer little climax that lay ahead. It was nearly sundown when something startling occurred. From the other side of a valley, far in front of us, a soldier, dressed in guerrilla uniform, suddenly sprang to his feet.

For a moment he appeared to study us intently. Then he turned
and fled in the opposite direction, whipping around the edge of
the mountain like a frightened stag. This seemed a little odd,
but we were by this time immune to curiosity. When, a few
moments later, we rounded the bend of the mountain, we saw
to the left of us and about half a mile away a cave village that was
inhabited. Standing in a flat meadow not far from us was the
soldier, and he was signaling frantically with his coat to the village above.

'What's going on?' we asked Colonel Tien.

'He is signal,' said the Colonel succinctly. He smirked to himself.

'Yes, of course,' we said. 'But what about?'

'About us. So that they telephone.'

'Telephone!' We were a little dazed.

'To Chihsien, the *hsien* city ahead a little. So that they know
we arrive there. All right?' went on the patient Colonel.

It was our first warning of what was to come. We noticed the
single telephone wire that had been strung across the wild country and we felt rather awed. An hour later as we were fording a
river, there was an abrupt clatter of hoofs and a rider on a pure
white stallion wheeled his horse from its solitary vigil on the opposite bank and rode away at a mad gallop. We eyed this
phenomenon in silence.

'He is messenger. Gone to announce mayor we are come. All
okey?' said Colonel Tien, with a touch of complacency. His face
by this time wore a permanent smile. But it seemed to him good
American university technique to keep us guessing.

So the mayor knew about us too! Probably he wished to prepare his tea table in advance. I thought back on all I had heard
of Chihsien. It was once the largest city in the county, a big
place of some seventy thousand citizens, with rich land and prosperous farmers all around its walls. That was before the Japanese

arrived. They had come over a year before, had burned the city, and executed about five hundred of the citizens. A week later the guerrillas had stormed and retaken Chihsien, driving the Japanese out of the county. The people had flocked back to their burned homes, determined to try again. New homes were built. The city boomed once more. Then in January the Japanese returned, this time with full mechanized units. But the citizens had become wise; they packed their belongings and furniture and children onto their donkeys and mules, and disappeared into the hidden valleys. The Japanese forces entered a totally deserted city, stripped bare of every removable article. They stayed three days this time before they finally burned the newly built homes and withdrew before the attacks of the Chinese. Then for the second time the people of Chihsien came back to their charred old city, to rebuild their houses, reopen their shops, and carry on as before with the Japanese still only twenty miles away. So ran the story of Chihsien as I had heard it, and hearing it had wondered for perhaps the hundredth time at the quiet perseverance of this race.

The drumming hoofs of the messenger's horse died away in the distance, and for some time we followed in silence. The sun settled red behind us. A whisper of cool wind crept through the thick spring heat. A moment later we crossed a bend in the river and saw before us the big mud walls of Chihsien, a mile down the valley.

We stopped our horses and simply gaped. It was not the familiar sight of a city wall that made us stare. It was the people. At least we supposed they were people — those little insect things gathered in a great black swarm outside the city gate and stretching toward us for half a mile along the road. It couldn't be! But it was. The entire city of Chihsien, come out to meet us! We stared with bulging eyes and perspired freely.

'That is reception committee come to meet,' said Colonel Tien happily. 'They wait in the sun since three o'clock. It is time now, I think, to get out and walk. All righty?'

We dismounted and, leading our horses, began to walk toward the waiting multitude. They had evidently seen us, for there was great confusion, calling of last-minute orders, assembling of ranks, and frenzied straightening of hats and banners. By the time we reached them the furor had ceased. They were lined up in perfect formation, four deep on either side of the road — the citizens of Chihsien, many thousand strong, dressed in their Sunday best.

A little group came forward to meet us, comprised of the mayor, the *hsien* magistrate, and a few leading citizens. Introductions, bowings and scrapings followed, while the long line of citizenry stood sternly to attention and tried not to crane their necks in our direction. Another delegation now approached us. They were the Christians of the city, forming a special welcoming committee of their own. And there was nothing polite or conventional about their wild joy at our coming. They had been carrying on by themselves since the war began, quietly assuming most of the responsibility for feeding the wounded and destitute and organizing relief work throughout the countryside. We were the first fellow Christians to come that way in two years of warfare and hard work. We shook hands carefully all around, and they smiled and smiled.

Followed by the welcoming committee, we started through the close-packed ranks toward the city gate. First in line were the able-bodied men, strong sun-blackened farmers, most of them, who grinned and saluted us awkwardly as we passed. All during that queer triumphal march, they shouted slogans. They sang songs of welcome. They even sang us a eulogy on American relief workers which had apparently been composed for the occasion and learned by the entire community. Thousands of voices proclaimed our praise, and I think we had the grace to blush.

Once a band of trumpeters greeted us with a splitting blast, each trumpeter embarking on a different melody. After the men came the women, who clapped and cheered as we went by. Last of all were the children, standing with heads back and stomachs out in self-conscious ranks, all the way from responsible middle-school graduates down to bowlegged two-year-olds in stiff padded jackets. The children joined in the singing and slogans, waved their banners, clapped their hands, and, for want of variety, simply shrieked.

I walked on and on between those cheering ranks, conscious of my incredibly dirty face, the dust over my uniform, the small rip in the seat of my pants. I wanted to tell these grinning, clamoring people that they were all wrong; that we were nobody important and deserved none of this and it must all be a mistake. I also, being hopelessly feminine, wanted to cry.

Through the city gate and along the main street we marched. Behind us the orderly ranks closed in and followed us in scrambling bedlam. Inside the city were massed the old and the feeble, the sick and the unimportant among Chihsien's citizens. These were also armed with flags and with excellent voice-power. They laughed and shouted as we went by, and their children broke away and ran beside us, grasping our hands and tugging us along.

On doors and walls and against the trunks of trees were plastered long bright banners of welcome. 'America is the Trunk of World Peace!' they proclaimed in graceful characters. 'Welcome to the Americans, the Long-Time Friends of the Chinese People'; or again, 'Our Deepest Gratitude to Miss Homer, Doctor Brown, and Mr. Roy, Who Have Come a Great Distance and Endured Many Hardships for Our Sakes!' We gasped as we saw our names. We gasped even more at the thought of enduring hardships. Were saddle sores hardships?

During that mile-long processional I looked about me with

some curiosity. A city twice burned and twice rebuilt was an absorbing business. Everywhere the blackened heaps had been cleaned up, the débris cleared away, the fallen tiles and bricks piled up in neat walls to shield the ruins. The new houses which lined the main street were made of mud walls and straw or tile roofs; not so easily burned as their wooden predecessors. Cosy little shops were open for business. Mud huts seemed to be springing up everywhere. Half-burned homes were sometimes occupied by several families. Every scrap of shelter was a home. Charred jagged walls were smoothed over and used again.

We walked on through that grotesque old city with her people marching and singing behind us. Looking down, I saw that the rough stone street had been washed that day, washed and scrubbed until it seemed to shine.

Even before we reached our lodgings, a crowd of soldiers led us into a ruined courtyard where a young guerrilla lay upon a pallet. A rifle bullet had fractured his thigh. Gangrene had already set in, and without surgical implements there was not much we could do. He was a startlingly handsome boy, flushed now with fever and half out of his head, but with an angular face that was strong and intelligent. He was the type of man one does not care to see die in battle. Skipper redressed his wound, while half the townspeople gathered round him. They trusted implicitly that the American could cure the wounded soldier with his foreign medicine. Only the soldier himself knew better, for he was an educated boy. As Skipper finished the dressing, he grew more and more embarrassed.

'Please, Hsien-sheng, do not stop so long over this wound. You are very tired. You must not stay with me. Please, Hsien-sheng, go now.'

We left him, feeling wholly abashed and helpless and angry. And the crowd stared at us wondering, not quite believing that we should desert him so.

They were a strange lot — the people of Chihsien. Of all the provinces of China, Shansi had suffered most. The highly organized guerrilla warfare of the Eighth Route Army which had operated in the north of the province since the first months of the war had made it a favorite victim of Japan's reprisals. Every Chinese raid brought with it the inevitable Japanese revenge of burned villages and slaughtered country people. Chihsien had had its full share of horror. The entire *hsien* had been ravaged with a thoroughness that was difficult to believe. Close to the city, we visited a cave village of twenty-eight inhabitants that had stood off the attacking Japanese army for five days. When the little place finally fell, the men and children were hacked to pieces and tossed into a heap, the women raped and thrown over the cliff's edge; one story which I was able personally to corroborate.

Yet here were the citizens of the county so high in morale, so efficiently organized, that it was difficult to tell a civilian from a soldier. The students sent out from Yen's universities were the experts in charge. They had divided the civilian population of the entire district into units, each unit to give a certain number of its working hours to the army. Farmers and merchants were trained as auxiliary defense corps; schoolchildren were drilled in emergency measures; men and women both were organized into stretcher units, medical and transport bodies. A small percentage of each farmer's crops and livestock was commandeered by the army, but taxes were almost eliminated and the people given a far better deal than they were accustomed to hope for in peace-time. The policy on the part of the Chinese army is universal throughout the country, and it is not based upon sentiment. Only by treating the civilians with courtesy and good will could it hope for their co-operation; and it is needless to point out that guerrilla warfare behind the enemy lines is dependent upon the active help of the people, who must feed the army, help to clothe

it, transport its goods, care for its wounded, back up the defense
line, and be trusted not to disclose the secret operations which are
the backbone of guerrilla tactics. Curiously enough, what started
out as a hard-headed policy of appeasement has grown into a
friendship between the soldier and civilian, an enthusiastic
brotherhood with fiery ideals of liberty and sacrifice. And since
every Japanese-occupied city is virtually under siege, an island
of resistance in the midst of a vast guerrilla country, Shansi is
today one of the strongholds of Chiang Kai-shek's China.

The following dawn saw us escorted on our way by more enthusiastic citizens of Chihsien. That day was dogged with a
series of incidents, a bad day all around. Andy Roy was the first
victim. His horse, in the act of fording a stream, decided to lie
down and have a good old-fashioned roll; it was especially unfortunate because it struck the rest of us as extremely funny.
Skipper did not laugh long; he crossed the same stream via a
narrow bridge that arched some ten feet above the brook. Both
he and his horse fell over sideways into the rushing water. Why
they were not both slaughtered on the sharp rocks I shall never
know; but as they emerged dripping, I could swear that the
horse was laughing, and Skipper was indulging in mild hysterics
and swallowing a large part of the stream.

My own turn came at noon. I was sitting in the shade of a
small straw-and-bamboo shelter eating my second and last meal
of the day (hard-boiled duck eggs), when a gust of wind simply
removed the shelter, setting it down in a dismal heap some ten
feet away and leaving me just sitting there with my eggs.

Our destination was to be the headquarters of the Sixty-First
Army, which was holding an attacking Japanese force at bay
outside the conquered city of Linfen. This army had already
made a name for itself in the annals of the war, and we were
anxious to study its technique. All along the route, that day, we
were given the same reception accorded us at Chihsien. Word

of our coming would precede us in some mysterious fashion. At
every village the citizens were lined up to receive us. There would
be more singing, more slogans, innumerable cups of tea. We
spoke at several mass meetings. It was an exhilarating business,
this: to sight a village in the distance and watch the villagers, who
had sighted us at the same moment, swarming down the hillsides
to the path, running hard, falling over themselves, in order to
form ranks and be ready for us by the time we reached the spot.
We began to feel rather like royalty on tour. Our reception in
China had been remarkable enough from the moment we set
foot upon Wenchow; but its climax was reached here in the
isolated province of Shansi. We were the first relief workers to
enter this part of the province; we were the first Americans most
of them had ever seen. Americans! The people were beside themselves, half-hysterical.

It was nearly dark when we reached the advance base of the
Sixty-First Army, where the officers were quartered. Its commander, General Chen, received us with embarrassing ceremony,
while the soldiers lined up by the thousands and cheered our arrival. Here, lodged in the ruins of an ancient temple, we made our
headquarters for the next week. In the adjoining valley, heavy
fighting went on day and night, as the Japanese tried to force
their way through to our base camp. We had to be prepared at
any moment for a fast evacuation, should the defending line give
way. In the cluster of homes and shops that surrounded the temple barracks, the village people went their chatty way as casually
as if this war had never been, as if they were in quiet peace instead of parked upon the edge of a major battle on an exception-
ally flimsy front. But all of them, civilians and soldiers alike,
were masters of the art of swift retreat; it is said that the guerrillas often covered two hundred _li_ (about sixty-five miles) in a
single march. Privately we hoped that we should be able to keep
up with them, and privately doubted it.

Certain things about this front-line camp taxed my credulity a little. Next to the walls of General Chen's private quarters lay a good clay tennis court, relic of anti-war days; the fat little General, Skipper, Andy, and I had some fast sets of doubles on that court. I never quite accumulated the courage to ask how it got there and why. Even more disturbing was a meeting of the General's staff which I attended one evening. They were not, on the whole, educated men; they were rather simple soldiers; but the main subject of dispute that night was the effect which Senator Pittman's neutrality amendment, now under discussion in the United States Senate, would have upon the Chinese and Japanese armies. The argument was hot; every angle of the question was aired and examined. I learned quite a lot that night about American legislation.

It was typical of this army that they should put on a show for us. A platform was rigged, decorations were strewn about like confetti, and one-act play after one-act play was strutted and stormed in front of us. A series of speeches lasted for two hours — an ordeal in which even I was forced to stand up there in my uniform before an assemblage of uncounted thousands of Chinese guerrillas and shriek happy phrases at them for some twenty minutes. Their songs amazed me. The part singing was quite good enough for American audiences, perhaps a little too good. I wondered idiotically if the Japanese in the next valley could hear them.

On our second morning at the camp, the guerrillas brought one prisoner, some small cannon, and two Japanese horses into camp. We tried out the horses, found them big and rangy and sure-gaited, and were forever soured against our own moth-eaten beasts. The Sixty-First Army was delighted with them, for some of the men quartered here were part of a cavalry division, and good horses were much in demand. The idea of guerrilla cavalry in Japanese territory amused me somehow; I had always pictured guerrilla warfare as a very furtive affair, a sneaking about at night, a slipping through the Japanese lines like shadows, a hiding in the hills by daytime. And here were the guerrillas riding around on cavalry horses, in uniform, taking their orders by radio direct from Chungking, playing tennis when they were not fighting, and more or less masters of the province. Naturally, every region presented a different picture; sometimes it was not so casual as all this; sometimes China's guerrilla warfare actually was a little nightwork on the side. But here in southwest Shansi, I should not have been at all surprised to see the whole Sixty-First Army sit down for a quiet game of bridge.

The prisoner caused quite a stir. I had long been aware that few prisoners are taken on either side in this war. To be honest about it, both Chinese and Japanese prefer to kill each other during the heat of battle. I was a little afraid for this prisoner, wondering what his fate was to be. I saw him first standing out in the temple's inner court surrounded by a craning mass of Chinese soldiery. An interpreter was questioning him and passing along the answers to the fascinated audience. The Japanese himself was a petty officer, apparently captured without a struggle; he was a big man, brown faced, a charcoal seller, they said. His features barely moved as he stood in the sun and gave his unemotional answers. It did not seem possible that a man could be so expressionless.

'What will happen to him?' I asked the interpreter.

'What will happen? Why, he will be sent to Chungking, perhaps to Yenan. There he will be fed excellent food and given the best bed to sleep in.' The officer spoke sardonically. He spoke the literal truth. Then he turned to the prisoner and repeated his words in Japanese, but if he had hoped for a sign of relief from the man he was disappointed. The prisoner stared at him unmoved.

A few hours later, I heard shouts of laughter coming from the room across the courtyard where the prisoner was billeted. For a moment I was nervous, thinking that the man was being tormented. I should, of course, have known better. When I peered into the room, I found the space jammed with a crowd of twenty or thirty guerrillas. In their center was the Japanese. He was teaching them ju-jitsu and wrestling tricks. The big man was taking on each slim little sandal-footed soldier, one at a time, and flooring him without much effort, while the rest held their sides in laughter and the prisoner himself grinned from ear to ear. By the next morning, he was the hero of the camp.

During the following days, we ranged far afield toward the north of the province, once to visit a university hidden there in the hills, again to call upon cave hospitals where the wounded hide out for months under the noses of the Japanese. In certain districts, we were nearly mobbed. Some of these villages had never before seen a foreigner and their people's curiosity outweighed even their enthusiasm. With a great deal of unembarrassed laughter, they would crowd about us, examine our features, peer behind our ears, feel our clothes, and very politely ask us intensely personal questions about our private habits. Like all their countrymen, their un-self-consciousness, anything but naïve and childlike, was so intensely sophisticated, so deliberate and calm and devastatingly civilized, that I longed to join them in their comfortable curiosity.

The university received us with feasting and song. It was so far from the beaten path that it had not yet been disturbed by the war around it. Had the near-by Japanese once guessed its existence here in the lonely hills, the result would have been slaughter. The fact that the secret was kept by virtually every country person in the district spoke well for their loyalty. The hospital was one of several like it in these guerrilla regions. They represented the one hope of the wounded for a chance to live. But their medical supplies were pathetically inadequate. All supplies in the province had to be brought in from Shensi by muleback; no wheeled vehicle could navigate these footpaths; raiding Japanese planes overhead added to the transportation troubles. Many of the wounded were men with frozen feet, received while fording a river during the heavy fighting of the preceding winter. Few of them would walk again. I thought of the straw sandals which they wore the year around, generally from choice, and I shivered a little. The superintendent of the little cave hospital was suffering from a glandular infection which, since he was the only doctor in the region, could not be lanced. Skipper obligingly did the job for him, and his gratitude nearly overwhelmed us.

On the way back from the hospital, with some twenty miles still ahead of us, a dust storm arose and developed into a serious gale. Loess dust accompanies every breath of wind in these dry Shansi mountains. But the storm that night was a more serious affair. It was just possible to breathe. As dark came down, the moon, all outlines of things, were blotted out. To open our eyes was a hazardous undertaking. And the wind screamed like a woman gone mad through the valleys of live dust. Skipper and I became separated from the rest of the party. Now, without a guerrilla escort to guide us, our new fear was that we should travel head-on into some Japanese troops. Our uniforms left no doubt as to just what our capture would mean. There was only one thing to do — give our horses their heads and trust them. We did just that. We even let them canter on the level stretches. And a few hours later, they casually deposited us in front of our temple door.

The most diverting occasions at camp were the taking up of Japanese rails from the near-by railroad and the bearing of them proudly into our village. The guerrillas accomplished this several times during our stay with them. The deed was done at night. The enemy-controlled railroad running between Linfen and Tai-

yuan was not too well guarded. Since the Japanese did not dare
allow their men outside of the city walls in anything but large
numbers, they could not post effective guards along their railroad
without using half the garrisons of Shansi with which to do it.
After the rails were spirited away during the night hours, our men
of the Sixty-First Army would placidly have them converted into
munitions. If they were discovered in the course of their rail-
lifting, they would dump the rails into the nearest stream as they
fled. Quite often the technique of stealing rails was varied by the
more exacting technique of blowing up Japanese troop trains.
At the time we were in Shansi, an average of several trains a week
were mined and destroyed by Yen's armies. While the fighting
that went on near us at Linfen was straightforward warfare, shelling, machine-gunning from hidden emplacements, and sniping,
by far the most telling and disturbing gains were made by these
night forays, when Japan's vital communications and her equally
important transport columns were destroyed.

A good deal of the present fighting was directed — or at least
advised — by a Russian advisor, sent out by Chiang Kai-shek
to lend his brains to the military efforts of General Chen's crack
troops. On all too many occasions, we heard him advising — he
dearly loved to advise. Knowing he was a Communist, I waited
patiently to hear at least a few words of Communist propaganda.
I was disappointed. His advice was localized and technical.
It contained no propaganda of any kind. In all of China, I heard
no word of Soviet proselytizing. One more careless supposition
of mine — that Soviet Russia was doing all she reasonably could
to communize China — went gradually up in smoke.

On the evening before we left on the long road back, the rotund
General Chen went strolling with us down the valley by a small
stream. Once he stopped and pointed dramatically to a slim
waterfall that had worn a deep gash in the boulders of the river bed.
'Look at the waterfall there,' he commanded. 'Do you see

how the water has worn away the rock beneath it? That is the
way in which we will defeat our enemies.'

For a moment I was impressed. The idea dovetailed in with
the popular notion that the Chinese would one day wear out the
Japanese by sheer perseverance, even perhaps absorb them. The
notion was, and still is, part of the Chinese conception of themselves. And after a moment's thought, I realized that it is this
very notion which has weakened China's chances of winning
the war. Call it perseverance, if you wish, or patience. But
it is also part of her vast national complacency: the complacency which a century ago led her to scorn and reject the
mechanical superiority of the West; the complacency which
caused the embattled armies of old civil wars to sit down after
every victory and have a feast about it; the complacency that
today makes her guerrillas wholly satisfied with rapier thrusts
and petty raids, with blown-up railroads and night ambushes,
with a wearing down process that might work with time — oh,
yes! — but one that has dedicated the people to a long and agonizing war. The mechanical reason behind the hit-and-run warfare, the failure to make any large-scale offensive was, naturally,
the lack of munitions, especially artillery and warplanes. Here
in Shansi, Yen's armies depended for their heavy arms upon
whatever they could capture from the Japanese; small arms were
imported from Szechwan and Shensi munitions factories and
were hand-made by local blacksmiths; fighting planes (rumored
at five hundred) owned at this time by the Chungking Government were used in the Yangtze Valley, in Lanchow, Szechwan,
and in the South. Clearly no large-scale offensive was practical
just now. Nevertheless, the waterfall-and-the-stone attitude,
the ever-present optimism of the Chinese, reduced to some extent the bite of their guerrilla tactics. They could have done
more. Given time and a chance to build up their munitions industry, they probably will.

To do them justice, they were laying in ashes the morale of the
Japanese garrisons. Neutral observers estimated that the Chinese
armies were accounting for an average of one thousand Japanese
a day — no mean casualty list. From the best authority and from
my personal observation, I guessed that their own casualties were
slightly smaller. In Shansi there were few wounded. The guerrillas seldom exposed themselves; they faded like wraiths into
the landscape after every sortie, their light khaki uniforms blend-
ing into the pale loess. A story-book thing to watch — this type
of warfare — and naggingly effective; but with potentialities
which the easily satisfied Chinese had not yet put to test. More
to be praised than their actual fighting tactics is the organization
which they have built up in Free China and behind the Japanese
lines, a co-ordination of all the armies and all the people so
toughened and sure that it can exist and feed upon itself and,
defiant of all enemy offensives, grow stronger with the passing of
war years.

A few dawns later, bidden farewell by the marching Sixty-
First in full throat, we started back the dusty trail to Shensi.
By this time we were a rather dreary company. The diet of the
past few weeks — two meals a day and quite peculiar meals at
that — had depressed us a good deal. Andy and Bill Djang were
both down with amoebic dysentery. Malaria chills and fever and
an inability to keep down any food were my own particular
problem; I weighed a little over forty pounds less than on the
day we had set out from Sian. That morning, for the first time,
I had to be lifted on my horse, a very blushing process.

We passed through Chihsien once more on the return journey.
The people welcomed us, not with stiff lines, but as old friends.
There were only a few more speeches; and I was presented with a
bouquet of flowers picked from a near-by hillside by a contingent
of young girl teachers who nearly passed away in their embarrassment.

When I awoke early the next morning, I found a crowd outside our door, absorbed and intensely excited over something they were making. They had decided that I must be very tired of horses (as I was) and should therefore ride the remaining day in a sedan chair. Without more ado they had persuaded four young farmers to act as chairmen and were rigging up a chair on heavy poles. There were no ready-made sedan chairs in the city; but their determination knew not defeat. I looked at the contraption. It was an ancient wooden armchair with one arm and half its back broken off. As I stared at this instrument of torture, Skipper saw and interpreted my gaze.

'Don't say anything,' he warned me hurriedly. 'It's the only chair in the city that wasn't burned.'

An hour later we started forth, the rest on their horses, I in my dreadful chair borne by four bouncing farmers. It was sunrise and the streets were almost deserted. But this was because, for the last time, Chihsien had gathered beyond the wall to see us off. Once more the citizens were lined up, many thousand strong, outside the South Gate. Once more they cheered and sang their farewell songs. My chairmen bore me proudly in the procession, joined in the singing, strode forward as though to a coronation.

Later, as we rounded the curve of the mountain a mile away, I took one backward glance. There was the ragged old city with its queer half-ruins. There was the river and the early sun. The people had begun to flock back through the gate, but they were still singing because they felt like it. The tune was easy to remember. It swung in our ears and rhythmed our horses' hoofs through all the curling dust and sweat of the long day.

(10)

THE COMMUNISTS

ANDY in the front seat yelled: 'That's it straight ahead! See the walls?'

The bare loess hills rolled back in yellow humps from a small river, and upon one high bank, there at the bend of the stream, stood Yenan — stronghold of Red China. The gray stone bank went right up another fifty feet to form the massive city wall. So high was the wall that nothing showed within. It looked like an ogre's castle. The gate was designed as though for triumphal marching hordes.

We stared at the place and grinned in mutual relief. The past week's journey from Chihsien had been back-breaking and frequently muddy. Sudden downpours had turned the steep loess paths into chute-the-chutes of yellow slime. We scrambled up them on hands and knees. Behind us, our ponies were more often down than up. Descending, both we and the ponies slid rapidly upon our rears, landing in a sea of mud and mild hysterics. Eventually we grew so weak from laughter that we nearly bogged down in Shansi altogether.

The same dog-eared ferryboat bore us leakily across the Yellow River. The same long road to Yen's headquarters confounded us, led us miles out of our way, and finally deposited us limply in our same cool cave. The next two days, designed almost as a prologue to Yenan, gave us something new to think about. They were spent in the guest-caves of Yen's universities, hidden in the west Shensi hills some twenty miles from his headquarters. Fifty thousand students were in training here. Their units honeycombed the hills like termites. Mountain after mountain had been layered into cave communities. These were political universities, turning out the young organizers whom we had met in Shansi and who had converted the people of both Shansi and Hopeh into such a strong backbone for the armies. Their job was to educate the people, teach the illiterate to read and write, give them classes in the history of China, the origins of the present conflict, and conditions in China today. Besides this, the men, women, and even children of the land must be organized into auxiliary defense and relief units to co-operate with the armies. The universities were very recent. Marshal Yen, in telling us about them, frankly admitted that they were patterned upon the great Communist universities of Yenan, though far from Communist in political philosophy.

We found the students a well-educated lot, modern young men and girls, most of them bursting with ideals and the importance of their job. They formed mass meetings for our benefit and listened to our speeches with grave, intent faces. Because the region was barren and so remote that supplies could not easily be brought in, their meals were painfully inadequate. Most of them had walked to this place from Chungking and even farther south. When they arrived, semi-exhausted, the fare was not large enough to build them up. Now almost thirty per cent of the students were seriously ill. Marshal Yen had warned us of this and of his difficulty in coping with the epidemics. During our two-day visit, Skipper and Bill Djang had a very satisfying time together arranging for the special transportation of medical supplies and nourishing foods into the isolated district.

The students were lucky in having near-by a convenient refugee institution, the Linfen Medical College. The college was doing surprisingly good work. It had escaped from Linfen a few hours before the city fell to the Japanese. But the conquering army pursued the little college and its donkey supply train containing their equipment all the way to the Yellow River.

'Our students crossed just in time,' the small and overworked dean of the college told us. 'One or two donkeys were in the ferry too, and their loads were saved. But the rest of our supplies were captured by the enemy.'

We walked through the dark caves where the students were bent over their books. We watched an anatomy class working over a dead goat with a small assortment of instruments. We peered through the one precious microscope that had been saved. The dozen or so American textbooks and Chinese translations were so tattered with use that they almost crumbled in our hands. But Skipper watched some of the interns operating in a near-by hospital.

'They're good doctors,' he told me. 'The standards of this place have always been high. Even now with their one microscope and handful of instruments, the students have to complete the full four-year course and two years of internship. Probably the experience they're getting around here will make them first-class surgeons before they're through.'

'This must be some contrast to the old life in Linfen.'

'Yes,' Skipper said. 'They had a fine school there. The best equipment. I wonder exactly what keeps them going ahead like this?'

The question was rhetorical, for we both knew. But though we knew, we could not cease to wonder.

Several thousand students waved us on our way one cold dawn. Colonel Tien was bid a fond farewell. Once more the big army truck toiled over that unmentionable road without disaster. At noon, Eva and Mr. Li met us at the junction where the Yenan road began. Eva was polished until she shone, and so was Mr. Li. The reunion was hilarious. The Chinese standing about stared at us as we pumped hands and patted backs all around like so many overexcited children.

Now, as the sunset of that day lit the mountains pink and dark rose, we sped dustily across the valley floor toward the waiting walls of Yenan. Through the gates we lurched and down the main street in search of presiding officialdom. But once inside the town, we stared in growing wonder. Yenan was the first city we had yet seen which could be described as wholly destroyed. In my three weeks there, I did not find one house undamaged. Most of the streets showed a few jagged fangs, drunken masonry, a negligent scattering of dead gray bricks — no more. The Japanese had not bothered to use incendiary bombs. Explosive bombs were quite enough to do a thorough job, for the city was small. Casualties were so high after the first raids that the thirty thousand or so inhabitants were not allowed to enter the city during daylight hours without special passes. Throughout the day, Yenan was a ghost city.

But at night, she came to life with a blaze and a clatter. Every house which could be patched up into anything at all became a crowded restaurant or a busy store. The main street grew a mushroom fringe of stalls and roadside markets. From a crumbling ruin, the little avenue blossomed into carnival splendor with the touch of dark. There was no rebuilding of bombed houses here, as we had found in Sian. An easier solution was at hand. Half a mile away, in a gully between the hills, a new cave-dwelling Yenan was under construction. When finished, it would look much like Marshal Yen's remarkable headquarters. Already a large part of Yenan's citizenry were moved into their private caves, and came into the city at night only for a bit of shopping or a bowl of tea.

At the noisiest restaurant in town we found the Reception Committee of the Communist Party deeply involved in a feast. The budget outlay for entertainment and publicity was large, we learned later, and the lucky members of the Committee were probably the only members of their Party who sometimes had enough to eat. Now they welcomed us with grins, jests, and innumerable toasts, although they had had no word of our coming and only a dim awareness of our identity. More and yet more food was ordered. We gorged ourselves on dishes called *san pu chang* ('three not stick,' to translate literally), and *hsueh tzai pu tsai* ('snow on the white vegetable,' which was nothing more nor less than sugar on fried spinach and a much tastier dish than it sounds).

The Reception Committee consisted of very young students in the blue-cotton uniform of the Eighth Route Army. They looked so much like children that my inclination was to pat them on the head; but they turned out to be quite important officials in the Party, most of them in their early twenties. The feasting done, they conducted us to a cave hotel halfway up a mountain and close to the city wall. The hotel was just that — a row of private caves, each with its *k'ang*, table, stool, and unfortunately a mirror. I had my first good look at myself in almost a month, and the sight was not reassuring. During that month we had all been sleeping in our clothes, thanks to the bitter nights and a complete lack of privacy. One or two baths in Shansi streams had helped, but not much. We had all lost weight to the point of emaciation, and we were all in need of a haircut. That night I spent a full hour before the mirror winding my hair into curls in one last desperate effort to appear beautiful.

The following day we drove many miles into the north to visit one of the Communists' model hospitals. In spite of ourselves we were impressed by the spick-and-span wards, laboratories, operating rooms, and especially by the X-ray apparatus. According to the doctors in charge, the one fly in the ointment was the small endowment from the Central Government which permitted the staff ten cents a day for food and spending money, and the patients not much more. I was puzzled at this.

'Do you mean,' I asked the doctor, 'that the Kuomintang pays for your upkeep?'

'Of course.' He was surprised. 'All the Communists are financed by the Central Government. Everyone in the Party and in the army gets a regular allowance or budget that is paid for by Chiang Kai-shek. If it were not for this, we would probably starve and most certainly freeze. It is most strange, because the Generalissimo has not very great love for us.'

An ever present headache, in Yenan and in all of China, was the lack of medical supplies, but here in the Communist areas medical personnel was surprisingly adequate. Besides the local Chinese doctors and the branch of the Red Cross, a Canadian doctor was at work with the army in Shansi. From his reports I gathered that he attended every major battle with a mobile operating unit, and was cutting down the rate of infection from wounds to a remarkable low of nineteen per cent. In the summer of 1940 he died on the job. Besides all this, a unit of volunteer Indian doctors from Bombay, brilliant young surgeons, had recently arrived in Chungking, and had at once been assigned to work in Yenan.

There was of course work enough for a hundred such units. Here in the Northwest, relapsing fever had reached epidemic proportions. The isolation hospitals in Sian were crowded to the doors with patients, most of them soldiers. Curiously enough, of all China's disagreeable diseases, probably the least virulent, though the most prolonged, was typhoid. Malaria and dysentery could be in some cases mild, in others fatal. In Shensi an outbreak of scarlet fever with its attendant complications was claiming a good many lives. Tuberculosis was of course the refugee's intimate friend and companion. Far more virulent than typhoid was its fellow, typhus, the very name of which was enough to

scare all of us badly. Probably more missionaries have died
of typhus during their years in China than of any other disease.

The fever which held for me a not altogether morbid fascination
was cholera. Without medical aid, the cholera patient seldom
lives more than a day or so. Sometimes he dies within a few hours.
But the treatment of cholera is close to magic. It was an oddly
exciting thing to see a cholera patient brought into a hospital.
Generally he would be unconscious, dried up, dehydrated, sometimes without pulse or sign of breath. It would seem incredible
that anyone so close to death could be brought alive again. Without an instant's delay, a doctor would appear at the bedside and
give the dying man an intravenous injection of saline — simple
salt and water. Within half an hour, perhaps within a few moments, the man's whole body and face and physical being would
change. Faster than a flower he would revive. Color and life
would grow in him with the speed of miracles. Soon he would be
conscious, growing stronger even as we stared at him. In an hour
he would be begging for a hearty meal.

An American doctor from Shanghai, superintendent of the
Yenan Red Cross unit, was glad to answer all my inquisitive questions.

'Venereal disease?' he asked. 'Yes, there's some of it here in
Yenan. Quite a lot more than in the rest of China. The students
in the universities have more liberty than they probably should
have. But you know, don't you, that compared to America and
Europe, there is almost no venereal disease in China. Perhaps it's
the way they're built. Probably it's because they don't have the
time or the inclination to be immoral. Even since they've given
up having more than one wife, they still keep their sex lives remarkably clean.'

While we were chatting together in his office, a messenger came
in with a note. The American doctor looked so worried over it, I
finally asked him, 'Is anything wrong?'

'Well — yes,' he said. 'It might be pretty bad. They claim that plague has broken out in a village near here.'

'Bubonic plague?'

'No — I wish it were. This happens to be pneumonic plague. It crops out mostly in Mongolia, but sometimes it slips through the Great Wall and gets down here into Shensi. In case you're interested, it's the worst disease known to man. About twice as bad as bubonic, and about twice as contagious. I don't think that there has ever been a known recovery from pneumonic. Usually it carries off whole villages and towns. It's rather like virulent pneumonia. The patient lives only two or three days.'

My healthy respect for China's diseases noticeably grew that day.

Nearly all the mountains around Yenan were man-made bee-hives. Over thirty thousand citizens and party leaders, soldiers and students, dwelt here in their caves. But in the year 1933, Yenan was a walled town of five thousand inhabitants, and the Communists still a thousand miles away. At that time they were engaged in their 'long march,' perhaps the most spectacular retreat in history. Fleeing before Chiang Kai-shek's larger forces, the Communist soldiers marched first into the South, then north through Szechwan and Shensi until in 1934, still undefeated, they settled in Yenan. The story is a familiar one: how Chiang continued his unsuccessful efforts to wipe out his Communist enemies; how the so-called 'red army' grew always more adept at guerrilla warfare, and Chiang more stubborn and intolerant; how in a visit to Sian, he was kidnaped and later released in an incomprehensible welter of apologies and face-saving tactics; how in 1937 an informal peace was declared with the Communists in the mutual struggle against Japan, and a few months later a non-aggression pact was signed with Russia. The story, blandly told by so many American writers, is one of the most compli-

cated ever played out on the human stage. It is shot through
with so many diplomatic mysteries and carefully guarded secrets
that the briefest statement about the Communists — in this
book and in every book — must be accepted as careful guess-
work, no more.

Even to the present day visitor, Yenan does not give away
much that is factually reliable. The little walled town of 1933 is
now the nerve center for the Communist Party's spheres of influence, granted them early in the war by the Kuomintang, which
include this section of northern Shensi and a small number of
hsien in Ninghsia and Kansu. In addition to this very limited
slice of territory, the Communist Eighth Route Army was
operating in north Shansi and Hopeh, and the new Communist
Fourth Route Army hard at work in the regions between Nanking
and Hangchow, although in the fall of 1940 it was disbanded.
Exact figures are available to no one beyond inner government
circles; but it is safe to say that there are less than a million actual
members of the Communist Party, a few hundred thousand men
in the Communist armies, and a very few million Chinese occupying the sparsely settled 'spheres of influence.' Virtually all the
Communists in China are segregated in the Communist districts.
The mental vision common to America of a warring China, under-
mined and overrun by Communists, is nothing more or less than
a popular fallacy. So is the vision of the war as fought largely by
Communists, although the former 'red armies' are China's best-
trained veterans.

Publicized to the saturation point, the Communists, queerly
enough, are the victims of a host of popular fallacies. I found no
Russians at all in Yenan, with the lone exception of a very homesick Russian photographer who had been sent out to bring back
propaganda pictures of Yenan. The American doctor partly corroborated my impression that fewer Russians strayed into the
Communist districts than into any other part of Free China. Rus-

sian munitions do not go to the Communists. All Russian imports reach China either at Chiang's stronghold of Lanchow or at Chiang's stronghold of Kunming. The small allotments that reach Yenan do so at Chiang's command. No motor road communicates between Russia and the Communist districts. Rumor has it that a dribble of munitions can occasionally get through from Lanchow to Yenan by muleback; but this hardly justifies the popular impression that Russia is sending direct military aid to China's Communists. It may also be noted here that in the event of a Chinese victory, Russia would still be unable to furnish the Communists with direct aid, except by permission of the Chinese Government.

In fact, Russia's relations with Yenan are a distinct puzzle to all concerned. The original Communist revolution that broke out in Canton in 1926 was financed and abetted by Russia. Afterward the combine became less intimate, and it is probable that Russia has to some extent lost interest in her Chinese protégés. The reverse is most certainly correct. From the day that I set foot in Yenan, I noticed a lukewarm attitude toward Russia on the part of students and young officials. Far more popular than Russia were America and Great Britain. At least once a day I was told, very earnestly, something like this:

'You must not confuse our Communism with the Communism of Russia. Long ago we broke away from Russia. Today we do our own thinking. In your country, you would probably call us Socialists. We believe in sacrifice for each other, and in hard work and love for all men. Almost it is like your Christianity.'

Nevertheless, the highest leaders in the Party have distinct relations with Russia. Cho En-lai and other chief executives have made one or more trips to Moscow by air, and Russia has negotiated diplomatically and paternally with Chungking on behalf of their Chinese fellows in Yenan and has obtained a monopoly of raw materials and a strong sphere of influence in the outlying province of Sinkiang. But it would seem that the average young party member is scarcely aware of Russian affiliations. Policy seems to have dictated those trips to Moscow — certainly not popular sentiment. For the two ideologies, the Communism of Russia and the Communism of China, are many miles apart.

How to explain Chinese Communism in a single page or a single chapter or a single book? It cannot be done. I do not fully understand it, nor do the Communists themselves. Physically, I found them a very young group, in thoughts as well as years: young, and inefficient, and carefree as the wind, and all on fire. They wore faded blue uniforms, caps set jauntily on their heads, hair sometimes long and self-conscious, sandals on their feet. Oh, yes, they were Bohemian. They were also a little like children in a summer camp, bursting with camp spirit but not quite capable yet of keeping their tents neat and their sneakers tied. They were elaborately informal, wrapped up in themselves. They were exasperating and ridiculous and lovable.

There was no denying their sincerity. Many of the officials and nearly all of the students had trekked here on foot from every province of China with ideals attached like wings to their heels. Afterward, given a chance to try out their Communism in the language of hard work and little-to-show-for-it, they surprisingly did so — and thrived upon it! I had always thought of Communist communities in general as groups of idealists and opportunists congregated together to the disillusionment of the former and the pleasant enrichment of the latter. Yenan — an unexpected exception — clung to its ideals. Possibly the opportunists were lacking. Perhaps the fire was kept burning because it was on the whole a creative one. The usual destructiveness of Communism was lacking here. Thoughts of advancement for the Party, sabotage, and overthrow of the Kuomintang had been at least temporarily eliminated by the hand-in-hand struggle against Japan.

So the students tilled the fields and gathered firewood, attended outdoor classes in bitter weather, cooked their own meals, worked harder than they had known it was possible to work, and (with a few malcontents to mar the picture) had quite a good time doing it. Watching them unseen, I noticed that they sang at their work; that they argued and laughed and rough-housed; that something of all this was in their blood. Over half were members of wealthy and educated families who gave up luxuries to revel in cotton pants and sandals and ideologies. Perhaps when the romance and novelty of being Communists wore off, when the thing became less of a lark and more of a lifetime's routine, they would turn back to their old homes. Perhaps not.

They dragged me enthusiastically about their cave campuses. Each cave housed some fifteen students, and was decorated with photographs and posters. Generally they worked, perched upon stools with their books and papers laid out upon the *k'ang*. Boys and girls dressed alike. Most of the girls wore Dutch bobs that gave them the gay, insouciant look of young pages. They were all eagerness to convert me.

'Did you know that our highest officials receive only ten dollars a month?'

'The country people in our districts pay us smaller taxes than in any other part of China.'

'We have actually raised the standards of living here.'

There was, I discovered from conversations with the aforementioned country people, some truth in what they said. Voluntary poverty found few exceptions in Yenan, but did not overdo itself. The villagers were sincerely fond of their Communist overlords. The reforms imposed upon them outnumbered the restrictions.

Once I made the mistake of asking a young girl student, 'What do you study here besides propaganda technique and organizing?'

'Why, that is all,' she said. 'That is all we have time for.'

'Don't you think you could fit in at least one academic subject?'
'Of course not! This is a crisis!' She was insulted.

In a sense, she had reason to be. The graduates of her 'university' were doing a thoroughly realistic job for China. Trained here in the Kongda or Anti-Japanese University as teachers and organizers, they were sent to the fronts of Shansi and Hopeh, behind the Japanese lines, where they took their lives in their hands to spread mass education and defense propaganda from the Yellow River to the sea, and sometimes to die for their pains.

My respect for China's students by now was built upon solid ground. They deserve something more of a eulogy than I know how to give them. Their energy and patience and courage are difficult to describe, being spectacular, being heroic.

Three days after our arrival in Yenan, Bill Djang, Andy Roy, the indomitable Mr. Li, and the indomitable Eva departed for Sian. Because we were anxious for a return visit to Shanghai, Skipper and I had decided to cross Shansi and try to reach Peking. So we stayed behind in Yenan, waiting for a truck that would carry us northward on the first lap of the journey. Although in the end the journey was never made, we were thankful for the opportunity to study Yenan in greater detail.

The next day I visited the Arts College, the one academic and creative branch of the University, and thereupon received the shock of my life. Only music and the fine arts were taught here — that much I had known. But just what kind of music and art it would be, I was afraid to visualize.

That morning a rehearsal was underway of an opera that had been composed in the college and was to be performed a few weeks hence. The rehearsal occupied a wide ledge in front of the cave mouths, halfway up a cliff-side. Grouped in a semicircle on the outer rim of the ledge was the chorus. It consisted of ninety mixed voices. Clustered in front of it was the orchestra — sixty-five pieces. Among the instruments I noted Occidental violins, 'cellos, clarinets, oboes, and Chinese violins, pipes, drums, all jumbled together in one vast and dubious ensemble. A bass viol was apparently unobtainable in Yenan, for I saw one that had been made from an empty gasoline tin. (Later I tried the instrument and found it to have quite a lovely tone.) All the musicians wore the casual blue cotton trousers and shirts in which Yenan went its cheerful way.

The rehearsal had just ended, but the group obligingly rehearsed all over again for my benefit. There on the mountain platform, the orchestra tuned itself noisily. The young composer of the opera, his soldier's cap on the back of his head and his sleeves rolled high, climbed upon a small ledge some twenty feet farther up the cliff. For a moment he stood as I had seen so many conductors stand in the hot waiting dark of an opera house, with arms above his head and baton poised. Then the arms snapped down and the orchestra crashed into the opening theme of the overture; I have not often heard music quite so beautiful.

Mentally I babbled to myself as in a trance: 'Modern French school. But not, thank God, discordant. Half a dozen melodies, all good. European music. No, there's the song of the trackers, the coolies. Chinese music. No. I don't know. But it's *exquisite...*'

And here I watched, half-dazed, upon this concert stage of blown dust, beneath this podium of loess, while a crowd of ragged kid soldiers made their music and a conductor's arms were stretched out above them and only the bare old Shensi mountains stood about to listen.

An hour later the crowd was gone. The conductor, his wife, and I sat in his workshop cave drinking tea. His name, I learned. was See Sing-hai and he was a graduate of the Paris Conservatory of Music, where he had studied seven years. His wife laughingly gave him away.

'My husband will not bother to tell you that his works have won prizes in France, that they have been played by many European orchestras.'

'No wonder!' I muttered, and he blushed. 'And you use the Occidental scale instead of the pentatonic!'

'Oh, yes, it gives much more freedom and harmony. My pupils are taught to sing and play both Chinese and Western music. It is good for them.'

'But your opera was a combination of both!'

'Yes,' he laughed, 'it took me a long time to learn that. To take Western music and give it Chinese melody, Chinese atmosphere and spirit. I thought I would go mad before I learned it.'

'So did I,' said his wife.

Anyone who has heard Chinese music knows how incomprehensible it can be to the Occidental listener. Musically, the East and the West are poles apart. Yet here was a man who had blended the two; had kept the best rules of Western form and harmony and combined them with the soft minor, enchanted, indescribable melodies of the East. Besides his opera, he had composed six symphonies and modern arrangements for five hundred Chinese folksongs which he had collected. For hours we pored over grimy scores. Happily we chatted of themes and expositions and recapitulations down to the last interminable coda.

His wife was a well-known young artist and teacher of painting at the College. The work of her students showed a remarkable hodgepodge of genres ranging from traditional scroll-painting all the way to French sur-realism and taking in nearly every stray school along the way. Square cubist figures from modern Russian art stood side by side with the fragile, gowned, and porcelain-faced maidens of the oldest dynasties. On the whole I was glad to see that China's ancient art, both here and in all the land, was still the predominant one, and only its technique improved by study of European schools.

'We are working toward a mixture,' See Sing-hai explained. 'A mixture of Chinese and Western cultures. We can learn much from you and use it too. But it is hard. It cannot be done at once.'

No, I thought. But the job is under way. It is going on in the middle of a war. Perhaps it is more important than the war.

That evening, as I was shopping for peanuts and safety-pins (one's shopping lists in China are apt to be like that) in the stalls that lined the main street, I struck up a casual conversation with two Chinese long-gowned gentlemen standing next to me. Casual conversations in this wonderful country may be carried on with whomever one wishes and wherever one pleases. So we discussed safety-pins and the weather and the fit of my Eighth Route Army uniform, which had been given me by the Kongda University students. But something about the conversation was not right. Listening carefully, I realized that these two men were speaking a Chinese almost as faulty as my own. Suddenly I knew what was the matter. In fact, I was so astonished that I virtually shrieked at them.

'You're Japanese!'

The two men held on to their sides and roared at me. In no time, a crowd collected about us, grinning collectively at the foreign T'ai T'ai's embarrassment.

'But, how . . . ?'

'We have lived here almost two years, T'ai T'ai,' one of them told me. 'We were taken prisoners, you understand. But we have lived here and become good citizens. There are nine of us in the city. I and my friend are both married, and my friend is the father of a boy.'

'You work here too?'

'Of course. I am a blacksmith. This man owns a small farm outside the city wall.'

'But can you not escape?'

'We can. Why should we do so?'

By this time, the crowd about us was overwhelmed with joy over the whole incident. They began patting the two men on the shoulders and pleading with me.

'They are good men, these Japanese that live with us.'

'You must not mind because they are of the enemy.'

'They are honorable friends.'

I laughed and reassured them. But as I wandered off, I felt a little dazed. All this in Yenan, the most war-minded city in Free China! I had already heard something of the Eighth Route Army's treatment of prisoners. Quite often they were taken back to the guerrilla camp, shown exactly how Communism works out in army life, how the highest officer lives the same life and eats the same food as his humblest private; for about two days the prisoner is given a courteous and persistent dose of Communism; then, because a Japanese soldier may not be absent as prisoner more than three days without suffering the death penalty at the hands of his own men, the Communists politely conduct him back toward his lines and release him. This comic-opera procedure is not as naïve as it sounds. The morale of the Japanese is low, to begin with. The conversion and subsequent release of prisoners have accounted for many desertions.

But there was something wonderfully carefree, almost debonair, in the idea of Japanese soldiers trotting about, free and popular, in a crumpled little city of Free China. Thinking backward, I remembered the Japanese pilot in the Hengyang hospital; and the prisoner that was brought into the camp of the Sixty-First Army in the middle of Shansi. I remembered other things: the fact that a good many Japanese residents of Free China had been going right on with their work since the outbreak of war. Nurses, relief workers, even government officials! At least one Japanese occupied a high place in the Kuomintang.

Wandering up the path toward my private cave, I muttered 'Damn!' to the mountain air; and 'Perhaps I'm crazy'; and finally, 'There's more wholesale bitterness toward Japan at home in America than out here in Free China.'

Like every Communist group that I had encountered, the Communists of China were governed by a small clique of men, most of them brilliant strategists and willing enough to live out a Communist way of life in terms of simple food, dress, and hard work, as well as in declaration of principles. The military commander, Chu Teh, was leading his armies near Wutai, in the north of Shansi. Cho En-lai was in Chungking, representing the Communists in the Kuomintang. But the acknowledged head of China's Communists, Mao Tze-tung, was here in Yenan.

'Mao is a genius,' was the statement I had heard in many parts of China. 'Aside from Chiang, he's probably the brightest gentleman in the country.'

I had visualized an earnest, rigid individual. Instead I found him a humorous man, boyish-looking, rather round-cheeked in spite of his constant battle with tuberculosis, and possessed of a wit that automatically made constant joke with the world. He had about him that moist, naïve, and happy look that one sees in men like Einstein. But his mind was sharp and flexible as steel.

Skipper and I badgered him with questions that were much too abrupt, on a night when we sat about a candlelit table with wine at our elbows.

'Do you permit Christians to become members of your Party?'

'No, that we cannot do,' he said, speaking in Chinese, for he knew no English. 'You see, they are unable to give absolute allegiance to our cause. But they are honored members of our

community. Quite a few of our students are Christians. Probably you remember that as a group we were once very anti-
Christian and committed atrocities against your missionaries.
Now we are grateful for the help you give us. It is more than politics, this gratitude. We consider your way of life and thought
closer to our own than any other single philosophy.'

My own investigations among the Christians of Yenan somewhat bore out his words. The old anti-foreign attitude had apparently died a natural death.

One problem stood out above all others in its importance to
China: the problem of the Communist's future in the nation.
The place of Communism after the war was a perpetual headache in official circles. At present the Communists were isolated
in their special districts, and masters of those districts. After
the war, what to do with them? Most Kuomintang officials would
prefer to scatter them throughout China, disband their army, and
let them act as a minority party to the Central Government, instead of an isolated group backed up by its own military forces.
It was obvious to everyone that Communism as an ideology
would never gain strength amongst the Chinese as a whole, to
whom personal freedom and individuality is a religion. Still,
there might be a place for Communism in post-war China — a
useful place, though certain anti-Communist officials in the Central Government were in favor of sterner measures. But meanwhile, the relations between Yenan and Chungking were in constant mysterious flux. Reports of friction were plentiful, though
I had seen no signs of it myself but only active and spontaneous
co-operation. An old feud of words and jealousies existed between Yenan and the provincial officials at Sian, who resented
the publicity and praise bestowed on their Communist neighbors
to the north. Nevertheless, the bickerings between the Communists and the Central Government have, even to this day, remained bickerings, occasional clashes, constant negotiations,

with the Communists impatiently working to enlarge their spheres of influence, their allotment of munitions, and the size of their budget.

These clashes (some real, some merely Japanese-sponsored fiction) have been given a spectacular hearing in the American press for the very elementary reason that a rebellion is news and a thousand loyalties are not. Correspondents in China have a pretty hard time picking up stories important enough for publication in America, for China during the last few years has been poor copy; they may be excused for seizing upon each clash, rumored or proven, between the Kuomintang and the Communists as news which will at least be printed. The fact that the skirmishes are localized personality disputes — inevitable, petty, stupid, but scarcely ominous — is, of course, not mentioned in their dispatches. Consequently, the American public receives the impression that Free China is forever hovering on the verge of civil war. The most serious break was the battle in the fall of 1940 between Kuomintang forces and units of the Communist Fourth Route Army; there was undoubtedly a certain amount of fighting and, in the end, the Fourth Route Army was disbanded, though the causes and details will never be known. But the impression that crept into American press reports and editorials of a serious revolt coming to a head within the ranks of the Red armies was based upon no factual evidence at all. It was based, instead, upon our ignorance of Chinese psychology, our assumption that the refusal of an army to obey orders must indicate widespread and growing unrest, our excusable unawareness of the fact that in China a local rebellion, though harmful to her war efforts and perfectly open to blame, is generally a personal quarrel involving pride, 'face,' pig-headedness on the part of one or two leaders. China's poor communications alone would be enough to prevent the spread of public opinion among the Communists or any other group.

During the past few weeks, I had seen many instances of co-operation and friendship between Central Government forces and the Communists in regions where active fighting between the two was at that moment supposed to be in progress. I had found the Communists as a whole, from the Party leaders down to the last small young soldier, even more uncompromising in their atti-tude toward Japan, more determined to win their war, than their non-Communist neighbors. It is almost laughable to sup-pose that the entire group (and it is an intelligent group) would kill its own cause for the sake of a personal grievance. Now that the romance and novelty of fighting side by side with the Central Government have worn off, there will be inevitable squabbles and local disputes — even, occasionally, physical skirmishes. But for each case of rebellion there will be a thousand cases of unity. The two one-time enemies, always sparring, wary of each other still, are nevertheless cemented in uncomfortable but dependable partnership by the cold knowledge that they must battle together or be defeated.

The future of the Communist Party in the event of victory is not quite so dependable a matter. I brazenly brought the subject up before Mao Tze-tung, knowing that his answer could not be wholly frank.

'What does your Party intend to do after the war, General Mao? Will you still be financed by the Central Govern-ment?'

He laughed at my bland inquisitiveness.

'We hope that our armies may be paid salaries by Chiang, for as you know, they are excellent armies.'

My eyebrows rose, for I knew that few members of the Kuo-mintang would permit a minority party to control an army in peace-time, especially the incomprehensible Communists.

'But your men are such good fighters,' I said. 'Will they be content to be strong and yet peaceful?'

He laughed again.

'Possibly not,' was the frank answer. 'But since we are too poor to feed and clothe ourselves without the help of the Generalissimo, and since his armies will be, after the war, as well trained and many times as strong as our own, I wonder if we will have very much choice.'

'You hope to preserve unity?'

'For our own sakes, we must preserve unity,' he corrected me. 'For our own sakes we must be content to be a small and very loud minority in our government.'

His answer was far more reassuring than would have been a declaration of faith in the Central Government, put on for my benefit. Perhaps after all there was room in China for the Communist Party, a good nagging minority. Perhaps it would give life and energy to the Government, instead of civil war.

On the night before we were to leave on the long trek through the lines to Peking, we celebrated with considerable feasting. But in the middle of the festivities, a sudden buzz of voices from a table in the corner of the room grew loud and invaded the little restaurant like the roll of drums. We stopped breathing as we froze to listen. The phrases came tumbling out.

'Ten thousand killed! That's what they say.'

'The first raid burned half the city.'

'Three weeks ago. The news just got through.'

'Bound to happen in Chungking ...'

Chungking! The raids had begun.

Wide-eyed, the crowd begged for news. But the details were not known. Only that on May 3 and 4 and many times since, the Japanese had flayed the city and burned it and that many thousands were reported dead.

'Any foreigners killed or injured?' This was Skipper, thinking of Brownie.

No one knew. Yes, someone thought that one man had been injured.

'Was Dai Chia Hang hit?' This was I, with my heart in my mouth.

'We cannot tell yet. It is the barest news. Just that much of the city burned and many thousands died.'

Oh, no! *No!* It was an exaggeration. Of *course* it was an exaggeration! Feeling curiously numb, I stumbled outside with my hands in my pockets. The darkness was good to me just then. For perhaps an hour I wandered through the lonely ruins, past the half-standing walls, then crouched finally beside a drunken doorway and cried hard for a long time.

Skipper and I scarcely spoke a word to one another that night. But when morning came, we quietly set about arranging a return ride to Sian; a return to Chungking. Both of us felt a curious guilt in our hearts, as if we had deserted the old city when she most needed us. For almost a week we waited. During that week, no more news came through.

At last a caravan of trucks was ready to depart. Into the back of the last truck we climbed, along with twenty-two soldiers of the Eighth Route Army on their way to the Honan front. Heavy wooden crates already filled the rear of the truck, and we learned the dreary fact that they contained hand grenades and small artillery. At dawn we started, perched upon our hand grenades and so jammed in that the process of scratching one's nose was an undertaking, an untangling of arms and elbows, and a frantic holding on with one hand while the truck bucked and howled. Every vehicle was similarly loaded. It seemed faintly incredible that so much of the human race could be stowed into such small and precarious space.

For three days we rode like this from dawn to late night. They were by all odds the most horrible three days in my fairly brief life. To keep from being thrown out, we had to sit upright and clutch with both hands. We had to do this for fifteen and sixteen hours a day with scarcely a break in the routine. The sun was merciless, and by the end of the first day, three soldiers in our truck were seriously ill from sunstroke. Worse even than the sun was the plague of dust. It curled up in giant clouds from our rear tires, and, in the narrow sunken roads, the air suction swept it over us. Our faces and clothes became so coated with loess that it was impossible to tell one of us from another. My blue cotton uniform of the Eighth Route Army that I had worn in honor of my Communist hosts turned so yellow that no hint of blue showed through. The dust finally did such incredible things to our appearance that it became a standing joke amongst the crowd.

'You have become a member of the yellow race,' the soldiers taunted me. 'Be careful that you are not drafted into our army.'

I grew increasingly fond of the Communist soldiers during these three days of nightmare. Under the pressure of dust and sun and misery, their ideals and their sense of humor stood by them. Some of them managed to read during the trip — small Communist pamphlets tattered with much use. Others tried to improve my use of Chinese and my knowledge of the country. Every half-hour or so, they would break into an army song. Other truckloads would take up the tune and the song would echo through the dusty land. Once we passed a band of boys and girls, marching toward Yenan. They too were singing. Our soldiers cheered them as we passed.

'They are students on their way to join the Communists,' I was told. 'They walk all the distance. Perhaps a thousand miles.'

Oh, yes, they are pugnacious — China's Communists. They are stubborn and young and laughably immature and they wear sandals and long hair and talk of equality. But they are good human material. They are ablaze with something which is not naïve; which may be a valuable thing for old China.

Their crazy spirits pulled me through the next three days. Each night we put up in a local inn; each dawn, at five-thirty, we were on the road again. A high fever which was not wholly malaria and my forty missing pounds now made themselves felt. By darkness of the first night, I was sick, much too sick to eat. Skipper too was close to exhaustion. The next two days passed as in a violent dream. All of us in the rear of that blundering truck soon reached the point where we laughed at everything we saw and did, and could not always stop. Eventually, the combination of miseries grew to such a point that the whole affair dissolved into pure comedy.

At dusk of the third day, we sighted far in the distance the medieval walls of Sian standing against the flat horizon.

'It is almost over, little sister,' said the soldier upon whose shoulder I had been happily resting.

'Skipper, we're here! I'm a sight. Skipper, where's your handkerchief?'

We must have made quite a picture as we crawled into the English Hospital compound and up the steps of the familiar little house; I half-carried by Skipper and a coolie, both of us so choked with dust that we were long since unrecognizable. Fortunately the house was empty and we were able to creep quietly into our beds unseen.

The next morning we wobbled about town, searching for news of planes bound for Chungking. Yes, we were told, an airplane was coming up from Chengtu tomorrow and would return at once; probably the last plane in many weeks, for all but one of the commercial planes able to clear the high Shensi mountain ranges had been shot down by the Japanese. The next day we waited for six agonized hours at the airport and then were told that the plane could not come because of near-by enemy bombers.

I crawled back home and into bed, and this time I could not get up again. Skipper diagnosed the trouble correctly.

'You may be interested to know,' he said cheerfully, 'that you have scarlet fever.'

And as I howled and pulled the bedclothes over my head, the air-raid alarm began.

BOMBS, BIRTHS, AND FEVERS

MY FOUR weeks of quarantine crawled feebly along. Only the first week was pleasant, because I was not very much aware of it. Meanwhile the English Hospital was forced to move into an empty middle school outside the city wall in the East suburb. Air raids had reduced most of it to a pile of rubble and had killed some of the Chinese staff. From my bed in the residence house I could look out upon the stiff skeleton of what had once been the operating room, the X-ray room, and several wards. The view was good because the glass in my windows had long since been blown out by a bomb that exploded just outside in the garden. Now the raids upon the open city showed no signs of abating; so the hospital moved. Perforce I stayed behind. Skipper and another doctor, a Canadian woman, took turns in punching my pillow and feeling my pulse; and the Chinese cook, very small and ancient *da su fu*, stood loyally by, proudly serving me meals in stubborn defiance of both bombs and germs because, as he blandly informed me, he figured God wanted him to.

At the end of the first week, I was well enough to be brought out to the new hospital quarters. The moving process was extremely *au naturel*. Four coolies merely entered the room and without a flicker of expression picked up my bed with myself inside, set it across their shoulders, and marched out of the house.

Through the crowded city they swung, while Skipper strode gleefully behind us, making personal remarks about my appearance in a choked voice. I tried stuffing the bedclothes under my chin and only succeeded in looking foolish. To make matters worse, one of the coolies began to shake in utterly silent laughter so that the northwest corner of the bed rose and fell hysterically. But since this was China, where anything can happen and generally does, we drew scarcely a bored glance from the crowds.

With nothing to keep him in Sian and no passenger plane in sight, Skipper left the next morning aboard a mail truck for Chengtu and Chungking, in a final effort to reach his wife. For three weeks, then, the only visitor permitted to see me was the Canadian doctor and a very large and English nurse who did much to cheer my soul. But Chinese nurses can make good company. They could speak no English and were bent upon improving my Chinese. Every day, Miss Cho, sleek and pretty in immaculate white uniform, would bring me the morning paper and read me the all too graphic accounts of the Chungking air raids.

'The Methodist Hospital,' her voice would drone cheerfully on, 'and the surrounding residence houses' (that would be Dai Chia Hang) 'were ...' And then a series of mysterious phrases.

'What?' I would yell in English. 'What was that?'

'*Mai yu tza-la,*' Miss Cho would explain patiently with a small grin. 'Not bombed.'

'Oh-hhh! ...'

'But the great fires burned up to the walls upon three sides. On May 4 it was surrounded by flames and had not the wind changed, all within might have perished.'

'Good night!'

Fortunately for my sanity during those three weeks, I had my work to do. Article after article sprawled itself upon grimy sheets and the backs of envelopes held above my head against

limp newspapers. I had had no way of knowing whether any of
my dispatches had reached my New York office. As yet, only
one batch of mail had arrived for me since I left Los Angeles,
almost a year ago, and that contained letters written before
Christmas of 1938 and brought to me in Chungking some five
months before. Since then, I had received no message of any kind
from the outside world. In desperation, finally, I cabled my
employers and begged for instructions.

During those last three weeks of isolation, some blessed small
god put an end to all air raids. Only once was there a diversion —
when a small city a few miles to the north of us was bombed, and
a Japanese bomber, as it left the scene of the raid, was forced
down by engine trouble into a near-by wheatfield. Although the
field was small and rough, the plane was scarcely damaged and
the crew unhurt. But they soon found out that they had landed
almost in the midst of a group of Chinese soldiers, who straightway attacked. The Japanese were about to die heroically for their
country. Just then the eight remaining bombers in the flight
circled back to the scene, and swooping low began to machine-gun
the Chinese troops. At the same time, one bomber detached
itself from the others. Running a serious risk of a crack-up on
the stubbly field, it swooped down to land beside its crippled
companion. Under a shielding hail of gunfire from the rest of the
squadron, the crew of the damaged plane transferred to their
fellow bomber. With its doubled load it took off from the field,
and joining the formation sped onward toward the home base.

Miss Cho told me the story. She omitted none of the details.
And as she spoke, her eyes shone with admiration for the courage
of her enemies.

On a day in early July I emerged at last, scrubbed, disinfected,
into the blazing sunlight of the compound yard. My new weight
of ninety pounds made me feel light as a feather; as if I could

leave the ground merely by lifting my arms, and drift up gracefully into the nearest tree. Perhaps in deference to my new-found
health, the raids began once more that day. Eighteen bombers
flew low, directly over our heads, and obligingly dropped their
bombs somewhere beyond us. But watching the silver of sun
upon their wings, I felt a queer return as from some cloistered
dream into the good breath-taking uncertainty of China's
war. Had it not been for the memory of the death that would
flower beneath those raiders, I should have been unashamedly
happy.

That night a cable arrived from my employers in New York.
It asked me to continue my work in China for at least another
three months. Feeling like a prisoner reprieved, almost smug
with the knowledge that my work had been acceptable, I cabled
the news to Bill. The world was very pleasant.

Almost a week passed before I found an opportunity to leave
Sian. During that week, I bore my wraith-like self from one end
of the city to the other and back again. Of all the strongholds of
China, Sian was the most ancient and the most surprising. We
had only to dig a trench in the hospital compound in order to
unearth bronze of the Han Dynasty and bits of pottery (not all
of it broken) dating from the third millennium B.C. If we needed
a soap dish or ash tray, the yard was littered with suitable glazed
ware of the Sung Dynasty. The Bell Tower and Drum Tower,
upreared in the heart of the city, were monsters of age, witness
to no one knew how many dynasties of violence and beauty.
Meanwhile, half the Chinese who passed beneath them wore pith
helmets, the latest fashion. In fact, the pith helmet had taken
the town by storm. Not far off, an ice factory had recently
opened, and now every fifth or sixth shop along the wide streets
was an ice-cream parlor. Ice cream had also taken Sian by
storm.

After dark, when raids could not plague us, we attended feasts in Sian's restaurants. Probably no *carte du jour* is as elaborate as China's national menu, and those feasts would have warmed the heart of the most unreasonable gourmet. Only in famine zones is food scarce, though refugees starve, as they do in every land, from insufficient money to buy food. Even the village restaurant can conjure up for the passing traveler any one of a hundred dishes that he might mention. Virtually every item of food known to the Western world may be had in China, and a vast array of exotic ones to boot. If you are foolish enough to wish spinach, you may have it; but you may also order up some jelly-fish, ancient eggs, shark's fins, fish stomach, pigeon eggs, wildcat (if you are so inclined), duck livers, sea slugs, and any number of choice and terrifying items, most of them delicious. A good restaurant chef, true epicure, will know several hundred ways of cooking duck and chicken. He adds to the allure of his con-coctions by giving them esoteric names. A certain quite humble spinach and mushroom soup, for instance, is known as 'black fungus soup with dragons' guts.' 'Peking duck,' properly cooked, will sometimes take four days to prepare. The firewood must be scented, the duck spiced in a dozen subtle ways. And when the crisp brown skin is served at last between pancakes light as spindrift, you will decide for perhaps the thousandth time that no culture can compare with the mellow arts of China.

One day I went to call upon Edward Bear. Until the hospital was forced to move, he had lived in the compound garden, where he dined on the best milk, swung perilously and blissfully from trees, and squinted with open and devastating scorn toward the thunder of near-by bombs. While the hospital was settling down in its new quarters, Edward had been boarded out with a railroad employee who owned several animals, among them a gentle but full-grown Himalayan bear. 'Good company for Edward,' we had thought, forgetting for a moment the quixotic character of

Edward himself. Today I called upon his temporary keeper. I found the man plunged in gloom.

'Edward,' he began slowly, the English name sounding doubly dignified from his lips, 'Edward *su-la*.'

'Dead!'

'Yes, T'ai T'ai,' was the sad reply. 'Yesterday we introduced him to the large bear, you understand? This Edward took but a single glance at the extremely large bear and sprang straightway at his throat. We mourn him greatly, this small Edward.'

'Oh, Edward,' I thought, 'you would!' But his passing upset us rather absurdly for anything as humble as a very young bear.

The hospital clinic these days averaged over two hundred patients a day. Many were air-raid victims with festering wounds. Every available bed in the hospital was full, the aisles crammed with cots, the staff white with acute exhaustion. More agonizing for them than the hard work was the necessity of turning away people who desperately needed a bed there, children with gangrene-blackened arms and legs, women with heavy tumors and eroded lungs who would not live long. It was a matter of pick and choose, familiar to relief workers, perhaps, except that in this case to be turned away can quite often be a summons to die — life and death resting upon a hair-trigger decision.

One morning I stood by while a baby was born during an air raid. Bombings, to this English hospital, were not altogether the same as bombings in other places and other lands, for the Japanese were then engaged in their first anti-British drive, and the hospital was the favorite target of their raiding planes. I decided to wait and see what would happen.

The mother looked no more than eighteen years old. It was her first child, and her body was slender and her pain quite horrible. Unlike the people of certain nations, the Chinese have as difficult a labor as white women. Here in Sian, sedatives were too precious to spare upon childbirth. But I noticed that through it all, the girl uttered no sound at all. Her face remained calm. Only her body arched and betrayed the agony.

As the child was about to be born, the air-raid siren blared forth from the Drum Tower within the city. The girl on the table sighed. As for the English and Chinese nurses who attended her, they merely laughed ruefully and went about their business. No hospital routine was permitted to stop during a raid. The climax of the birth arrived just as the undertone of planes began. Still the rhythm of it went on unmoved in the small room where death was overhead and underneath a new life forced its small way into the world. Very gently above the roar of the bombers, the nurses spoke their encouragement, and with strong, sure motions, with no injury to the mother, eased the baby's sudden entry into its noisy universe. It was a boy, visibly no different from any newborn son in any land. For a moment his squalls rivaled the shake and smash of exploding bombs. Then, with a laugh, the English nurse sponged him off and gathered him into his blankets. The mother, wrapped for a moment in the pain of afterbirth, nevertheless caught sight of the boy, and through the driving agony, scarcely aware of the hideous din about her in the enchantment of the moment, she smiled and smiled.

A few days later, word came of a small passenger plane that was to arrive the next noon from Chengtu and return to its Szechwan base the same afternoon. True, I was not bound for Chengtu; but a plane left Chengtu every morning for Chungking. It was the chance I had waited for — the first passenger plane to leave Sian in four months. I was luckier than I knew. It was to be the last for many months to come.

The plane itself was not exactly prepossessing. It was an ancient Douglas, seating four passengers, that had been bought extremely second-hand by the Chinese Government eight years before and had seen almost daily service ever since. But it was the only plane sufficiently old and feeble to spare for the difficult flight to Sian, where nearly all the Junkers in Free China had been shot down or burned. Moreover it could, with coaxing, build up enough altitude to clear the Shensi mountain passes. Our pilot was Chinese and one of the best airmen of any nationality in China; and a well-trained Chinese flyer is as safe a pilot as one can wish for.

Into the small close cabin we crawled — I and three other passengers. For an hour the pilot labored for altitude, circling the wide plain where Sian lay like a brown postage stamp on the greener surface of the land. Sometime during that hour I bade a mental farewell to the ponderous, tattered old city and to the dust and the space and the grandeur of the Northwest.

At last the nose of the plane swung toward the layers of white-tipped peaks to the southwest. We cleared the first range by less than a thousand feet. Others piled up below us. The nearest emergency landing field was four hundred miles away in Han-chung. Thirty minutes later, without any warning, we drove into a storm. A world of cotton wool closed in about us. Sleet fingered a quick tattoo upon the wings and windows. Instantly the plane began to buck, at first gently, then horribly as ice formed upon the wings and air pockets sucked it down toward the invisible peaks. Opening a partition into the cabin, the pilot leaned through and bellowed an order that I did not understand. At once the three passengers began to adjust their safety belts. I lost no time in following suit.

As I clicked the belt in place, I fell forward against it hard, incomprehensibly. Something must be wrong inside my head. No, it was the plane that was doing this. The plane was in a spin. Perhaps it was the ice upon the wings — I do not know. For a few split seconds the air poured whining past us. Handbags and magazines slapped wildly about the cabin. The belt cut me first

on the left, then on the right, then the back of the seat pressed
me hard. Emotionally paralyzed, I could think no coherent
thought just then; I could only see a picture within my mind and
stare queerly at it — a picture of mountain-tops. We *could* not
fall far.

Still nosing downward, the plane gradually came out of its
spin. But it could not seem to level out. Abruptly we dived out
of the storm and the sleet no longer stippled the windowpane.
From out of the opaque whiteness that shrouded us, a brown
shadow gathered with startling speed and grew clear and dark.
Now it was spiked like the heads of trees. But they *were* trees!
In that small second, unbreathing, we watched them rush up at
us. Then the pilot gunned the motor. Sideslipping, the plane
roared down the mountain slope parallel with the trees, and so
close we could have counted the branches. Deep into the valley
we thundered, its floor rising obliquely toward us. But by that
time the pilot had worked up enough speed and control to pull
the ship out of her dive and into a steep climb. The valley was
long and wide and we followed it, sometimes circling to gain
altitude. Then, once more in a position to clear the peaks, we
leveled off and headed due south toward Chengtu.

Many times since I have wished that I knew some rudiments of
flying, just enough to explain exactly what occurred above that
mountain range.

It was good to see Chengtu once more, and sad too, for on a
day in June, incendiary bombs had rained upon the graceful old
city. Wide stretches of wasteland had opened up in the heart of
the town. Five hundred men and women and children had died.
Even the big campus had been bombed and students killed and
wounded. It seemed to me almost as if the bombing had stiffened
the morale of Chengtu, and that the people walked with a firmer
stride and a wiser look. My one-day visit there was a preliminary
warning of what awaited me in Chungking, where the raids still
blasted and burned.

I was able to book passage on a mail plane leaving the next dawn for Chungking. During that hour's flight, I was half-sick with fear — fear, not of what would happen, but of what I should find there. So strong was the personality of Chungking, so humorous and big and rowdy, so full of new hopes and booming programs, that it had become for some of us a personal friend. Now a sentence of death had been decreed. Already the massive old stronghold had suffered and I had not been there to do my part.

The chorus of a song ran foolishly through my mind: the Chungking Rotary Club's theme song, sung by its Chinese and foreign members in full and mellow throat every Thursday night.

> Oh, it's Chungking,
> Famous Chungking!
> Of all the world's cities,
> The most unique thing.
> Some folks call it hilly,
> But we think that's silly.
> So we'll all sing,
> 'Here's to Chungking!'

The small green mail plane purred lazily toward the place where far below two rivers met. Between them lay the bumpy city-laden promontory that had caught my eye so many months ago on the flight from Kweilin. As we circled lower, I could make out Chungking's roof-tops, her filaments of streets; and for a moment I thought, 'Why, it's hardly touched!' Then I noticed that upon certain wide sections of the city lay a queer leprous scab of dirty white.

$$\overline{}\left(\,12\,\right)\overline{}$$

CHUNGKING ON FIRE

ONCE again, in mocking repetition, my plane settled light as dust upon its island sandbar. 'Return to Chungking!' I thought bitterly, remembering the gay confidence and jubilance that ran riot in the city on that day in March when we rode out upon the Chengtu road. Leaving my luggage at a friend's house, I started out in a ricksha, telling the boy to take me to Dai Chia Hang. At first we passed through a section that was very little damaged. The high gray blocks looked tattered and scratched-up, but the buildings still stood and the gay banners and signs still hung from their doorways. Only the streets, I noticed, were different. They were almost empty. Afterward I learned that of Chungking's seven hundred thousand inhabitants, a hundred and fifty thousand were left within the city. Forced evacuation as well as raids had cleared the town. I blessed my special military passport, signed by the Generalissimo, and the small additional Chungking passport with my picture on it which permitted me to enter the city. But I missed the crowds, the careening rickshas, the booming shops. Not even at dawn had the old Chungking been so still, so spiritless and lonely.

The noon sun was high as we wheeled through the silent streets, past the boarded-up store fronts, past the little park in the center of town where the branches of the trees looked oddly blackened.

Without warning, we came to the end of the city. Before us, as far as the eye could reach, Chungking had disappeared. In its place was a wasteland, a monstrous twisted dump. Hardly any wall stood up to mar the view. The fallen bricks made lumpy mounds, white with dead ashes. Nothing looked very much like a house. The fire had been too hot. It was impossible to tell one street from another. For a mile we passed through the white desert that had been the proud shopping and business center of Chungking. Soon I could not be sure what part of the town stood before me.

> Of all the world's cities
> The most unique thing.

Exactly. No city had even looked quite like this. Just ahead there lay like a plump oasis a group of buildings that had miraculously survived the fire. A small crumbled alleyway led into their midst, the alley itself fringed with white ruin. At the mouth of the alley, my ricksha boy unaccountably stopped.

'Please do not stop,' I told him. 'I wish to go to Dai Chia Hang.'

'This Dai Chia Hang,' he said. And again, 'This Dai Chia Hang.'

My last weeks in Chungking were a strange blend of violence and peace. Half the time was spent with Mrs. Brown, who was keeping house in a Canadian mission residence on the far side of the Yangtze. (Skipper had long since arrived, seen that his wife was safely moved out of the city, and then gone on by plane to Hongkong and Shanghai with plans to return later in the summer.) The strangest days and nights for me were those spent within the city. I had much work to do here with the government information bureau, checking on a multitude of facts and statistics. Dozens of films must be taken of the ruins and the reconstruction. After the first raids, the foreign population had largely moved out into the hills to their summer cottages. But I found five or six old friends still living in the city, men whose mission work forced them to brave out the bombings. Most of us boarded at my old home on Dai Chia Hang. The place still hung together, although bombs had ringed it in on several occasions. It was in the heart of the burned areas. Every time I entered or left the house, I had to pass by the unrecognizable ruins of the shops we had once known so well — the tailor's small establishment, the barber shop where my hair had been elegantly waved, the dim, crowded little restaurant that had been a meeting-place for all hours. The Americans who lived here had more than once saved the mission from incendiary bombs, and in the process had come uncomfortably close to death. Whenever the air-raid alarm sounded, they would grow restless and troubled. But not very much was said. We had long ago filled the garden with round holes, four or five feet deep, with trap doors made of bamboo to pull down over our heads. Unfortunately we looked so foolish inside them, so embarrassingly like prairie dogs, that we never quite had the courage to use them. True, there were dugouts belonging to the near-by hospital. But I for one was deathly afraid of dugouts. Concussion alone was often enough to collapse them and bury the occupants alive in suffocating dirt. I have not yet dared enter one. Raids on Chungking were in a class by themselves. They were, in brief, violent rains of bombs upon a small river-bound promontory. The men living and working here within the city knew that there was slim hope of perpetual escape; that probably one day their turn would come.

My own fear of the city that had chilled me through the winter was of a specialized sort — a simple animal fear of fire. Hemmed in by rivers on three sides, Chungking was born to be a firetrap. Bombs were something else. In a sense, they were exhilarating. Now that great fire lanes had been opened out within the city and the danger of being trapped was over, my fear left me. I cherished every moment I could spend here. The big mutilated town was the friendliest place in the world. Some life still went on within her walls. In late afternoon, the restaurants and shops opened. As in Yenan, there was a blossoming in the night hours which even the moonlight raids could not dampen. Most of the government offices had moved out of the city before spring; now the rest had followed. Beyond the neck of the promontory and for twenty miles around, the Kuomintang carried on its work for Free China. In serene disregard for the bombings, new fireproof buildings were springing up by the dozen outside the city, new roads were under construction. The business of reconstruction went blithely on its way. In a curious sense, Chungking was still a boom town. Let the Japanese bomb and burn the old city and lay her in her grave! The new one, decentralized, spread out upon the countryside, was indestructible.

Gradually I picked up the details of the raid on May 4 which had started the worst fires. Like Kweilin, Chungking was good fuel. One fire, a mile in length, had swept through the heart of the city, others had roared up the one main road leading from the promontory. Apparently there had been little panic. Although the people had massed up helplessly in the streets, they had moved along steadily and surely to the safer waterfront. There had been no pushing or trampling. But in too many cases, the fire had been swift and the streets narrow. The people had been trapped. Only the work of the firemen in finally putting out the conflagrations saved the greater mass of the population from burning alive. As it was, several thousand died that night.

The panic came afterward, when with the dawn the fires began to die down and the people who had fled the conflagration came back to their devastated homes. For a few hours, chaos and hysteria ruled the city, while men and women searched in panic for their lost families, children who had become separated in the mêlée wandered weeping in the smoky streets, wounded in the

ruins screamed for help while the fire crept toward them and
there was no one near to dig them out.

Now, with nearly every raid, more and more of the city was
given to the flames. Fire engines were handicapped by the fact
that most of the streets were steps, and most of the fires could
not be reached.

> Some folks call it hilly,
> But we think that's silly....

But casualties were no longer large. Great tunnels that had
been blasted fifty feet below the surface of the rock were long
enough to shelter the remaining population. Order had been
restored out of chaos, and something very like peace had settled
over the city. Not a physical peace, of course, but a psychological
one. Japan's bombs were destroying Chungking, obliterating her.
By the fall of 1940, not one section of the promontory was to be
left standing. But in some impossible way, Chungking had survived her own death. She had proven herself immortal. The
people knew this. They saw their government operating without
fuss, almost without notice of the burning of its capital. They
saw reforms continue, education increase, relief centers spring
up, refugee villages come into being overnight. True, there was
much suffering, most of it conducting itself quietly in the hills
and country districts where one would not notice. But on the
whole Chungking, that had lived so many months in terror and
fear of destruction, had now tasted destruction and found it not
quite fatal. With a sense almost of relief, the people went about
their business. Chiang's Central Government had chalked up
one more important victory.

Even the new-found unity and selfless enthusiasm within the
Kuomintang had survived the trial by fire. During my first visit
to the city in January, the worst dissenter I found there within
government circles was Wang Ching-wei, who, with his clique, was
even then threatening discord His flight from Chungking a month

later and the cleaning out of his henchmen from officialdom had
cleared the air. Today, the Communists were too occupied with
a fight for the freedom of China to make serious trouble for the
Kuomintang. In Yunnan, Governor Lung, an old-school war lord
and virtual dictator of his province, who had never quite committed himself to loyalty, was being gradually drawn into the
fold, and gave promise of becoming one of Chiang's strongest
allies. True, there must have been some quiet grumbling on the
part of officials at the hectic conditions under which they lived.
But more important still, they continued to do their work and to
do it well. A certain buoyancy and devil-may-care spirit was carrying Chungking through the bitter months of summer and no fog.

The job of rebuilding China upon firm ground went on unperturbed. One afternoon in mid-July, I was taken by the
mountainous Colonel Huang on a New Life Movement carnival
tour. It was just that — a carnival. The Colonel was born to be
a circus barker. His years in America had made of him a publicity genius of the first order, and his system of instilling in the
Chinese villagers the New Life Movement's ideals of sanitation
and Spartan living would have done credit to a P. T. Barnum.
We set off that afternoon in a truck that was outfitted with
moving-picture apparatus, sound projector, quantities of posters
and decorations, stacks of booklets, a mobile medical clinic and
personnel. Outside the city, we passed through suburb after
suburb so crowded that it was a wonder we passed through them
at all. Here a large part of Chungking's exiled population had
settled down for the summer months. Farther on, the Colonel
proudly conducted me through some of the mat-shed villages that
the government had built for the city's refugees. At last we drew
up before the soccer field of a large middle school.

'We do this with our sound trucks all over West China,'
Colonel Huang told me with justifiable pride. 'Watch and see
what happens.'

Within half an hour, the soccer field had been transformed into a parade ground. Posters of every kind floated to the breezes. Most of them bore comic-strip episodes in gaily colored pictures: stories of ailing young men who learned just too late or just in time the wonders of modern medicine; of young mothers who absorbed modern hygiene and just too late or just in time saved the lives of their babies; of gentlemen who became great by giving up their pet vices; of little boys who became governors by working hard at school; of a whole host of people who curbed various plagues by learning not to spit on the streets. The tales were imposing. So were the pictures.

'What do you think of it?' Colonel Huang's deep-throated bellow hit me like the blow of a fist.

'Wonderful!' I told him. 'I am almost moved to give up my opium-smoking and my spitting on the streets.'

'Wait till you see the rest,' he roared.

Meanwhile, at the side of the field, the medical clinic was holding forth. Business was good. Several hundred people were inoculated against cholera and typhoid in the course of a few hours. As soon as it grew dark, Colonel Huang set up his moving pictures and the show began. Some of the films were national propaganda pictures dealing with the reforms that were sweeping the country and the joys of reconstruction. Others were films on Western medicine and personal hygiene. They were not bad at all. I found myself gaping at them like any movie-struck female. The sound commentary did not satisfy the energetic Colonel, who rained his own remarks like manna upon the hungry audience. Between the films he made a speech that held us spellbound. For the thousandth time I blessed the man for a genius. Had he been born an American, he would have been either an actor or a campaign manager. Here in China, as the overtaxed head of the New Life Movement, the Officers' Moral Endeavor Society, the Wounded Soldiers' Bonus, and three or four other relief organizations, he was probably doing a somewhat more constructive job of work.

At least a thousand people listened to our program. And I could swear that the town went to bed that night a chastened but uplifted town.

Meanwhile life flowed on amongst the foreign population across the Yangtze. Brownie was dashing about these days on a score of relief jobs; but her household was amusingly normal, her coffee excellent, and her garden parties large and hilarious. Five explosive and incendiary bombs that had collapsed her gate house and dug up her lawn had failed to interrupt the placidity of the establishment. I admired the foreign colony for its refusal to be ruffled. Embassy secretaries, Standard Oil employees, Navy men aboard the American gunboat *Tutuila*, worked hard in the sickly heat and somehow held on to their courtesy. *Cherchez la femme* had taken on new meaning here. As far as I could judge, I was the one unmarried American maiden in the capital.

For the preservation of our sanity, we formed a 'Suicide Club' which met every Sunday for some relaxation. Usually we climbed aboard our shaggy Tibetan or Kweichow ponies and made for the hills. Buried far back in the Second Range was a swimming-pool where we could gather a few moments of semi-coolness. The word 'suicide' sprang from the incredible personalities of our ponies, who would go so far as to fling themselves off small cliffs in order to dislodge us. The paths among the mountains and riverbanks were generally stone steps, slightly steeper than the average household stairs. Our talented ponies would climb the steps with loud grunts and descend them at a dead run, quite often landing in a scrambled heap at the foot. During each excursion, at least two or three members of the party returned with assorted sprains and bruises. The ponies were our only vehicles of transportation aside from sedan chairs. We went calling, even dancing, on pony-back. Brownie's private animal, whose name was Stanley Napoleon, bore me nobly during these weeks. He only fell down with me twice. It seemed quite natural to trot out to lunch with friends who lived deep in the mountains and five miles away. By this time I was thoroughly used to not very sure-footed ponies on precarious paths.

But I never failed to clutch myself in terror at the almost daily trips I was forced to take on Chungking's steam ferries. They were lowly scows. Generally they were so crowded that the river water lapped over the floor boards at my feet. With passengers standing in the type of jam found in New York express subways, the groaning craft would head out into the Yangtze's current and, tearing sideways down the river, begin a lumbering, swaying motion not at all proper in ferries. Now and then an overloaded ferry would turn turtle, and since the current did not permit even the stoutest swimmer an opportunity to swim, the possibility was disturbing. More often, they blew up. Each crossing took forty minutes and aged me considerably.

One gray afternoon, I started to cross by ferry to Brownie's home, only to find that the ferries were not running that day. No explanation was given. In some remote part of my brain, I noticed that the Yangtze seemed higher than usual and the current roaring in a way I had not heard before. Much later, I learned that sudden thaws in the mountains of Tibet had raised the river level slightly over fifteen feet in the past two hours. The old Yangtze was in flood. In the space of an afternoon, her surface had become a sheet of rapids. For three days she was unnavigable. But no one had thought to warn me of the Yangtze's sudden moods. I decided to take a sampan. The refusal of one boatman after another to brave the river only made me more stubborn. Had they told me the reason for their refusal, I might have had more caution. But I went blithely ahead with my efforts and thereby drew as near to leaving this earth as I shall, God willing, ever come.

At last a boatman agreed to make the trip. Several other marooned citizens, seeing us about to start, decided to join us. A moment later we shoved out into the gray water.

Twenty feet from shore, the current caught us. Like a toy in a maelstrom, our boat was swept sideways down the river at a speed that was not wholly believable. Behind us the city fled past. The boatman, sculling at the stern, began yelling unintelligible orders to his two oarsmen at the bow. They dug in their oars and tried to bring the flat little boat about and make for the shore we had just left. The boat did not respond because it was out of control. With my heart pounding in my ears, I reached down and unlaced my shoes, and at the same time offered up a small prayer to what powers there might be. A moment later, the boat slipped into a sucking whirlpool. Instantly it began to spin in a wide circle. Panic caught us all simultaneously. Only the boatmen kept their heads and made constant and futile stabs at the soft swollen current. The boat began to keel, slowly at first, then faster until one gunwale slid under the surface and water began to pour in upon us. We had barely presence of mind enough to climb onto the other gunwale, where our combined weights held the sampan at this crazy angle for a few precious moments. An eternity passed and the boat slipped out of the whirlpool, and slowly righting herself sped on down the river.

For twenty minutes we were alone upon the flood. No more eddies caught us, and the floating wreckage that marred the surface of the river passed us by. The boatmen plowed the water always in the direction of the far shore. Within the first ten minutes we had left the junction of the two rivers and the city upon her promontory far behind. When at last, many miles below Chungking, we drew near the farther shore, it did not seem possible that we could land at such a speed, for there was no way to check the sampan on her drunken sidelong course. But by this time the boatmen were laughing at the whole affair, making scornful remarks about the river. As the docks rushed up at us, they leaned far out with their boathooks, dug in, and, bracing their legs hard, hung on. Instantly the hooks were jerked out of their hands and they sprawled backward. But the momentary reduction of speed was enough to send us slamming sideways at the pier. The crowd that waited there caught at the sampan as she hit. They held her, though the impact knocked all of us into the well of the boat and stove in her side. One by one we climbed out, wet, scared, shaky. But we were across.

It was a night of terror on the river. When I reached home at last, I found officers from the *Tutuila* marooned there, unable to navigate the hundred feet of water that separated the anchored gunboat from the shore. As the dark closed in, we set out for the officers' canteen, a much-loved clubhouse perched a mile away upon the riverbank and overlooking the gunboat. I rode there in a borrowed sedan chair, high on the shoulders of four chair coolies. The chair was an ornate box borne upon heavy poles, carved with serpent shapes and gaudy with paint. The uniformed coolies were but slightly less spectacular. They padded up and down the winding steps that led through the cluttered waterfront blocks, and their chanting rose above the thunder of the Yangtze. Beneath dim archways we moved, our lanterns swaying. Slum quarters stood tier upon tier, with a way of life that had not changed very much with the passing of the centuries. Silent figures brushed us by. Through open doorways, I could see now and then a fire burning, and perhaps a group of forms crouched intent upon their rice bowls. Within this rabbit-warren, the darkness was complete. Only now and then a strip of sky stood above us, gay with stars; and below us the big river showed its teeth in white rapids. Its voice smothered out all sounds of the crowded, gusty life that went on here.

No sooner were we settled on the balcony of the canteen than a flurry of yells drifted in from the river. A large junk had broken

loose from its moorings somewhere upstream, and we could see
it now coming fast down the flood. Not much of it showed above
the water, for it was sinking. Thirty or forty dark forms clung
to the forward deck, waiting for the end to come. Behind the
junk a sampan rode the current, its crew poised at the bow with
boathooks held ready. We learned afterward that the sampan's
crew had seen the doomed junk and had deliberately pushed off
to try and pick up the men and women aboard her. Both craft
were sweeping down the river a hundred feet offshore. They were
bearing directly down upon the *Tutuila*. The seconds passed.
For a moment it looked as if the junk would clear the gunboat.
Then it struck her glancingly, stove in one of her portholes, and
instantly sank. By some miracle the *Tutuila's* moorings held.
At once we could see the crowds of American seamen busy
at her rails. Hooks and ropes were lowered and three or four
black forms were pulled over the side of the ship. Of the rest, no
sign was ever seen. At the same moment, the gallant little sampan struck the bow of the gunboat and capsized. One of her crew
was caught and rescued as he swept past. I saw another sucked
under the bow of the *Tutuila*. Seconds later he bobbed up again
below her stern, still struggling. Then the dark and the river
swallowed him and he was gone.

An hour passed. The sight of that mass drowning was still in
my brain. We were sitting inside the canteen trying to be gay.
Suddenly all conversation stopped and we froze in immobility.
There it came again, this time very clear, a yell from the *Tutuila:*
'Man overboard!'

The sound of that phrase above the roaring of the river held a
quality of ice. It meant that an American sailor was overboard.
It meant that he had not very much chance to live.

Perhaps three seconds passed while we ran to the balcony.
At the end of those three seconds the searchlight at the gunboat's
bridge flashed on. It cut across the dark surface of the river.

Almost at once it picked up a blacker speck drifting rapidly down the current. Five seconds later we heard the deep roar of the *Tutuila's* speedboat, the one craft which could hope to battle the current. The powerful racer thrust out from the gunboat's flank and, circling, thundered downstream toward the place, now much farther away, where the pencil of light met the river's surface. Then we could no longer see the bobbing head. Pretty soon we could not even find the motorboat. We could only stand there silently.

Again an hour passed. It took the speedboat that long to fight the current back. The officers with me yelled across, and after an eternity or so the reply came, 'Got him!'

Several days passed before we could learn the whole story. The crew member, marooned on shore, had unwisely tried to cross that hundred-foot strip of current in a sampan. He had started well upstream and had reached the *Tutuila,* but the force of the impact as he struck the gunboat had caused the sampan to capsize. The motorboat that went after him caught him at last just above a stretch of rapids that would have pulled him under. Had the man chosen any section of the river for his impromptu ducking other than the side of his gunboat, he would not have been heard of again. As matters stood, the rescue was a spectacular bit of co-ordination and nerve, and scarcely caused the crew of the *Tutuila* to flicker an eyelash.

The days passed and the heat grew worse. Hidden in the suburbs and in the hills between Chungking and Chengtu, the great mass of the city's exiled population suffered quietly and without complaint. Occasionally death came out into the open, for the well-organized relief efforts on the part of the Kuomintang and missionaries could not wholly stem the epidemics. One morning I passed a group of thin young recruits clustered on Chungking's foreshore, awaiting their marching orders. Three of the boys were stretched out on the steps; a fourth lay crumpled in an unused sedan chair. I went up and spoke to one of them, but he did not answer. He was dead. A single glance was enough to tell me that he had died of cholera. Another was still conscious and gasping hard for breath, but not quite able to lift his head from the stones. When I knelt down to feel his pulse, he grinned at me in intense embarrassment. But even as I held his wrist lightly, the heartbeat stopped and the smile froze foolishly upon his face.

The mission hospitals were doing the impossible these days, for the municipal hospitals within the city had been long since obliterated. Only the Methodist Hospital at Dai Chia Hang, a bulky brick refuge in a desert of white ruin, carried on emergency clinics for the wounded. Others outside the city worked to stem the agony and death that infected the countryside. Mission doctors were white with fatigue.

And still the heat grew and we sagged limply about our small affairs. A letter had arrived for me from my New York employers asking me to continue my work through the summer and fall, and return from China before Christmas to lecture in the United States. My articles and press releases, even my photographs, had come through all right, and were raising money for relief. At once I made tentative reservations for the next possible plane to Hongkong, thinking to tour Japanese-occupied territory and return to Chungking for a brief visit in the fall.

Meanwhile I watched, justifiably wide-eyed, at the resilience of the Chinese Government in its battered stronghold. The Kuomintang's finances were still strong. True, the exchange value of the Central Government currency was dropping, thanks partly to Shanghai's incurable love of speculation and manipulation and the various brands of military Yen with which the Japanese were flooding the market. Silver reserves in America and England were low, but soon to be increased by further stabilization loans. The Western world had discovered China to be a conscientious bor-

rower, and stood increasingly ready to back her with loans that
are even now being paid off by export shipments of tungsten and
wood oil.

As for the internal economy, it was based upon the possibility
of many years of battle. Financially, the Kuomintang long before
the war had kept itself rigidly conservative. Issues of banknotes
were maintained well below the saturation point. The very word
'inflation' would have caused a ripple of horror among the astute
bankers of the land. Because of the country's low per capita
wealth, the national income had leaned heavily upon customs
duties and such indirect taxes as the salt tax and consolidation
tax. But it had been backed up by a hinterland wildly rich in
natural resources and with a basically strong agriculture.

Since the outbreak of war, the Kuomintang has clung like
death to its conservative ways. With a feeling that time alone
could defeat the Japanese and that only a fiscal policy capable of
growing old gracefully could cope with the difficult years ahead,
Chungking's ministry of finance has turned its back on excessive
inflation. The increase of note issues has been relatively slight.
The floating of government loans has been moderate. Even the
taxes have been kept in most cases as they were, and in the case
of war sufferers and budding industries, they have been reduced
or eliminated altogether. Financially China has pulled her
punches. She can afford to do so, for she has resources that
Japan cannot claim. Instead of running her war wholly on cash,
she has tapped her hidden wealth of minerals, speeded up her
industry and food production by loans of raw materials and tools,
co-ordinated her man power into co-operative units that may
some day make the nation self-sufficient. More than anything
else, she has won the confidence of her own people. Voluntary
giving has become a national pastime. Men are willing to invest
and banks to loan; and funds pour in from overseas Chinese.

The situation is anything but perfect. Prices have risen

enormously in certain interior cities, chiefly from poor transportation facilities and the inadequacy of supply to meet the increased demand. All too often, the exorbitant price of rice and other staple commodities has resulted from hoarding and deliberate price inflation on the part of certain uncharming individuals who like the feel of money in their pockets. The recent execution of Mayor Yang of Chengtu on the charge of hoarding may mean that the Kuomintang has lost patience with the gentlemen. But for all this, China's internal economy stands moderately firm. It may even improve with time, should transportation continue to be stepped up at its present rate of speed and hoarding to be stamped out. As long as the Burma Road remains open, passage to the sea is assured, and consequent backing from England and the United States. The strange truth remains that hard-pressed China, as yet unburdened by an enormous war debt, is financially stronger than her enemy.

Politically the Government hangs together with deceptive tenacity. Even more surprising, it has held on to some measure of its democracy — no easy feat in wartime — and the evidence of this democracy lies not in the glib and highly democratic slogans which I heard on every side but, more reliably, in the physical bone structure of the Central Government and its day-to-day control of Free China. Before the war, the Kuomintang was definitely the party in power and not to be dislodged except by force. Since the outbreak of war, it has been formulating plans for a far more liberal democracy based upon popular vote, to be put into operation with the coming of peace. Whether or not this government-of-the-future will live to see the light rests upon a multitude of 'ifs' and 'perhaps.'

The present government divides its labors amongst a confusing conglomerate of councils and *Yuans*, meaning 'organizations.' While the war is in progress, the highest authority will be held by the Supreme National Defense Council, although unlike most military cliques, its deeds are open to criticism and pressure from other groups within the Government. Corresponding to our Cabinet is the Executive Yuan; and our Congress has its counterpart in the Kuomintang's Legislative Yuan, which does not, however, have the power of impeachment. All impeachment duties are relegated to the Control Yuan, which spends its days happily investigating Kuomintang officials. The principal agency of non-military legislation is the Judicial Yuan. The Examination Yuan is the Central Government's personnel bureau for officialdom. The most democratic group within the Central Government is the People's Political Council, its two hundred-odd members chosen from every province, including Mongolia and Tibet. Laymen including many professional men, they are elected by various provincial and municipal boards. Once a year they convene at Chungking to receive reports upon the proposed policies of the Kuomintang and to deliberate upon them. They have no absolute power of veto, but their opinions bring considerable weight to bear upon the Government.

Though it is the party in power, the Kuomintang is astonishingly democratic in spirit. Over 60 per cent of the officials working for the Central Government are not members of the Kuomintang. One of them, for instance, is Doctor Hu Shih. The Communists' representative in Chungking, Cho En-lai, holds a definite position in the Government. Any man of ability who is willing to work with and not against the Kuomintang, regardless of his political views, is welcome. Tolerance is still a part of life in Chungking. Students are allowed unbelievable freedom of expression, and frequently take advantage of the fact. Occasionally, when criticism becomes too sharp, restrictions are ordered, but only to be relaxed later on. There is definite censorship of the press — and one which cannot compare to the rigid censorship that exists in England and the Continent; it serves, however, to arouse the indignation of American pressmen who feel that the

Central Government should trust them without question. Passes are required to travel about the country, but on only two or three occasions was I called upon to produce one. There is nowhere the sense of the heavy hand, the perpetually kibitzing Government, that has laid its pall of fear and suspicion over Europe.

Oddly enough, the chairman of the National Government is not Chiang Kai-shek, but a certain gentleman by the name of Lin Sen. Chiang's positions are numerous and give him at least a finger in every pie. He is head of the Kuomintang Party, Commander-in-Chief of the Army, Navy, and Air Force, Chairman of the People's Political Council, of the governing boards of the four leading banks, of the Military Council. But his powers are definitely limited. He is by no means a dictator, as some, distrustful of the term 'Generalissimo,' would suppose. He cannot make laws, control currency or finance, choose his own henchmen. He cannot, in fact, do anything at all without putting the matter before the proper group of men. He can put nothing into effect *per se*. In the time-honored system used by the Quakers, every proposed act must be placed before the round table, examined, rejected or accepted according to the weight of opinion. Quite naturally, the power of the Generalissimo is great in that his officials regard his ideas with deference, recognizing in him the highest hope of victory and respecting him as their leader with a respect that is pretty spontaneous. But they can and sometimes do override his wishes. It may be stated with absolute certainty that he has no love of personal power.

Chiang's reputation in Free China is a curious one. He is little publicized. Far more often does the picture of Sun Yat-Sen appear on official walls. No halo is painted in about Chiang's head, no eulogies spread at his feet. But every farmer and housewife and beggar and priest and child knows all about the Generalissimo. He is the leader who is pulling China together and holding the Japanese in check. In all my months with the people there, months of small conversations and a thousand questions, I could find no man or woman willing to speak critically of Chiang Kai-shek or of his Government. Nor could I find one who would acknowledge the possibility of defeat.

Morale was not won there with trick statements or with false propaganda. There was propaganda, true; and I was startled to find it mild and strangely truthful. On the whole, Chinese reports upon their military activities are fairly accurate. Pamphlets and wall posters, though sometimes violent, are more apt to cry a note of tolerance. Madame Chiang, almost as American as she is Chinese, is more uncompromising in her attitude toward the Japanese. She has the bitterness which we in America would feel were our country invaded. But her husband is pure Chinese. He may call his people to victory against the invader; he may bid them fight for their country; but the blasting recriminations common to military leaders are just not there. His attitude, and the tone of his propaganda, is wholly realistic: a simple statement that the Japanese people are not responsible for this war, that they are scarcely aware of what is happening in China, that even the soldiers fight because they are forced to do so. The guilt, says Chiang Kai-shek and his people, lies upon the heads of the Japanese military. 'Fight, Resist, Rebuild Nation!' — it is Free China's official slogan. No mention of blame. It gives one a confidence in the Generalissimo that is not at all naïve. The tone of his propaganda points directly to the fact that he is preparing now for peace; that he knows that the Japanese, once free of their military clique, could be turned from enemies into good neighbors, that they need free trade and some economic concessions in China which might be actually beneficial if justly handled, and that without them, Japan will rise again and the whole miserable business will repeat itself. By keeping his people free of bitterness, he is preparing now for a sometime friendship with Japan. In a sense, the future peace and harmony of the East hinges upon whether or not he will have his way.

On the afternoon of July 24 I received my flying orders. A booking had been made for me, said a message, on a C.N.A.C. passenger plane leaving the next afternoon for Hongkong. The warning was short, because planes come and go rather furtively in Free China. On the Hongkong flight they must pass directly over Japanese-occupied territory in the region of Canton, and the gentlemen of Japan are only too pleased to down them. Already several passenger planes had been shot down and many others chased through the clouds. Chungking's transports could leave for Hongkong only in comparatively bad weather — a state of affairs typical of this peculiar war.

I tucked the message into my purse and hauled forth my suitcase from under Brownie's bed. It was just as well, perhaps, that I did not know that I was preparing to leave Chungking for the last time.

My packing was rudely interrupted. For almost ten days we had had no air raids. Tonight at dusk, as if to bestow upon me a fitting send-off, the sirens screamed the approach of enemy planes. Probably an hour would pass before their arrival. This amazing city frequently knew the exact moment in which Japanese bombers in Hankow were being loaded. I finished packing and sat down to write a letter, wondering somewhere in my mind whether Brownie's house was scheduled once more to play host to some Japanese bombs. There was a small dugout near the gate. By sitting near the doorway I could look down upon the whole of Chungking and still be ready to duck should matters grow uncomfortable. Meanwhile, I was alone in the house. Pretty soon the lights flickered off and I went to fetch a candle.

Half an hour later the urgent warning broke in upon the clack of my typewriter. At the same moment the roar of planes began, the high falsetto of Chinese pursuits taking off to meet the oncoming enemy. I wandered out into the dark garden. Coolies and servants sat in clusters near the door of the dugout, quietly smoking or chatting, just visible by the half-moon. Below us the river lay in a pale glow and beyond it the promontory, wholly dark. There was no betraying flicker of light. No city showed upon its apparently wild night slopes. But within the darkness, the city and the people waited.

Now the cicada hum about us grew louder, now more guttural, and a wedge of nine black shapes swept low, directly over our heads, so low that we took it to be a squadron of Chinese pursuits and did not know that enemy bombers were passing us by. In the same second a dozen searchlights thrust upward at the night sky, probing the dark, and then caught the planes in a prism of light and changed them into whitened ghosts.

Far down the river a row of bright small flowers blossomed along the shore. A second flight of eighteen bombers were sweeping up upon the city from the south, dropping their bombs as they came. Anti-aircraft guns swung into action and streaked a pattern of fox fire across the sky. The two flights of bombers met over the city, merged, and circled back. For just a moment, the section of Chungking over which they passed remained dark and still — the new city beyond the promontory and the Chang Pei district on the far bank of the little Kialing River. Then thunder rolled out in staccato bursts and a hundred flaming polyps thrust their arms upward as bombs raddled the city. For just a moment, the promontory was bright as day.

Now the twenty-seven bombers were over the river, spearing toward us and flying low, their shapes silvered by the wheeling searchlights. Even as we watched, without any warning at all, a group of ten smaller planes materialized from the darker sky above them, coming at a fast dive. Chinese pursuits! Fast little black crosses, they swooped down upon their ponderous enemies and broke up the formation. The fight was on. Weaving back and forth they went, almost above our heads, up against the moon and held by a dozen searchlights. The anti-aircraft fire was silent, but the exhaust of each war plane lumined its course and red tracer bullets cut a filigree of fire across the night. I followed a Chinese fighter plane in its flight through the bedeviled sky, saw it dive, sideslip, climb straight up for altitude without bothering to circle, duck through the shifting cloud of black shapes, then dive once more with guns spitting sparks.

For almost ten minutes they fought their moonstruck battle above the river. Now and then a plane sped across the moon's face. The night was growing oddly red, almost molten. Looking down I saw that Chang Pei was burning, sending a glow that was almost a sunrise across the sky. At last the dogfight swept over the mainland to the north of us and a final load of bombs burst in crisp slaps upon our bank of the river. Still fighting, the host of planes slipped from sight beyond the hills, the jazzy din faded out, and we were alone with each other and with our burning city.

For a long time I watched the fire spread. At first a round chrysalis of flame, it began to lengthen, to send out bright arteries and smaller capillaries until a fragile network of flickering light stretched across the densely packed town. I guess the wind caught it then, for it began to grow high. It churned up over a hill, and after that it became a half-mile cascade of fire that engulfed block upon block in long arms and streamers of flames and fled across the city in a hot red wave. It was roaring now, thrusting up its giddy flames in bright antic shapes. The sky above our heads grew dark red.

Brownie and I did our best to sleep that night. Unfortunately my cot was out upon an upstairs porch where I could watch every leap and flick of fire from the burning city. When I closed my eyes, the glare stayed against my eyeballs, pulsing and shifting as the fire shifted. At midnight, worn out from resting there, I slipped out of bed, climbed into ancient slacks and shirt, and shouldering my camera set out for Chang Pei.

At the riverbank, I was lucky enough to find a sampan that

would scull me across. In midstream we could feel the first breath
of heat. A moment later, I was climbing slowly up the avenue of
steps that I had trod once before in first-aid duty after that long-
ago January raid. The houses near the waterfront had escaped
the fire. But on the crest of the hill, the tortured flames still lingered. They burned slowly as in old heaps of rubbish, and I was
able to walk through the streets and see on either side the glowing
skeleton of Chang Pei. Except for workmen fighting the dying
fire, I saw no one there at all. Now and then a wall crashed down,
spitting sparks in a fragile cloud. Small flames lapped at window
sills and blackened doorways, curled about the charred legs of
tables, sucked briefly at a sprawled pair of chopsticks and a
child's silken cap, left the chopsticks pure black and the cap a
feathery round ash. Very few walls stood firm. Most of the region was an uneven heaping of bricks and black rubble where fire
lurked.

A phrase of poetry wandered into my thoughts from somewhere out of my childhood — a phrase from Byron:

Man marks the earth with ruin ...

Gradually the people came back. They went through the step
streets slowly, as I did, stopping to gaze or to kick at a burning
fragment. As the fire cooled, men, and women too, and even
children, began to pry tentatively through the smoky pyres; and
I was reminded of Kweilin and the upheaval of work that began
there at the moment when the last flame died.

Once I passed a house that had partly escaped the conflagration. By some freak of fire, the kitchen at the back of the home
was still standing, though I could look across the ruins and directly into it as though it were a stage. In the foreground, the
humped débris of the gutted house glowed with sudden and shifting flames. And within that small kitchen, I saw a man and a
woman and two children. They were crouched about a brazier

in the middle of the floor, and with rice bowls and chopsticks in hand they partook of their early morning meal while the rest of their home still flamed and smoldered about them ...

Darkness was bleaching into white foggy dawn when I started up the last row of terraced fields toward home. Each curve of the steps, each sudden tree, corn patch and graveyard and anonymous small shack was fingered by the mist, a dim ghost of a landscape. Below, somewhere, the river coiled, and above was the piling up of hills. For no very great reason, I left the steps and began to climb up through the terraced fields. In a moment I would see my own house, so I stopped because I did not want to reach home. I wanted to stay here where it was still China. I sat down on a clump of weeds and watched a brown figure slip by me down the fog, stripped to the waist, two heavy wooden buckets swinging from a pole across his shoulder. A coolie emptying slops. He hummed a tune to his running walk, and the tune stayed for a long time after he had vanished in the woolly light.

Queer to think that in no other land but China could I wander alone through the night hours in such sure and absolute safety. There was nothing here so strange, not any other place so friendly. I stretched out almost flat with my head against the bank, my elbows digging into the soil, a clump of moss beneath my hand, feeling ridiculously comforted and cared for by this foggy field. The Byron poem. What was it? ...

And laid my hand upon thy mane — as I do here.

I tried to make my thoughts on Free China profound and impressive, as befitting the solemn occasion of farewell, and contrived merely to collapse into emotion. Later, from a vantage point, I would look back on this odd jumble that was China and, if I were unwise, draw some weighty conclusions like hot plums out of the mysterious pie. But stretched here on my shoulder blades against a prickly bank, watching Chungking slowly materialize like Valhalla from her cloudbank, I could not think but only feel.

I am alone here and never lonely, because every coolie and farmer and shopkeeper is a companion with whom to chat away the hours. Each village is my refuge, a place of good tea and small inns and a dozen lazy conversations. The dark of a narrow alley at midnight is a comfortable and pleasant dark, full of smells. Should I ask for help on a street-corner, a dozen friends would be around me like magic. For I may wander the land alone, as idly and surely as though I wandered in my own garden. And what of that Old China I had heard of once — that mysterious China, that dangerous and remote China, that bandit-ridden interior? Not, certainly, this queer, crowded, solicitous, amused old place?

'All sentiment aside,' I thought, 'you'll probably never have a closer friend. You'll come back here for peace some day. Peace. That's pretty funny.'

I found myself unconsciously and foolishly stroking the moss beside me with my hand.

(13)

CHINA UNDER JAPAN

IT HAD taken us well over a month to travel from Shanghai to Chungking. My return trip was completed in exactly five days. Because the island air field was under water, a Commodore hydroplane carried my fellow passengers and me twenty miles or so outside Chungking to the military landing field. Transferring to a Douglas, we left in much secrecy with blinds down. But I raised them in time to see for the last time the bumpy promontory of Chungking with its scaly white patches, and a new patch in Chang Pei, move past beneath me and out of sight.

At ten o'clock that night, we passed over Japanese territory, flying at fifteen thousand feet, with lights out and motors barely humming. Minutes later, we began to lose altitude, drifting down very gradually through the darkness and through cotton clouds. At three thousand feet, we glided through the floor of the cloud-bank and suddenly we were above Hongkong. I have not yet dreamed of anything more spectacular. We burst upon the city without warning, and I had forgotten the tales I had heard about Hongkong's harbor and her lights like jewels. In one blinding flash they were below us, necklaces and bracelets of lights, red and green and yellow and blue, coils of them, rubies, sapphires, long looping strings of pearls, emeralds caught between diamonds, flower clusters of amber and bloodstone, strewn upon the black velvet of the shore, mirrored in the harbor, set cunningly at the base of the high peaks.

It is eternally to my discredit that I saw so little of Hongkong. In the two or three days that I spent there, waiting for a coastal boat to Shanghai, I could do nothing but wander in a daze from soda fountain to grocery store to soda fountain to French restaurant and on to soda fountain, consuming large and sticky things. I was a female uncontrolled, and it is a wonder that I survived at all. Butter! Cream! Lucky Strikes! The best English ale! When some friends took me out to dinner and hurled lobster and thick steaks upon my plate, I thought that I should break down and cry. Ham and eggs for breakfast! Orange juice! Well, that was Hongkong . . .

Three days later I was in Shanghai. Eight months had passed since I sailed away on that leaky German river boat, and both the city and I were a little leaner but much the same. Skipper was in town, just polishing up his business and ready to start on a visit to his old mission station, Wuhu, sixty miles up the Yangtze from Nanking. He knew that my New York office wished me to study Japanese-occupied territory, and almost the first thing he did was to present me with a Japanese military pass to Wuhu, made out in my name. We were on the road again.

This time I did take a few days out to catch my breath, send off some copy, and deliver reports, lectures, and press interviews that did stimulating things to my ego. Then we set out once more, we two — but this time our hosts were to be the soldiers of Japan.

From the moment that our station-bound taxi nosed through the barbed-wire border that separated the International Settlement from Japanese-occupied Hongkew, our hosts were with us. They inspected our passes at every available opportunity. Before we boarded the train, they sprayed our legs with a disinfectant scarcely strong enough to kill the most enfeebled germ. They crowded the train, their swords hanging neatly from hooks. We could tell a Japanese soldier from a long way off because of his inevitable rooster way of throwing out his legs when he walked. The reason for this was not so much hauteur as the weight of his thick army shoes, which replaced the sandals and clogs that had been a part of life back home. Two or three Japanese women boarded the Nanking train with us, their bright, voluptuous houri coats and *obis* seeming strangely out of place.

At every station, guards stood by in round concrete pillboxes. Here and there along the track, old gaunt ruins, half buried in a three years' growth of grass, turned vacant eyes at the passing scene. Most of them had been the homes of farmers and countrymen. But about and around them, life went on as before. Here in the valley of the Yangtze, the rice was a dark green, and so tall that it hid the land in a high-banked, rippling sea. Each village had become a small island of trees and curling roofs. Children sprawled brown and naked and supremely comfortable upon the backs of their obedient water buffalo, while the enormous beasts waded and wallowed in the deep paddies.

A night with friends in Nanking. More pass inspection and baggage inspection and a good spray of disinfectant. Then at last we were being driven through the big walled port of Wuhu, and a half-mile beyond the city to the hill where Robert Brown's gleaming brick hospital towered high and proud above the Yangtze. There must have been close to a hundred people, Americans and Chinese, massed at the compound gate to welcome him. Others crowded the winding road that led up the slope and blackened the lawn upon the hilltop. It was a spectacular homecoming and quite worthy of the Skipper, who was vastly pleased.

As the days at Wuhu lengthened into weeks, the feeling grew upon me that in going from Free China into occupied territory I had stepped from bright sunlight into the darkest of cellars.

Jubilation, zest, buoyancy, new life and new vitality — they
were things of the past. Quietly the people of this conquered city
went about their business, enduring with an unshakable passivity
the misery and humiliation of the waking hours. Their poverty
was beyond anything which they had yet known; at this time,
the average monthly wage in Nanking (perhaps even less in
Wuhu) was eleven dollars per family, and prices were exorbitant.
Even now after a three years' occupation, the atrocities continued
on a smaller scale. The occupation of Wuhu on December 9, a
few days before the fall of Nanking, had been a bloodthirsty
prophecy to the world that Nanking might expect no mercy.
Skipper and his staff had been forced to see fleeing men and
women shot down in the streets. Girls of eleven and twelve were
brought into the hospital so torn by constant rape that in most
cases they did not live. There had never been any question as to
the truth of the stories; the most remarkable proof lay in photographs taken by the Japanese soldiers which showed them proudly
thrusting swords into men in civilian clothing and holding
women naked upon the ground. The snapshots had fallen into
the hands of missionaries and told, more graphically than any
words, exactly what happened.

Although the citizens of Wuhu went about the streets almost
mechanically, as in a prolonged nightmare, they somehow clung
to their sense of humor. It amused me to stand near a Japanese
sentry on a street-corner and watch the Chinese who were forced
to bow before him as they passed. They knew he could not understand their language. And with serious and reverent faces they
made remarks.

'Now bow to your ancestor, my child.'

'Has he not a charming thick neck, this wonderful ancestor?
I can scarcely wait to grasp it.'

'I think that you shall not have to wait long.'

'Do you suppose the poor man is ticklish?'

And so it went. Only once did I catch a glimpse of the fervency and hope that I had left behind me in Free China — on the occasion when the Japanese proclaimed a forced 'military schooling' for all the young people of the city, girls as well as boys. 'Military schooling' was no more or less than drafting into the Japanese army as mercenaries. A quiet but determined whisper spread across the city, and by nightfall it was known to us that the youth of Wuhu were planning a mass exodus into Free China, there to fight and work for their government. On the far bank of the Yangtze was guerrilla territory; they had only to cross the Yangtze. Luck was with them and no one gave the plot away. One night before dawn we watched them go, ferrying back and forth across the river in stolen sampans under the cover of an absolute darkness. Two of our hospital nurses had decided to join them, and the excitement of saying good-bye almost gave the institution a combined nervous breakdown. By morning there was scarcely a handful of young people left within the walls of Wuhu.

On our third day in the city, Skipper went to bed as a patient in his own hospital. Before leaving Shanghai he had had several severe sinus operations and then, with a horrible masculine stubbornness, had refused to take proper care of himself. Without any warning, one evening, he began to have a series of hemorrhages. The days passed and he grew weaker, and still the hemorrhages continued and would not be checked. When the staff held a special prayer service one morning, I began to be scared. Finally one evening the doctors told us that another attack would quite definitely be too much for him. On that night and on the next day and the next night we paced the halls, conversing in low, dramatic whispers like a house-party of nervous ghosts. But I might have known that Skipper would not be so unoriginal as to die. By the time that the next attack came, he was strong enough to live through it, and as the hemorrhages gradually stopped, he became a thoroughly unmanageable and indignant patient. When at last he was well enough to get about, we would gladly have thrown him out of his hospital.

Toward the end of his convalescence, the Japanese officials in the city came to him in a body, apparently to call. Their arch-enemy was confined to his bed, and they may be pardoned an uncontrollable urge to gloat. They did more than that: they refused to extend his return pass to Shanghai that had lapsed during his illness. It was two weeks before they allowed him to leave Wuhu, and after he had departed they refused to permit his return. Skipper was unperturbed. He did not love the Japanese. To work under them was far from his thoughts. Today he is holder of numerous honorary positions in Free China, and superintendent of the new hospital recently completed in Chengtu to supplement the West China Union University's medical school. It is a three-hundred-and-fifty-bed institution and the largest mission hospital in China. Skipper is content.

Our entire relationship with the Japanese of Wuhu reminded me of an apparently amiable fencing match in which the tips had inadvertently been left off the swords. Early in our visit, the American gunboat *Wahoo* (pronounced drunkenly, like 'Wuhu') had tied up at Wuhu's *bund* for a stay of several weeks. Immediately we brought down the ire of the Japanese military by our unconventional way of calling the *Wahoo's* doctor up to the hospital hill whenever he was needed. A woman doctor had boned up on her Morse code, and would save a mile's journey simply by stationing herself on the hospital's roof garden, flash-light in hand, and blinking out a series of requests and occasion-ally personal remarks. To the military of Japan, this was rank spying. Flashing flashlights from hospital roofs could be nothing else *but* spying. After every such episode, they would appear at the gate of the compound and demand that we cease spying at once.

One night they won a well-earned revenge. The hospital's foreign staff, including myself, had received invitations to attend some quite modern moving pictures aboard the *Wahoo* — an old custom of the Yangtze patrol. We jammed ourselves into several dilapidated Ford cars and proceeded in the direction of the gunboat, only to find that the Japanese had politely and happily closed every road leading to the *bund*. 'Just for the evening. We hope you will forgive us.' Route after route we tried, only to be confronted by a group of sentries whose tendency was to smile broadly from ear to ear. I could imagine just how they felt. Foreigners must be utterly exasperating to the Japanese military, rather like having someone's else children in their home who cannot be disciplined or even ordered about. We are so annoyingly outspoken in demanding our rights, so gloriously eager to complain to Washington or London. We are in such a pleasantly inviolable position, since Japan has not yet declared her war against China; and we take such placid advantage of that position. It did not often happen that the long-suffering military could so neatly get the better of us. So the sentries grinned and almost patted us on the back, and we argued and threatened and finally retired to our beds with great loss of face. Another international Incident had slipped into history.

It was in Wuhu that I began to realize more and more how remarkably unoccupied is Japan's so-called conquered territory. Directly across the river was a great tract of territory that lay wholly in the hands of Chiang Kai-shek. But matters did not stop there. On an average of two or three nights a week, I could sit out on my hospital balcony and watch the fighting that went on in the fields less than a mile away. Rifle shots cracked the night air, occasional cannon boomed near by. It was war upon a small scale, but quite definitely war. During our visit, the guerrillas of the Fourth Route Army broke into Wuhu (for the third time), put a number of Chinese puppet officials to the sword, and departed. Puppets were the number one enemies. But these biweekly raids called for revenge from the harassed Japanese. One night we had to shut our ears against the screams and frenzied barking of dogs, and close our eyes to the glare, as a village close to the walls was burned and the inhabitants were slaughtered. It was common knowledge that all about Wuhu lay guerrilla territory in which constant small battles were taking place. All too often adults and children were brought into the hospital with bullets in them. An interesting spectacle was afforded by the battered wrecks of Japanese freighters (the only freight boats allowed to ply the Yangtze) that sometimes drifted down the river, blasted by Chinese artillery or Russian flyers somewhere in the upper reaches. Small observations like this lent strength to China's faith in herself, and reduced Japan's claim over the territory she had entered to something of a farce.

Once I tested all too intimately the daring of Free China's guerrillas, and also the perverse loyalty of her coolie class which almost brought me to an untimely and rather sticky end. A mission on the far side of the city was possessed of an excellent tennis court. One evening we played until dusk and sat about in lazy and exhausted conversation until well after dark. Embarrassingly late for dinner, I hailed a ricksha and, telling the boy to hurry, started back toward the hospital hill. Soon we were well away from the friendly glare of the city in a narrow short-cut through the fields and graveyards. The path was barely visible in the late twilight. Once a motorcycle carrying two Japanese soldiers passed us in a cloud of dust, nearly forcing us into the ditch. We swore comfortably together — the coolie and I. But hardly had the sputtering roar faded in the distance when it again grew louder. 'Coming back,' muttered my coolie in a depressed tone. The motorcycle swept around a curve of the road in front of us, accelerator open wide. And as it thundered down upon us, the soldier perched upon the rear seat suddenly twisted around

and with a heavy pistol fired two shots into the half-darkness. It was a signal for the night to come alive. As if some giant fuse had short-circuited, the ditches and dim fields on either side of us spat and crackled with sound and with bright sparks. A raiding party of guerrillas had been discovered and the battle was on. At first the rifle fire came only from the far side of us, but not for long. In perhaps three seconds' time, before either I or my coolie had time to flex our frozen persons, answering shots blazed from the direction of the city, to be joined by the softer and deadlier purr of machine-gun fire. We were neatly caught between the two lines of fire. Even as I scrambled out with undignified haste, I heard a sharp *ping* on the metal fender beside me and softer thuds in the banks on either side of us. Probably we could not be easily seen. Probably they were wild bullets. I devoutly hoped so.

In the ensuing seconds, my coolie and I enacted a small scene which must have resembled something out of a comic opera. With mutual accord we started for the ditch. But at the extreme edge, we simultaneously braked to a skidding halt. The ditch was filled with a deep black slime. It occurred to me too that should we be found by either warring party, slaughter would come first and investigations afterward. For an instant we poised there on the lip of the ditch. Then I wheeled and started to run down the road, my tennis shorts lending wings to my heels. But before I had progressed fifty feet, the imperious voice of my coolie split the air behind me.

'Come back! Come back! You late for dinner.'

I looked over my shoulder and saw the shadowy outline of the coolie standing patiently between the shafts of the ricksha, while all about him were the red flashes of rifle fire. It was useless to argue. He would stand there until doomsday or until I returned and climbed once more into his ricksha. Feeling a little like Don Quixote in one of his anticlimactic *gestes*, I started back with a speed I did not know I possessed, while the guns spat about our ears. The line of flashes from the direction of the city was now almost upon us, as the Japanese advanced and the guerrillas slowly drew back through the fields. The din was deafening. And still I could see no sign of movement. I wondered if they were shooting blind, or if they could actually see a target there in the dim light. Were we one of the targets? I hurled myself into the ricksha, mentally cursing every coolie in the land. Then the boy ran. I had heard somewhere that ricksha coolies could out-distance the fastest sprinter by riding the shafts of their rickshas, and now I can swear to it. The boy literally flew through the air, his feet barely touching the ground. Although by now the gunfire was beginning to die out, we were beyond earshot in a matter of minutes.

Sweating, heaving, but unaccountably grinning, the coolie deposited me at the hospital compound. I tried hard to account for that grin, and finally remembered what a fascinating sight I must have made to the enchanted boy as I fled wildly down the road, leaving my perfectly useful ricksha behind; what glorious loss of face! A little shooting and the foreigner ran away! I could almost hear him mentally preparing the story for the entertainment of his bosom friends.

I paid him off and started through the gate, thanking him with great gusto for bringing me home to dinner on time. And the last I saw of him, he was ambling away, the ricksha dragged behind him, and his shoulders were shaking in unmistakable and private laughter.

On August 18, a cable was handed to me at Wuhu, duly forwarded from my office in Shanghai. It read neatly, briefly, and astonishingly:

ARRIVING SHANGHAI ABOARD EMPRESS
OF JAPAN AUGUST TWENTY-SECOND

BILL

With knees that felt curiously weak, I sped about Wuhu arranging transportation to Shanghai. Skipper had to be left behind; he possessed neither the strength nor the required military pass to make the trip. So it happened that on the following day, I departed alone for the coast.

A day's stop-over at Nanking gave me a glimpse of the city that was to be confirmed by later visits; but my first impressions were indelible. Probably there is not anywhere a more tragic place. It was once a graceful city — Nanking — spread out over many square miles of park and garden, with wide, proud avenues open to the sun in an abundance of space and light. Constructed by artists as well as architects, the giant government buildings might have been called beautiful. Although many had been gutted by the fires of December, 1937 (some set by the Japanese, some by the retreating Chinese), the charred empty walls still showed traces of pastel color where stone and metal had been fashioned into palaces in the days when Nanking was the new young capital of China.

Most of the city was still intact, though half-alive. The principal stores were wayside stands that had sprung up like weeds along the once-modern streets, and now conducted a thriving trade with anyone fortunate enough to own money. Japanese trucks and light tanks thundered down the deserted avenues in eruptions of dust. Japanese olive-drab uniforms were everywhere.

Nanking bore tragic witness to Japan's foolishly heavy hand in China. The few Chinese officials who before the war were inclined to be pro-Japanese were quickly alienated by the needless brutality of the invaders, while the hearts of people were kindled into sullen and unsmotherable fire. Blame for Japan's failure in her treatment of China may be placed squarely upon the shoulders of a limited group within her army who chafed under so strong a hatred of the Kuomintang that they actively incited their troops (already on edge with fear and disillusionment and lost pride) to kill and rape at will; in some cases, ordered them to do so. The moderate element within the military were helpless to prevent the débâcle, and won some measure of control only after the earlier outrages proved a boomerang against their perpetrators, stiffening and uniting the Chinese armies and arousing the wholesale wrath of the Western world. Later occupations became more orderly, though hardly benign.

But to speak of the innate brutality of the Japanese soldier as the cause of the atrocities is unjust. Both the Japanese and Chinese are capable, when aroused, of a very special and horrible kind of cruelty. Western capabilities along that line are not far behind; witness the systematic and uncontrolled looting of Peking by American, British, and other Western troops, at the end of the Boxer siege of the legations. Too many neutral witnesses in China have testified to the fact that the man in charge of a city's occupation can make that occupation a massacre or a blessing. Some of China's conquered towns are undergoing a continuous and almost medieval torture; others are under orderly control; now and then, the Japanese official in command happens to be a Christian, and a curiously benevolent atmosphere develops.

Yet it appears that Japan is incapable of learning a lesson and profiting by it. As if she must prove the wisdom of her policies and show this hypercritical Western world that she is justified in her acts, she continues to antagonize the Chinese, to treat them as bothersome delinquents, to close schools and colleges, to burn villages and massacre civilians in reprisal raids, to imprison students, to appropriate goods and grain, to permit the wholesale rape of women, and — most damaging of all — deliberately to turn them into drug addicts. The sale of heroin and cocaine (far more destructive than opium) began in 1932 after the seizure of Manchuria, when Japanese and Korean drug smugglers of a gangster type cluttered the trains leading into North China and, setting up their

drug shops about the walls of the cities, defied the Chinese authorities under the protection of extra-territoriality. Until then, drugs
had been almost unknown in China, and opium half-eliminated.
Now, nine years later, drugs are sold openly in the stores and on
the street-corners. Opium is the principal source of income for
the Nanking puppet government. And, to Japan's eternal sorrow,
her soldiers are bringing the drug habit back to her own cities and
villages where it had never before been known.

At the time of my visit, her most recent mistake was embodied
in the person of Mr. Wang Ching-wei. When, in February, he
had fled with many of his followers from Chungking, that city
had sighed in something very like relief. During his stormy political career, he had been universally admired for his genius and
hated for his treachery. By nature he could take orders from no
man; and although a close friend of Chiang Kai-shek, more than
once he had betrayed his Party. His abrupt departure from the
ranks of the Kuomintang was in the nature of a purge. Now, in
the summer of 1939, he was being coddled here in Nanking by
Japanese who hoped that his prestige would win him a ponderous
and impressive following. But they forgot his unfortunate background. Even the Chinese puppet officials who had openly worked
with the Japanese, although impressed by Mr. Wang, were
frankly wary of him. And the average citizen detested him and
branded him as a traitor. The chances of a strong clique under
Wang became a wistful Japanese dream; his own followers would
not trust him. By the time a year had rolled around, Wang
Ching-wei's potentialities had melted into intrigue and farce, and
the Japanese themselves were thoroughly sick of him. But, ironically, the enthusiastic publicity that had been showered upon the
man by Japan's own press, and the high faith which her people at
home placed in him, forced her willy-nilly to set him up with some
pretense of a Government.

Blunder after blunder — this was Japan's record in China.

Her military campaigns had bogged down in the unwieldly interior. Crop failures and the active resistance of countless farmers who, preferring starvation, refused to seed their land, had put an end to her high hopes of profit from the rich cotton crops of the northern provinces. Her occupied cities and railroads were in a virtual state of siege. The people of China were united against her with a grimness and purpose that seemed to increase even as their sufferings increased.

These are not matters over which to gloat. For the Japanese, they spell tragedy. Some will say that Japan deserves small sympathy, and it is quite true that her troubles are of her own making. But there are many Japanese in conquered China — business men, army officers, clergymen, officials — who are perfectly sincere in their wish to help China as well as Japan. There are many who love and admire the Chinese, who are sickened by the damage that has been done their 'cause' in China, who chafe in misery over their inability to reach the hearts of her people. They must stand by and see the riff-raff of their country, the criminals and the profiteers, invade China like a plundering horde and by their example bring down the anger of China and of the world upon their heads.

I once talked for many hours with a Japanese Christian pastor, one of many who had been sent to China by the Japanese Government in the interests of appeasement. He was a weary little man and his words were an expression of personal tragedy — a viewpoint, seldom acknowledged, that is held by certain Japanese in all parts of the world today. 'We Japanese are paying now for the brutality of a few men. Our ideals and hopes for our country and for China have been turned into — what is the word? — jests? Bad jokes? Many of us came hoping to do good here, and we have brought nothing but misery. The world condemns us and loyalty will not permit us to speak of our mistakes. So we grow more and more prideful. And more troubled.'

14

FLOOD!

I SAW from my office window the *Empress of Japan* swing around a bend in the sunny Whangpoo and point her high aristocratic nose toward the Shanghai *bund*. Armed with a pass which allowed me to board the boat at her preliminary docking in Hongkew, I fled up the gangplank into her dim interior, suffering from acute palpitations of the heart and a curious inability to breathe. I found him at last. We tried to be casual.

'Hello, Bill.'

'Hello, little fish . . .'

Then I spoiled it by weeping profusely upon his overcoat and the immaculate and very crowded lobby, because I guess I had not been sure that I would see him again.

Almost at once Bill began to learn Chinese, and within a few weeks could take care of himself very nicely and order an elegant meal. His work carried him from one end of the city to the other in the violent headlong rush which is his usual progress through life. Within a week, he knew more about Shanghai than an average person would expect to learn in a year. His tall blondness was a continual delight to the Chinese, especially to the country people, who like their foreigners as bizarre as possible. It was not until long afterward that I learned that Bill, when he cabled me from mid-ocean, had not received my last letter; that he had not.

in fact, the slightest idea in what part of China he would find me. He had simply come.

Early September arrived and suddenly the world was at war. In occupied China, already war-weary to the point of bitterness, the news was received with a curious apathy. On the morning that war was declared, the foreign population in Shanghai went about its business very silent, a little numb. Not until the German offensive in the spring of 1940 did the war lend itself to Shanghai's small talk. China was still the supreme topic of the day. Europe's war seemed remote and unnatural. For many months it scarcely ruffled the surface of the Far East.

Meanwhile in North China came the flood. It started in Tientsin and raged through the provinces of Hopei and Shantung. 'Worst flood in history!' the newspapers yelled, not knowing that they spoke the literal truth. At the same time, a letter from my employers expressed the gentle hope that I would cover all floods and famines, and see as much as possible of conditions in occupied territory. I remembered the Sian hospital's orders — that I was to proceed at once to the big Peking Union Medical School hospital and be checked over. My hopes of another visit to Free China crumbled at last into dust. If I were to obey orders and return to New York before Christmas, there would be time only for a survey of the flood. Peking it was to be, then. The harbor at Tangku was closed because of the flood, and there was not a soul in Shanghai able to tell us whether or not we could get through from Dairen via the Manchurian Railroad. So we bought our tickets to Dairen on faith alone, with a shrug and a small prayer. But before we sailed, we said good-bye to a certain gentleman by the name of Robert Brown who was on his way to Rangoon, back to Free China, back to bombings and crumbling roads and flooded rivers. Yet somehow I was not at all worried about Skipper. His own little god of luck perched day and night upon his shoulder. Should a five-hundred-pound bomb fall directly at his feet, it would inevitably turn out to be a dud.

Our little steamer bore us elegantly up the China Coast, first to the once German-held port of Tsingtao, where we wandered the streets in the lazy sun and sampled the local menus, then on to Dairen, which is a city indescribable. So many nationalities have had a hand in Dairen that the place has lost all of its character and is nothing but a large gathering of neat colorless stone and brick buildings along wide colorless avenues, and filled with Japanese and White Russians and Chinese and Siberians and Koreans and English and quite a few other people. The American Consul informed us cheerfully that the railroad to Peking had opened only the day before, when a washed-out bridge was finally repaired and a trial engine sent across it.

'Of course the bridge collapsed under the engine,' he went on with a faint, sardonic smile, 'but it's quite all right because they have now repaired the bridge once more.'

We thanked him drearily and went off to catch our train. But it seemed that we were not to go to Peking that night; and the reason for this was the Japan Tourist Bureau. I like to think that the Japan Tourist Bureau did it on purpose. Just before we left, it sold us our tickets, checked our passes and visas, and sent us happily on our way. All went well until, a few hours outside of Dairen and quite some time after sundown, a Japanese official inspected our passports and informed us coldly that we did not possess a transit visa for Manchukuo.

'Oh, you mean Manchuria?' I asked, sounding not very bright.

'Madame,' he said, drawing himself into himself, 'Manchukuo. You cannot pass. You should not have crossed the border at all. I will have to put you from the train where you can return to Dairen and procure you the needful pass.'

He did, too. We found ourselves marooned with all our baggage on a microscopic station platform somewhere in the midst of Manchuria. Fortunately a train was to leave in an hour for Dairen. But it so happened that the train was a single car running on a gasoline engine, and fifty miles outside of Dairen, in the dead of night, it broke down. The engineer stepped on the self-starter and nothing occurred. He ground the gears in a huff and stepped on the starter again, but still nothing occurred. He tinkered with the engine and tried it again, with less result than before. He even took up the floor boards under our feet and virtually everybody in sight began tinkering with the engine. Meanwhile, the unmistakable sounds of an automobile emerging from a train continued to entrance us. At last the engineer and his now numerous assistants did the only sensible thing. They got out and pushed. At once the engine started. Everybody beamed.

We saw embarrassingly little of Manchuria. Before darkness fell on each of our successive train rides, we had time to note that the countryside, here in the south, was rich and cultivated down to the last available square inch, a fertile loamy land, quite unlike the barren expanses that for some reason I had expected to see. After that, we scarcely noticed Manchuria; the third-class bunks were exceedingly comfortable, and we slept.

On the following day we entered the flood. At first we saw only a whitening wetness in the fields. It was at Tangku, where the track leaves the coast and turns inland, that we first met this fellow Flood and his specialized kind of deviltry. Tangku, the neighboring port of Tientsin, was now a muddy, bedraggled little town where each stretch of high land was blotted out with freight cars, lorries, salvaged goods, and quite a few thousand refugees. The refugees slept under the cars on the sidings; they put up mat sheds — acres of mat sheds — cluttering the dry ground about the railroad station; they scrambled for shreds of bark that fell from passing timber loads in order to eat them.

Once when the train stopped beside a mat-shed city, a group of refugee children began crowding up to the windows, awkward in their new rôle of beggars. Up and down the length of the train the windows opened and bits of food, coppers, and even clothing

were handed down to the upflung waiting arms. To the smallest
boy we threw some money. His face turned radiant and he rushed
away with his prize, back to his mother's tent only a few yards
away. Apparently she was upset for fear that her son had not
thanked us properly, for we could see her demonstrating to him
exactly how the correct bow should be made. Then she sent him
back and he bowed reverently before our train window.

We did not yet know that we were witness to one of the greatest
floods in human history; so we were not prepared for the sight that
met us beyond Tangku. Here a sheet of water stretched from horizon to horizon. Sometimes there was nothing protruding above
this flood — nothing at all. It was an inland ocean, upon which
the high railroad embankment coiled as a greedy serpent upon the
waters. Occasionally a clump of trees, taller than their fellows,
would stick round, surprised heads above the surface, and the tops
of telephone poles looked foolishly stunted, close beside us. Only
once did we see a sign of the myriad villages that had clustered
here, scarcely two hundred yards or so apart; and that was a single
piece of wall which thrust its ragged shoulder up out of the flood
and refused to crumble. For hours, as the train crawled across the
false sea, I stared and stared at first one horizon, then another,
hoping to see something — anything at all — that would break
this pale monotony.

In places the flood rose higher than the embankment and rails
and was kept back only by makeshift dikes of sandbags. Brown-
sailed junks cruised across the waters. Around them a host of
carved wooden coffins, sluiced from their shallow graves, bobbed
idly on the small waves and crowded the edge of the embankment
like a fleet of ghostly ships. Sometimes they had broken apart
and their contents were spilled clumsily over the rim. A good
many thousands had died in this district, and now and then we
saw their bodies, the skin bloated and drawn tight, sprawled face
down by the water's edge, gleaming in the sunlight.

Meanwhile, along this eight-foot-wide strip of railroad embankment we watched as strange a crowd as I shall hope to see. Here were all those thousands who had managed to escape the flood. Unable to cross the makeshift trellises along the railroad track, they were marooned; and because the railroad itself belonged to Japan, no relief could be brought to them. They had been here for approximately three weeks. The flood had come so quickly and there had been no way to tell which way to go or from whence the water came or how far it reached. It seemed to rise out of the earth. They probably waited as long as they dared, watching their homes, anxiously watching their tools and fields, thinking of looters. Then when the walls began to crumble and the thatched roof settled with a splash, they gathered the family and a few treasured belongings together on a raft and started wading through the rising yellow water. As in previous floods, the one sure refuge was the railroad embankment. But this year, the flood was not the same. It did not go down. Gradually their supply of food dwindled and was gone, and still they were marooned and still the waters rose higher.

There was scarcely room to move about, so great was the crowd beside the tracks. Mile upon mile the black line stretched. Perhaps after all they numbered in the millions. The children were potbellied from drinking floodwater and eating dirt to stop the pain. We saw no sign of food or cooking as we crawled slowly past, hour by hour. Low mat-shed tents had been put up here and there, but the people used the precarious space economically, lying close together on the ground or in the tents. They were keeping very quiet, and using little or no energy, trying to prolong life without food. They scarcely glanced at the train as it crept by. Occasionally a man would be fishing for tiny silver minnows with a dip net, a woman hanging mats or nursing her child. A few gaunt dogs with bare ribs and festering hides prowled about the huts, and once I saw a donkey, reduced to fur and bones, wobbling at his tether. There was a puzzled, weary look on the faces of the people as the train rumbled by.

There was silence on the flooded countryside. The white herons and fat Chinese crows feasted well on fish and human carrion; but they made little noise. Even the clamoring locusts that had plagued the land until the coming of the waters, rising in black clouds above the unprotected grain, were drowned together with the crops they had devoured.

At last we saw in the distance the beginning of Tientsin, where the brick walls of flooded factories protruded above the horizon. And at the same moment, leaning out of the windows we sighted the newly repaired bridge which the American Consul in Dairen had so jovially called to our attention. The temporary span was of wood, perhaps a hundred feet in length, and resting on girders that in their turn rested, unbelievably, upon sampans and junks moored in the flood. The current swept through the wide break in the embankment, the little boats strained at their moorings, and the girders swayed. It was the kind of bridge one should encounter only in a nightmare and describe in loud tones at the breakfast table.

The engine nosed up to the edge of the bridge and stopped while men ran up and down the track shouting orders and what may have been encouraging remarks. At last the heavy engine and its long line of cars took a deep breath and started to crawl almost imperceptibly out upon the span. Simultaneously Bill and I noted that though our own window was open, those across the aisle were firmly closed, and there was no telling upon which side the train would tumble into the flood. We stared down at the rushing waters beneath us and tried to act as if nothing untoward was occurring. The train spent a good five minutes in crossing that bridge, and it was by all odds the longest five minutes I have yet encountered. The span shook and trembled and even bobbed up and down a little, and I felt very sorry for it and even sorrier for myself. But by some miracle it held. Either the luck or the engineering genius of the Japanese was strong that day.

Beyond Tientsin, the fields were dry. But I could not wash out of my mind the picture of that gigantic army of human beings, rich as well as poor, farmers and students and priests and beggars and young wives and young babies, waiting there upon an eight-foot strand for the falling of the waters. They could not have known that many weeks were to pass before the flood went down. There is no describing what must have happened there.

Peking lay sprawled, big and square on the North China plain, very alive in the sharp September air, castellated, timeless, half-ringed, as always, by her Western Hills. I had not known that the city would be quite so beautiful, her gatehouses and temples so massive and full of mellow color. Although Peking had had her full share of tense moments and fighting had gone on within a few miles of her outer gates, she was thrice blessed of China's cities in that the war had passed her by. Not a shot had been fired within her walls. She had been given over intact to the Japanese, and for three years life had conducted itself there with some semblance of peace. The wide avenues were busy with rickshas and laden donkeys, camel trains, Peking carts: they were gay with banners and bright signs. After dark, colored lights plastered the walls, shining upon balconies and painted dragons and fairy shapes and graceful red and green characters. Con-quered Peking was still the imperial city.

But as time passed and we grew more and more familiar with the old place, I learned to suspect the apparent peace, the icing of calm, that lay upon the people. I began to wonder if, perhaps, Peking was not one of the most tragic cities in the land. Blame it on her beauty, that the Chinese who remained here felt the intru-sion of the Japanese with a terrible and personal agony. They went about the streets with expressionless faces, but they spoke their minds with an all-consuming bitterness that startled me. I was still accustomed to the patient, realistic tolerance that is the password of Free China. I think that should Chiang Kai-shek have marched victoriously into Peking, the people of the city would have risen in a body and massacred every Japanese man, woman, and child within her walls. It is a fortunate thing for Chiang, and for the Japanese, that so small a percentage of China's population is under the direct and daily rule of their conquerors.

Japanese soldiers in uniform made up a large part of the street crowds. Usually they rode in rickshas, and they would not always tolerate traffic laws and red lights, and sometimes they beat their coolies. There were Japanese women, too, in the bright costumes of their land. A Japanese civilian population of some fifty thousand were living in the city, and more were coming each day. The principal sightseers at the Forbidden City and the Lama Temple and the Winter Palace — in fact, at every historic spot in Peking — were Japanese soldiers in uniform who examined the great temples reverently and worshipfully. Accustomed to beauty as a part of life, the miniature beauty of Japan, they must have felt lost and homesick in this vast dusty city on its flat plain. So they spent most of their leisure hours amongst the temples and palaces, drinking in each familiar scene that they had read about at home, stretching on the grass with an upward gaze of wonder at the loveliness of the thing.

At the time of our visit, Peking, and in fact all of North China, was in the throes of its Japanese-sponsored anti-British movement. Already twenty-three desperately needed British hospitals had had to be evacuated from interior cities because of hired mobs and threatened tortures from Japanese officials. British in blockaded Tientsin were being stripped and searched by Japanese guards, although Americans were treated with vast courtesy. Fortunately the movement had received small credence from the

Chinese masses, who, being practical of mind, could look about them and see what the so-called imperialist British were up to with their free clinics and good schools.

Only once did I encounter any active hostility. My ricksha boy happened to take me past a street crowd composed of some Chinese and slightly more Japanese who were apparently listening to a soapbox lecture upon the sins of the British Empire. The crowd, already stirred up, caught sight of us as we drew abreast of it, and took me for one of the outrageous Britishers. An ugly mutter began, and grew into a mob sound that is a chilling thing to hear. But though they started toward us in a body, my ricksha boy was past them and gone like a flash on flying feet.

Shortly before our arrival in Peking, a huge anti-British demonstration was put on in the city of Peitaiho, the foreign colony's chief summer resort. Announcements were posted throughout the town to the effect that anyone wishing to march in the protest parade would receive 40 cents per hour and unlimited free lemonade. The parade went off in fine shape. Everyone had quite a good time. But the Japanese sponsors failed to notice that at least half a dozen British children bearing anti-British posters of their own design marched quietly in the parade, received their 40 cents an hour, and consumed untold quantitites of free lemonade.

Though the first city in China to be conquered, Peking is a storm center for guerrilla activities. Units of the Eighth Route Army are stationed within a few miles of the walls. I was enchanted to learn that the guerrilla leader in the region had recently come into Peking and had had his tonsils out in the big P.U.M.C. hospital. Once during our visit a guerrilla raiding party actually smashed its way into the city in the dead of night, shot up some Japanese troops within a block of the Language School where Bill was boarding, and retired without losing a man. Two days later, as we sipped tea at the Empress Dowager's Summer

Palace a few miles outside the city, a battle got under way just out of sight behind a near-by hill. For hours the ground shook to the beat of shell fire and the deeper roar of bursting bombs. Planes dipped and swooped gracefully overhead. In our small teahouse, the windows, chairs, dishes rattled protestingly. Our waiter was particularly upset because the tea was spilt.

During our stay in Peking, the famous drive on Changsha began. The Japanese-controlled Peking *Chronicle* was full of the good news that almost any day now the mighty metropolis of Changsha would be in the hands of Japan. As its fall became imminent, a large balloon was floated above Peking, the same balloon which is sent up with every approaching Japanese victory; at the exact moment when the imperiled city falls, a sign is hoisted to it proclaiming the news to the supposedly cheering population. For two days, the fall of Changsha was to be expected daily, hourly, half-hourly. Then one morning at dawn, the balloon was quietly withdrawn. For three days the subject was not mentioned, although the news of the Chinese victory had spread like wildfire by word of mouth amongst the Chinese population. At last the *Chronicle* came duly forth with the announcement that the Japanese army in Hunan had completed its mopping-up operations amongst the guerrillas in the Changsha district with great success, and having accomplished their purpose, had returned victoriously to Yochow.

As soon as my hospital tests were over and we were able to leave Peking, we set out for Tientsin and the flood. The waters, we were told, in the foreign concessions of the big industrial city were at last gone, but the Chinese city was still flooded. So as soon as we arrived at the station, we ordered our ricksha boys to take us to the Methodist Mission on the outskirts of the Chinese city. For a while they wheeled us along dry streets, past the barbed-wire blockades that proclaimed the enforced siege of the concessions, up a wide avenue of shops, and into a narrow alley. And there, a hundred feet in front of us, the flood began. I had expected to see water, but not this thick black slime aglint with scum. Like some devilish dark cauldron it was alive with floating things, refuse, dead animals, occasionally parts of what had once been human beings. Underfoot, it was soft, coagulated mud filled with long-sunken and nameless objects. Now only two feet deep, it left a dark line high against the walls on either side of the alley, where the crest of the flood had been. Below that line, houses, walls, dim interiors, small cluttered back yards — all were coated in mud. Worse than the slime itself was the mordant stench which rose and filled the city, thickening the air. The smell was new to me and I shall not forget it. It stayed in our mouths and our nostrils for the next few weeks, and long after we had left the flooded city far behind.

Our coolies hitched up their trousers and plunged into the deep ooze. For an hour they struggled with their rickshas through street after street, bogging down, hoisting, shoving, laughing, sweating. Sampans sculled past us up and down the narrow alleys. Once we passed a garbage dump high enough to rise above the flood and now almost hidden by the weight of mat sheds where refugees had taken shelter. The mission, we found, was just emerging from its three weeks' bath, though the streets around it and the lower ground within the compound were still under water. The alleyway between the residence home and the big brick hospital lay four feet deep in the black stuff. At one end of the mission lay a dike, and on the far side of the dike the flood was still from eight to fifteen feet in depth. As for the main residence house, the lower floor would never be quite the same again. Other homes in the compound were still coated with mud. For almost a month, the American staff had been camping on their second floors, cooking from impromptu stoves, and living a strange life together. Within the first few days of the flood, they had organized a great fleet of sampans and had poled through

the city, day after day, taking the sick to shelter, handing out food and bread, and holding small roof-top clinics. Great fires had started as the waters rose, and their hospital had only just escaped the flames. Hundreds of refugees had been housed in the upper stories of their big middle school. Inside their own main residence house, the water had risen close to the level of the second floor. They kept their private sampan moored to the top of the staircase, and each morning they stepped into it and sailed calmly out the front door.

It was now Bill's turn to experience China's germ power. The day after our arrival we put him to bed in the hospital with a virulent streptococcus infection which, by the time we found out about it, had reduced him to an extremely sick man. The Methodist Hospital was not equipped to care for foreign patients, and for eight days he lived on Chinese rice gruel in a half-flooded building, cared for by Chinese nurses who could speak no English, unable to read by the dim light of the vegetable oil lamp, yet somehow incredibly cheerful. In order to visit him, I had to cross the flooded alleys on a long spindly bridge of single boards that more than once deposited me in the slime. To make matters even more confusing, the guerrillas on several occasions staged raids upon our section of the city, and there was shooting about the hospital walls. Then for a few days the flood waters started to rise again and it seemed as if the whole affair would repeat itself. Probably no man has been ill in a hospital under more peculiar circumstances.

Fortunately for my own sanity, I had much work to do. Articles had to be written and smuggled out to the coast, innumerable photographs taken. Generally we set forth in the morning, a nurse or two and a boatman and I, to join in the rescue work. Our sampan was kept moored to the far side of the dike. Loading it with food, padded garments, and medical supplies, we would shove out into the water and scull through the deeply flooded streets. In the suburbs the water was close up under the eaves of the houses. Whole blocks had collapsed, the débris dimly visible beneath the surface. In all of Tientsin, a minimum estimate of ten thousand had drowned in the early days of the flood, and the deaths still went on. Here the entire population was living on their roof-tops, clinging there by the hundreds like strange flocks of birds or creeping animals. They had been here a month, in most cases, without any food except the weekly allowance of two lumps of bread the size of a man's fist which we and other rescue workers were able to hand up to them. The flood had come quickly and they were not prepared.

Some of them were in bad shape. For hours we would crawl about the roof-tops, bandaging infected wounds, handing out medicines, doing what we could. The worst cases would be brought back to the hospital. It was queer that they could live at all. Time and again we would approach a block of buildings, the roofs dark with crouching forms.

'Have you any food?' the nurse beside me would call up.

An old man or woman would lean over the edge of the roof and, grinning down at us, would act as spokesman for the group.

'No, no food. A week ago it was gone. You are the first boat that has come to us.'

'We have bread here for you. Have you a basket?'

A straw basket would quickly be lowered on a rope, the allotment of round bread lumps, or *mon tow*, placed within, and the load drawn up. Then:

'Do you have water?'

'A strange question, T'ai T'ai. Look about you!' and the group would smile at the jest.

'Do you mean that you drink the flood water?'

'We must. There is no other way.'

'And have you a fire? Can you boil it first?'

'No, T'ai T'ai. We have no fuel. We must drink it as it is.'

I could not repress a shudder.

'And have you sickness among you?'

Again the heads that crowded the edge of the roof grinned at the question. Was there sickness! Better to say, was there health?

'The small child here. He is very sick with the dysentery and we do not think that he shall be well without help. And his oldest brother shivers and cannot stand.'

Up would go our ladder and several of us would swarm onto the roof. A moment later and the clinic would be under way as we sat there, our medical supplies between our knees, straddling the ridge.

Sometimes we would run out of supplies early in the day, and then we would have to pole for home, past the scores of roof-dwellers who called and called us. Once we reached the mission compound long after dark only to find that the dike, which virtually surrounded the place, had been pronounced forbidden territory by the Japanese. No one was to land or cross that dike. The sentry shouted at us in abominable Chinese, angry that we should so much as dream of crossing the dike in order to reach home. Something had to be done. We poled quietly around the block and, as silently as possible in the darkness, approached the dike a hundred yards below the spot where the sentry stood. If we could creep along without being seen and slip through the mission gate behind him, all to the good. And if he saw us, well . . . Feeling ridiculously furtive, we beached the boat without a sound, and bending low, stole along the dike in the direction of the sentry. But the atmosphere of dark intrigue was too much for us. Half-way to our gate, both the nurse and I developed a violent and uncontrollable case of the giggles. We made so many small squeaks and heaves that we knew the game was up, and throwing caution to the wind, made a dash for it. The sentry turned with a startled mutter, just as we dived under the closed gate and collapsed behind the bullet-proof compound wall in limp hysterics.

Our experiences with the dike were not always so light-headed. Hospital employees would often forget the new regulation, trespass upon the dike and be badly beaten for their pains. Once I was crossing over toward the hospital when a boy ran past me shouting that a coolie on the dike was being clubbed to death by a sentry. I stared up the alley toward the place where, a hundred yards from me, the little street ended at the foot of the dike. There on the top a Japanese soldier stood, swinging his rifle barrel high in the air above him and bringing it down with splintering force upon something that lay beyond my field of vision at his feet. Every blow was enough to crush a man's skull. I ran toward the dike, too angry to know exactly what I planned to do. By the time I had scrambled up the slippery sides, the sentry stood alone, and the body of a young boy was being dragged off by a Chinese policeman. There was a streamer of blood on the ground, and from where I stood it looked as if the boy's head had been battered in. I turned and foolishly started toward the sentry. He said no word at all, but raised his rifle to his shoulder and pointed it at the center of my body. I stopped dead and the scene stiffened into immobility. His face remained without expression as he stared at me over the sights.

I said, 'You killed him,' speaking in Chinese.

No flicker of movement crossed the man's face. His unemotional silence unnerved me far more than his gun. Then his thumb moved and something in the gun clicked. I tried to think calmly of the proper thing to do, but my mind seemed dead; to run would be an invitation for a bullet. I must preserve the illusion that foreigners were not to be shot down. Somehow keeping the panic out of my muscles, I turned very slowly, and with a crawling sensation between my shoulder blades, started to walk toward the compound gate. I had not gone three steps before the rifle roared, and my heart and everything inside of me rose up to choke me. But no missile struck near. Probably he fired in the air to frighten me. If I ran now, he might not be so kind. For two hundred yards, I stalked with infinite deliberation down the alley, and I did not know that it could be so difficult to walk instead of run. Then I was through the gate and safely out of sight. The shot had passed unnoticed by the people of the mission, so rather than create an incident, I said nothing about it. But I did not again go near that dike.

The day before our return to Peking was the Methodist middle school's opening day of the fall term. A large part of the compound was still under several feet of water, and the school building itself was only just in the process of drying off. Some of the ground floor rooms were inches thick in mud that extended up close to the ceilings. The missionaries were laughingly curious to see how many of their pupils would turn up for the opening day of classes. Most of them lived in villages and suburbs where the flood was still high. But as the day dawned, they began to arrive, at first in twos and threes and then in scores, some in boats piled high with books and luggage, some wading through the flood with parcels on their heads. By nightfall, all but four students had arrived; and although the school was primarily a day school, the pupils, obviously unable to ferry themselves back and forth each day through the water, had stubbornly and blandly come to stay, bag and baggage. They moved in that evening, and, side by side with their teachers, went uproariously to work cleaning out the sticky mud and fixing up communal bedrooms for themselves. Throughout most of the night, loud runnings and shovelings, hoots and snatches of song and suppressed giggles floated from the open windows of the building where one of America's mission schools was getting under way in the middle of a flood.

It was with a very definite sigh of relief that Bill and I left the foul, bedraggled city far behind us and returned to Peking. After a series of committee meetings, we arranged to have questionnaires sent out to every *hsien* in Hopei and Shantung in an effort to plot the extent of the flood in maps and statistics and work out some definite relief plans for the winter. When the reports came in at last, it was shown that approximately three quarters of Hopei had been at some time under water, and nearly as much of Shantung. Some of the old China hands called it the worst flood in their experience, others the greatest flood in human history. During an investigating trip into the north of the province, Bill found that in regions where the water had gone down, famine had already set in, the leaves and bark already eaten from the trees; and winter had not yet begun. No one will ever know the number of casualties that resulted from this flood. The lowest calculation states that at least five millions died during the winter months. But in the United States the matter was quite simple, because the flood was called merely the Tientsin Flood and reported for two or three days in the leading newspapers and straightway forgotten.

November was at hand. If I were to reach home by Christmas, as my New York office suggested, it seemed high time that we return to Shanghai and cast about for an American-bound ship. A visit to our old friend, the Japan Tourist Bureau, revealed the fact that we could progress to Shanghai either by railroad or by one of the Japanese coastal boats even then waiting off the Tangku bar. True, the railroad to Nanking and Shanghai had only been open for the space of three days because of the flood, but train service was now regular. Both Bill and I had business in Tsinan and Süchowfu, stop-offs on the line; but there was the disconcerting fact that quite a few trains, especially between Tsinan and Süchowfu, had been mined and blown to bits by the guerrillas, and their surviving Japanese military contents machine-gunned to pieces. Foreigners who preferred to live just were not using the railroad these days. Still, there was the work to be done.

I said, 'We've *got* to go by train. We have no choice!'

Bill merely laughed at me. 'Be honest!' he said. 'Admit we're curious and *want* to go by train.'

'All right, two tickets to Shanghai.'

Again a tortuous journey across the flood, again the inland sea. Near the city of Tsinan the land was dry again, though some of it was ruined by a thick layer of sandy silt. In one region, a branch of the Grand Canal had overflowed one of its banks, flooding the fields, while beyond the other bank drought had set in, burning the crops to crisp, dry, useless stubs. Flood and drought met there at the riverbank.

Two nights in Tsinan were sufficient for the exchange of flood reports and statistics with local American experts. Tsinan's big Cheeloo University had moved to the West, but a skeleton staff still carried on a limited number of classes on the old campus. In fact, the city seemed grimly peaceful under its Japanese overlords, who had captured the place early in the war, with scarcely a shot fired.

The countryside about its wall was said to be guerrilla-free and almost serene, and that is why, on our last afternoon in Tsinan, we set out for a walk among the villages. We have not to this day mentioned the events of that afternoon, partly for fear of creating an unnecessary Incident, partly for fear the news would reach the press and upset my family. But it was a strange afternoon for the two of us. Feeling free and light-headed after the somber weeks of flood, we trailed the paths that led out through the low hills, between sunny fields. Locusts buzzed in the cornstalks. Here a half-naked farmer with the sweat gleaming on his sun-blackened skin worked half-hidden in a patch of high grain. After a while, the fields gave way to stubbly hills, moth-eaten, bare, deserted. They seemed to go for endless miles, these hills. And discouraged, we turned back toward the farmland.

We had gone perhaps a dozen steps when to the north of us a flurry of gunshots snapped in the clear air. We froze in our tracks and stared. Scarcely three hundred yards from us, two Japanese soldiers crouched behind a clump of weeds; one was apparently loading a gun and the other held something to his shoulder, either a sub-machine gun or a repeating rifle, from which he fired short bursts of shots. A moment later, two or three answering shots cracked from somewhere far back of the rolling hills in front of them. There was no high grain, no cover for us.

Bill whispered: 'Don't move. They haven't seen us yet.'

But just then, one of the brown-capped Japanese heads turned our way. Instantly two guns swung their muzzles toward us. Without a word, Bill sent me flying in a one-handed shove, and flattened down beside me. The guns cracked at the same moment, the rifle once, the repeating gun in a flurry of shots. But we must have moved at the same moment that the shots were fired, for I heard no bullets strike near us. A few yards away there was a declivity in the ground, and with one accord we squirmed toward it. We reached it, too, but not before a bullet had spattered up dirt beneath Bill's half-raised chin, and another had caromed from a rock beside his moving foot with a high, shivering rasp of sound. The dent in the ground gave us momentary cover. For a moment or two the Japanese clipped the edge with a burst of rapid fire that spattered us with dirt, but finding it useless they stopped, and for the space of a few unbreathing seconds there was absolute silence within the hills. Then apparently they decided that whoever we might be, we were unarmed, for we heard the sound of heavy boots thumping the earth in a quick run and coming toward us. My heart rose into my throat.

Bill pointed and said: 'Run for that knoll. Try to get behind it.' And, as we started up, he yelled once more, 'Don't zigzag!'

I ran straight and as fast as I knew how, aware that Bill was carefully running directly behind me. Before we were fairly on our feet, the shots began. But this time I was far too occupied to notice whether or not they struck near us. It did not seem probable that the two men could miss forever at this comparatively close range. Just then, another crackling of shots broke out from the guerrillas hidden in the hills. Bill risked a glance over his shoulder and said: 'It's all right. They're firing at each other now.' And my breath went out in a long sigh.

We ran, though, around the little hill, then trotting slower on and on until the peaceful fields were all about us and the only sound was the lazy hum of locusts. For a moment we stopped and rested on a dusty bank and grinned at each other in silent, inexplicable embarrassment. Perhaps the incident was too sensational for our tastes, too reminiscent of pulp-story adventure. For to this day, we have not talked of it together.

On the following morning, we boarded the train for the all too precarious trip to Süchowfu, wondering gloomily if somewhere along this rail-bed a thick load of dynamite was in wait for us. The carriages were certainly crowded with Japanese military of every description, one polite specimen of which shared our compartment with us. Almost at once, our train slowed down in the midst of a stretch of wild, bare hills, and the reason for it was a charred mass of engine, telescoped cars, contorted steel and wood, lying side to the ground, desolate, mutilated, almost unrecognizable as the wreck of a train. That was the beginning. Every hour or so for the rest of the trip, I would call to Bill, 'Another wreck!' Before we reached Süchowfu we had passed the remains of exactly seven troop trains, all dynamited within the last few days since the opening of the railroad. In several places, the track had been torn up by the explosion beyond the point of easy repair; and at each of these spots, new rails had been laid which led down on a slant from the embankment, skirted the snarled wreck, then calmly returned to the high roadbed. The effect of feeling one's train without any warning leave its bank and nose downward, slow motion, at a drunken tilt, run around a wreck, and slant tipsily up again, is a peculiar one. We never quite enjoyed the moments. Trains were not meant to do things like that. As night closed in we talked frantically and played parlor games in our compartment. For it was after dark that the guerrillas staged their mining operations, and it was many hours after dark before we pulled into Süchowfu. The last few hours were not pleasant. An eternity later, we dropped down on the night-shrouded station platform and watched our train puff slowly away; ten miles down the track it was mined and destroyed.

As long as I live, I shall not quite rid my mind of a shudder when I think of Süchowfu. A ghost story might have been staged here. Murder was the city's closest companion. Early in the war, the Chinese victory at Taierchwan had inflamed the Japanese to a dangerous pitch. Süchowfu, in their path and stoutly defended, bore the full brunt of their rage. Bombings, shellings, street fighting — it had been but the beginning of the city's saga, which continued for months and years to come. They say that every man, woman, and child left in the place was massacred during the occupation. The few thousand that trailed back afterward, hoping for peace, found none. Neither Chinese nor missionaries were permitted the use of electricity and telephones. A week after our departure, two American Catholic priests were shot by sentries — one of them killed.

We had hardly picked up our baggage and started for the station door when we were held up by a Japanese sentry who forced us, at his bayonet-point, to enter a small office somewhere in the station. Here our passports were examined by a Japanese officer who seemed much amused by us, and, through a sallow-faced Chinese interpreter who kept telling us sarcastically that he was Japanese, fired a round of questions at us. During the half an hour's examination, I noticed a Chinese, a gentleman of perhaps the wealthy merchant class, crouched in a kneeling position in the corner, quietly blubbering to himself. It is so seldom that a Chinese will cry out that I could not help staring at him. The Japanese, seeing the direction of my gaze, went across to the man and without any visible emotion on his face kicked him in the ribs three times with the full strength of his booted foot. The man crumpled up on the floor. I had already noticed that his lips and chin were stained with blood, perhaps from a blow on the mouth. Now I guessed that his lungs had been punctured. Twice more, while we were cooped up in that lamplit office, the man was kicked and beaten.

A little scared that Bill might lose his temper and start a fight, I asked the interpreter why the man was treated so, hoping for a reassuring answer.

The Chinese shrugged.

'An offender,' he said, and grinned abominably. It is no mere melodrama to speak of the feel of evil in that room. When at last we were permitted to leave, I was choking with humiliation and anger.

Rickshas carried us through the dark sleeping city toward the outskirts where the compound of the American hospital lay. The city's old ruins lay barely visible around us. Nothing else moved on the streets. No light showed anywhere. Every hundred yards or so, we would see suddenly a Japanese sentry standing still and dark in his appointed doorway, and all that showed of him in the half-moonlight were his bayonet and the white cornea of his eyes. As if to lend fleshy realism to the scene, each telephone wire that ran beside the roadway was weighted down with long, unbroken lines of carrion-eating crows, squatting there, fat and placid, making no sound or movement.

This was Süchowfu. We finished up our work in short order and did our best to leave on the dawn of the second day. Four o'clock in the bitter morning found us seated patiently on our baggage waiting for the one train which went through each day to Nanking. By seven it had not come. At last a Japanese guard appeared on the platform and began to shout orders at the crowd which was gathered there, at the same time laying about him with a club, and incidentally catching Bill a clip on the back of the head. The crowd scattered. I asked a Chinese station agent what had happened.

'*Ch'i ch'ei huai-la*,' he said, with a perfectly straight face. 'Your train has been spoiled.'

Later we were informed that our train had been blown up some thirty miles to the north and four hundred people killed.

The following dawn did at last see us on our way to Nanking. One more good look we had at the flood; this, when we passed through the flooded region around Pengpu where the Huai River, swelled by the waters of the Huang Ho, had burst its dikes. Here the flood was very deep, and was to last through most of the winter, enveloping the land in ice.

Near-by was the city of Showchow. A strange story had been circulating through China about Showchow. It concerned an American mission teacher by the name of Miss Mabel Jones, and later in Shanghai I was able to check the details of the story from that dry and matter-of-fact lady herself. It happened that during the summer months, she was the only foreigner remaining at the Showchow Presbyterian Mission. Quite early in the summer, she appeared in Shanghai with a request which she immediately put before the American Advisory Committee that allocates American-raised relief funds. The request was for thirty thousand Chinese dollars with which to rebuild the city wall of Showchow. After discussion of her plans and some dubious head-shaking and chin-pulling, the committee granted the sum and Miss Jones vanished once more into the interior. The reason for all this was, of course, flood prevention. She organized a committee of Chinese, put the mayor tactfully at their head, and stayed well in the background of the project, giving it a gentle shove when necessary. She says they did a good job of wall-building. About twelve hundred destitute coolies were put to work on the project; besides salary, they and their families were fed, clothed, and given mass-education classes — all this in addition to the business created for the sampan and junk men who were employed to bring in materials through the rising flood. Overnight Showchow became a boom town. And the wall was completed just in time. In the last few days of work, the crew managed to keep it a bare hand's-breadth above the rising flood, wall and water going up side by side. And when, at last, the flood had ceased to rise, one could climb up onto that high wall, kneel on the top, and wash one's hands on the other side.

Once, at the height of the flood, a strong east wind came up and at the same time the northeast wall began to give way. Had it collapsed, every man, woman, and child within the city would have been caught like so many rats and drowned outright. It was at this point that the Japanese garrison and civilians hired a fleet of sampans and evacuated the city in a body. They reserved a special sampan for Miss Jones, but Miss Jones guessed she wouldn't go. She was too busy. That night the entire city was mobilized, buildings were torn down for repair material, and the greater part of two hundred thousand people worked on that wall. They held it. Even today, as our train bore us slowly over the still flooded land, Showchow was the one city in the district without its burden of wholesale death and agony. And all because of three thousand American dollars and a lady.

The long journey was almost over. Up to now, I had felt fatalistic toward my work in China — not divinely protected because of any imagined altruism on my part, but somehow indifferent toward the outcome because the work had to be done and I was there to do it. I think I had taken it for granted that something actually *would* happen, that my luck could not hold forever. Therefore I had not dwelt upon the possibilities, had not even cared. Taking as many precautions as possible, I would merely

go where I had to go and do what I must, and let the end of the
thing come or not, as it wished. Now suddenly, with Bill beside
me here, with the last journey in sight, and a good chance that it
would, after all, come out right, I was terrified! The ferry that
brought us from Pukow to Nanking rocked and swayed, not at all
dangerously, in a heavy rain, and I was frozen with fear. Riding
about Nanking in rickshas for a day or so, I was as nervous as an
old hen. Although the trains between Nanking and Shanghai
were seldom mined by guerrillas, the trip left me in a cold sweat.
My new rabbity nervousness was too much for Bill; he did not
laugh — he merely marveled.

During our last three weeks in China, Bill and I grew increasingly fond of Shanghai, and for no reason that we could define.
For the Chinese there, life was, in a few cases, intensely profitable, and for the rest so frail that a breath could extinguish it.
The International Settlement went its way, a big, gaudy city of
huge department stores, shiny streets, laden with rickshas, cars,
and double-decker busses, elaborate hotels, skyscrapers, movie
houses; while about the edge stood what had once been the homes
of two million refugees. In Nantao, the Chinese city, we found
scarcely a building standing. The devastation stretched for many
miles. A few people who had straggled back here, too poor to rebuild their homes, lived as scavengers in the lonely ruins, selling
charcoal, searching the brick heaps for what they could find that
would sustain them. The rest tried to continue their lives within
the safer confines of the Settlement, and quite often they failed.
In 1940, some twenty-five thousand bodies were picked from the
streets, most of them on the winter mornings; twenty-one thousand were those of children. Meanwhile, the missionaries and foreign business men worked hard on committees and organized relief centers with insufficient money. They could not do so much,
because in America and England the cause lacked glamour and

sensationalism, and funds were hard to raise. But they tried. Each penny that came in was wisely spent.

Life for the big foreign populations in Shanghai had not greatly changed, except for the fact that business was at a standstill, and everyone about town gloomed into his drink and swore that the end of Shanghai was but a few days distant. It was a state of mind which had the redeeming quality of being excellent stuff for conversations. Their worries were not exaggerated, for the Japanese were making constant pecking encroachments upon the Settlement's freedom, rent and food prices were soaring, Chinese puppet officials were slaughtered almost daily in the streets, anti-Japanese newspaper offices were under attack by those worthies, an American news commentator was forced to wear a bullet-proof vest, and Shanghai, once the imperial shrine of Western capitalism, was a pretty terrible place in which to live.

By this time, all doubt as to Japan's intentions in China had been removed. Should she be victorious, foreigners would there and then please take themselves back across the Pacific where they belonged. It had been made clear now; everything Western was once and for all to be cleaned out of the Far East. The Pacific and all that bordered thereon was to be Japan's private preserve. And in the event of a Chinese victory? Some in Shanghai gloomily swore that Chiang would do exactly the same thing; that as soon as he became strong enough to rid himself of Japan, he would also rid himself of trespassing foreign investors, and the Open Door in China would be a dream of the past. It was an important question, this; vital to England and America. It had been answered for me many times out in Free China. Again and again, Kuomintang officials had said to me:

'It is after the war, more than today, that we shall need your American firms running their industries here to assist in our national recovery.' Or: 'If we can only persuade foreign investors to co-operate with us after the war, to pour money and technicians

into the country, our reconstruction work will be easier.' One
official put it perfectly frankly: 'The record of your business men
in China is not without stains. But because of the relief work
done by your people, you have grown close to us. Beside this,
after we have won the war we shall need foreign investors, workers, even monopolists from the West to help us in developing the
riches of our land.'

In America and in England, this realistic view on the part of
China should be well pondered.

On an evening in late November, Bill put me aboard a boat
bound for Japan. For the next two weeks, I was to do a strange
job of work there, while he finished up his writing in Shanghai
and joined me in Tokyo for the last voyage across the Pacific. I
locked my mind on emotion that night; and when before sunrise
the steamer slid gently out onto the Whangpoo and began a glid-
ing march down the river, which even then was crowded with its
dawn traffic, I was able to stare in a frozen trance at the shore and
the listing junks and the last that I was to see of China. The job
was done.

A picture of China was now burned into my brain for all time, a
picture that was curiously complex, that included both sides of the
battle-line, that depended not upon second-hand information,
but upon my own observations. Luck had given me a visual portrait of this war that few, if any, neutral observers had as yet
accumulated. I was no military expert; even if I were I would not
be fool enough to launch forth into predictions. Interpretations
and sweeping forecasts might bluff some into believing me, and
that is not good enough. But I could state the facts which I know
to be true and which I know to be important. I do so now.

On the debit side, China may list her lack of gasoline, fighting
planes, mechanics and pilots, demolition equipment, and sufficient
heavy artillery to stage an adequate offensive, a state of affairs

which will probably continue until her transportation facilities
are further improved and her imports and aid from abroad increased. It is doubtful whether the Burma Road can bear the
volume of large-scale importation; so far, the truck fleets are
bringing in only enough to keep Chiang's armies in condition for
defense fighting and small-scale attacks. Should the United
States or England send over fighting planes and allow them to be
flown into China from Rangoon or Hongkong along with foreign
crews and mechanics, should we send demolition experts, engineers, and technicians into Free China, the picture might change.
Further loans from abroad might step up internal industry and
aircraft production to the point where it actually could supply
the materials for the general offensive necessary to drive the
Japanese from China.

On the debit side, too, is the group of hoarders who are helping
to raise prices in the interior; the few remaining officials who are
out to enlarge their bank accounts; the hundred or so Chinese
millionaires who are sitting tight in Hongkong and Shanghai and
clinging like death to their millions; the long-corrupt Army
Medical Corps; the Far Eastern tradition of face-saving which
makes it difficult and sometimes impossible to get rid of a dis-
honest or stupid official; the lack of good communication and
transport facilities. Another debit item is the nation's tendency
towards complacency in military affairs, her easily satisfied ego,
her optimism.

Japan's worst mistake has been, of course, her treatment of
China. Had she used more wisdom, she might have gained for
herself every economic concession and monopoly that she wished
without a war, even without enmity. Second on the list is the
poor showing made by her army, a performance worthy of a third-
rate power. From what I saw of the work of her artillery units in
Nanchang, Szeshui, Wuhu, etc., I should judge them almost incapable of a direct hit upon their objective. True, the army has

hauled its mechanized units through the difficult mountain regions of Shanshi and Kwangsi when experts predicted that it
could not be done, and it has shown ingenuity and sometimes
brilliance in putting up makeshift bridges and crossing hazardous
terrains; but time and again a thaw, a cloudburst, a few days of
rain, have bogged down a Japanese advance in a helpless muddle
and left it easy prey for the mobile guerrillas, as in the big Japanese drive in southeastern Shansi during the summer of 1939.
Japan's bombing squadrons have proved efficient when the going
is easy; when faced with the unexpected they are often completely
demoralized. Today, morale is low among Japanese garrisons.
Soldiers are forced to leave the safe shelter of the cities with the
almost certain knowledge of death at the hands of unseen guerrillas waiting for them beyond the city walls. Sometimes we have
seen them weep. Japan's invasion of China has been a thrust of
long, vulnerable fingers into the country, a reticule of conquered
cities connected by beleaguered railroads and highways, surrounded by a resolute country people and a countryside which is
still Free China. Wuhu, Nanking, Peking, Tientsin — all are
small islands of occupation in a sea of resistance. During six
months of 1939, over two hundred battles were fought within a
two-mile radius of Shanghai. Outside the walls of virtually every
conquered city, the *hsiens* are administered by the officials of
Chiang Kai-shek, and pay their taxes directly into the Kuomintang treasury. Japan cannot collect taxes from the rural population for the simple reason that only a good-sized army would dare
venture outside the occupied towns in order to collect them. In
many conquered cities, the Japanese are in control during the
daytime; but at night, the garrisons retire to their barricaded
quarters and the guerrillas take possession of the place, wander
through the streets, do their shopping, chat with their friends, and
with the coming of dawn quietly retire to their positions beyond
the city walls. Japan's supply columns, her truck fleets and

trains, are under constant surprise attack. The nerves of her soldiers are frayed; there have been open rebellions among her troops at Hankow and in the harbor of Tientsin; the suicide roll among her officers mounts daily higher. She has shown herself capable of long, hard offensives; and each offensive leaves her more precariously strung out over the vast interior, more vulnerable to the Chinese, to whom the loss of territory matters very little and the weakening of Japan a great deal. Even her puppet governments have proved a failure, whenever they have survived long enough to prove anything at all. The life-span of a Chinese puppet official these days is very short, very short indeed.

Japan's strongest item in the credit column lies in her navy, a proud force which has seen almost no action in the China 'Incident' and which is eager enough to battle it out with somebody. However, the navy's one performance, during the struggle for Shanghai in the early months of the war, was a masterpiece of poor marksmanship, only surpassed by the Chinese themselves. Meanwhile, into Japan's bank account is pouring the money she receives from China's purloined customs duties and from the sale of drugs and opium, though the enormous profit which she had hoped to make from her conquest of North China has so far proved an idle dream. The conquered cities also provide a certain market for Japanese goods, and in the winter of 1940, confiscated rice from the already stricken provinces of the flooded north was exported to feed the people of Japan, whose rice crop had been below par.

The principal military strength of China lies in the very nature of her interior, where mountains, great rivers, rainy seasons, and few roads create a thousand headaches for an invading army. China's men under arms now number in the neighborhood of five million; of these about a third are in the field, a third in reserve, and a third in training. Her man power is far from being exhausted; she has so far utilized approximately one out of every

thirteen able-bodied potential fighters. Her munition factories
are able to supply enough small arms and light artillery to make
up for each day's loss; three small aircraft factories are operating
in Free China; meanwhile the Chinese are yearly becoming
stronger and more experienced soldiers. The guerrilla units are
well officered, well fed, and well uniformed men who receive their
orders by radio directly from Chungking.

The Chinese have proved themselves brilliant air men; as
many as eleven Japanese bombers have been shot down in a single
raid. They have also, to the surprise of the world, proved themselves thoroughly courageous and willing enough to die in battle.
From a military standpoint, China grows stronger with the passing of each month and each year.

An unexpected credit which must be set down on the Chinese
side of the ledger is her Christianity. Chalk it up to the work of
missionaries who have blundered in the past and clung intoler-
antly to petty creeds, but who in recent years have dropped their
mask of pious superiority and concentrated upon deeds instead of
sermons. But chalk it up to China, too, and her realistic turn of
mind. Not content with a string of comfortable beliefs and theories and high-sounding words, her Christians, now leaders in
government and education throughout the land, have an incurable habit of using their religion literally, as a secular way of life.
They go about calmly letting that man called 'Jei Su' teach them
how to live. And it is a startling thing to see this Christianity,
which we turn on and off like a faucet, suddenly undergo a sea-
change and take to itself a power beyond anything that we in the
complacent West can readily conceive. Usually we writers in
China blush to report on it, putting it down as 'missionary stuff.'
But there it is, one of the great contributary causes of the New
China, the headline which will never be printed: Christianity
Backs Up China's Resistance.

And is there need to summarize here the achievements of her

reconstruction and educational policies? I do not think so. China has set about the task of making herself internally and fundamentally strong enough to oust her invader and to take her place in the scheme of things; and she is doing it in the midst of a war. More than that, she is keeping herself deliberately democratic and deliberately tolerant in preparation for peace.

Strongest of all China's weapons today is the spirit and fire within her people. Japan finds herself fighting not an army but an entire population which has banded itself into one indestructible unit of men and women who can suffer for a period of many years, who carry on active resistence beneath the noses of their enemies, who are unwilling passively to 'absorb' the Japanese, but who will not rest until they may once again claim their lost territory and their potential greatness. China's new-found unity, her renaissance in the West, is no fable, no optimistic dream of those who love China and wishfully place their blind faith in her. It is a hard-driving, tempestuous, flaming reality. When in the summer of 1940 the British closed the Burma Road, then for a little while China's courage reached its lowest ebb and might have failed her. Today, with the vital road open and new loans from Britain and the United States already put to work, the people of Free China — the officials and the newsboys on the streets and the farmers and the merchants and the girls in their soldier uniforms, and the whole brawling, toiling mass of the population — are at work again with faith inside of them and one foot in the clouds.

15

STRANGE ASSIGNMENT

THE hardest part of my job lay ahead of me. I was to go to Japan for the express purpose of informing as many of her people as possible exactly what I had seen in China, including the actions and policies of her own army. I was to lecture privately to interested groups, and they who came to hear me would be taking their lives lightly in their hands. But the thing had to be done. Not even Europe could claim as rigid a censorship as that which existed within the boundaries of Japan. The Japanese are very thorough about these things. The educated classes and those inclined to doubt the newspaper versions of certain goings-on in China had no possible way of learning the truth except from the two or three of us who were willing to go and tell them bluntly the more unpleasant details of the China 'Incident.' I had stopped in Japan for a two weeks' visit on my way out to China and had at least a speaking acquaintance with the land and her people. They were anxious to have me return.

So it happened that a little over a year from the day that I sailed from Japan to China, I was once again a visitor on her shores, this time with a strange and even heart-breaking mission. Since my first visit in 1938, certain changes had come over the country. The third-class coach that took me from Kobe to Osaka and on to Tokyo was as crowded as before, but today there were more soldiers. As always in Japan, the train arrived at the Tokyo station on time to the second; but now there were no crowds on the platform waving red-balled flags and singing patriotic songs to departing troops. Superficially, Tokyo's streets were still wide and glistening, the department stores streamlined beyond anything Fifth Avenue can boast, the subway clean and comfortable; but there were significant differences. Busses were run on wood instead of by gasoline; they steamed pantingly up each small grade; there were not many of them. The subway, still beautiful, ran at a snail's pace because electricity was weak throughout the city. Trolley-cars were a rarity, and all vehicles so crowded that during rush hours people were often forced to walk many miles. There were fewer wounded, in their traditional white robes; rumor had it that they were not permitted to return to their homes for fear that they would spread discontent among the people — in short, give the flimsy show away. Because of the strict rationing of fuel and electricity, the foreign population could not always be sure of warming their houses, reading their books, or cooking their meals. The nation suffered horribly from the winter cold. (In the summer of 1940, many large factories in Osaka and other industrial centers were shut down altogether for weeks at a time in order to save precious fuel for the all-important munitions plants; some failed to reopen.) As for proud Tokyo, once a miracle of efficient and streamlined living — they told me that the city had turned the clock back twenty years; that conditions were much the same today as they were at the end of the first World War.

There were other changes too — a lack of buoyancy, a mood of patient waiting and inward unhappiness. Once on a Tokyo street I passed a mile-long line of horses which were being led slowly through the traffic. They were exquisite animals, big and rangy; and they had been recruited by the army and were now on their way to headquarters. At each horse's head was its owner, generally a man in farmer's clothes. One or two were very young boys. Nearly all of them had dressed their valuable beasts for the occasion, twisted ribbons in their manes, and braided their tails with bright streamers so that they might look proud and beautiful on their last journey. The horses, as if conscious of the solemnity and excitement of the moment, held their heads high and pranced the avenue. But quite a few of the men were weeping.

Tokyo's stores, these days, looked opulent, and the look was deceiving. Silk and woollen goods were almost unobtainable in the whole of Japan. Even cotton was scarce. The *obis* and kimonos were made of rayon. Other shortages included butter, milk, timber, drugs, rubber, leather, and a dozen more. Manufacturers, unable to buy the necessary raw materials at the exorbitant prices which had been fixed by the Government, were resorting to an underground market. Oddly enough, cash was all too plentiful. The Government has had no difficulty in raising money, but it cannot step up production fast enough to be able to spend it. The gold reserve was gradually dwindling and the note increase very high. Taxes were enormous and the nation's debt a staggering burden. As an economic boon, the conquered territories of China had proved a pipe dream; a vast amount of capital and greater control over the territory itself would be needed to develop the well-hidden resources of North China; so far, China had cost billions in investment and had paid back few dividends.

One reason for the shortage of such staple products as butter and rice and silk was the precarious position of Japan's foreign credit. Scarcely any measure was too extreme if it resulted in the purchase of foreign currency and the stabilization of trade, especially with the valuable United States. Consequently, butter and silk and other necessities were exported almost *in toto*, and Japan became impoverished in her own most prolific products. Conscription of men into the army and into the vital industries had caused a shortage of farm workers. Already the price of rice and tobacco had gone up, and the press had expressed its indignation in astonishingly frank terms. On a previous occasion in Japan's history when the price of rice went up, the famous and disastrous 'rice riots' swept the country — the first and last time that the country people openly rebelled.

Today, price rises are not yet disastrous, thanks to the temporary prosperity enjoyed by Japan's working classes. Because of the high selling price of rice and silk, I found the farmers flourishing; factory workers, too, were growing rich on overtime and increased wages. There was no thought of strikes. Everyone's income was on the rise. The worker's life, in fact, was so externally rosy that he scarcely noticed the increased regimentation under which he lived, the gradual control exercised by the Government over wages, hours, prices, and number of employees. The favoritism shown to all munitions plants caused many other factories to curl up and die a natural death, adding to the shortage of all products not essential to the waging of war.

Nearly all the government organizations and bodies were becoming more and more the tools of the inner military clique which was represented in the Cabinet, and which ran the war in China almost as it pleased. The Diet was now kept busy on internal legislation, forced to leave foreign policy and the China 'Incident' to more influential bodies, and in 1941 gave up all control over the Cabinet's decrees. Quite naturally the members were resentful, though few dared express themselves. But the feeling prevailed within the Diet that the Army was keeping things rather too closely to itself, and had failed to announce its future policies or even to account for its overwhelming demands. To put it briefly, nobody was telling anybody anything about it. So the Diet fussed quietly and futilely to itself. Only once did a member come right out and demand in effect: 'Just exactly what are you up to in China, anyway? Whatever it is, it does not appear very successful.' He threw the honorable assembly into something not far short of a nervous breakdown; later he was ordered to appear for trial, but being a popular gentleman, was released at the plea of his fellow legislators. Meanwhile, the Emperor continued to emerge now and then from his sanctuary, to live a quiet and, we hope, a peaceful life, and to be kept always in ignorance of what went on outside his palace walls. They claim that he is unhappy over his war. Probably no emperor in history has had less to say about it.

So the gradual drift toward complete military control went on, with ups and downs, with shifting of cabinets from lenient to stern and back to lenient, with a change of prime ministers like a change of petticoats, every few months. Continuous diplomatic skirmishing went on between the conservatives within the Government and their more ambitious army and navy. Many of Japan's officials felt thwarted and almost chained by their own military. A small Communist group was waiting underground for the possible collapse of their government, at which time they hoped to step in and take charge. Within the military itself there existed cliques. The majority of officers in North China had long been in favor of consolidating their gains in the north and letting the rest of the country take care of itself; many were violently against the Yangtze Valley and South China campaigns. But their more energetic brethren who happened to be in control on the spot more than once took matters into their own hands. True, there is not the complete chaos and lack of discipline in the Japanese Army that some observers would wistfully like to think; but military matters are quite often determined by what General So-and-So ate for breakfast rather than any formal orders he might have received from Tokyo. As for the Nanking atrocities and the more violent phases of the Japanese Army's policies in China — they have been mourned by Japan; officials in Tokyo are acutely conscious that lack of discipline and the uncertain temper of a few of their generals have made military hash of what might have been a promising and profitable campaign.

Meanwhile, the war situation has had its ups and downs. The summer of 1939 had brought the disastrous clash between Soviet and Japanese forces, during which each side allegedly shot down considerably more fighting planes than either side possessed; the Japanese admitted the loss of eighteen thousand men, which number, in view of Japan's usual accuracy in these matters, may be safely multiplied several times. Her losses in China had by now almost certainly passed the million mark, although the approximate number can never be known. Billions of yen had poured into the China campaigns. At this time, the capture of Nanning was a very definite boost to Japan in that it cut the road from Hanoi to West China and eliminated one of Chiang Kai-shek's routes to the sea; later, after the diplomatic coup within French Indo-China, Nanning and several other South China cities were to be evacuated, to free troops for use elsewhere, and also (though this was not mentioned in the Japanese communiqué) to give up positions which had been made almost untenable by the attacks of General Pai's men and also by virulent epidemics among the Nanning garrison. A year later, Ichang was captured after months of devastating air raids which laid the city in ruins. But except for those two victories, Japan's gains had apparently ended in a stalemate; her campaigns in southeastern Shansi collapsed in a sea of mud; her later offensives in Hupeh were a useless gesture. As the Chinese put it, she was on the tiger's back; and that is not the most comfortable place to be. It was quite natural that even in the fall of 1939 her government had begun to look to the south, to the rich islands of the Dutch East Indies and to Indo-China, for the replenishment of her ailing war machine. Today, with the subsequent fall of Holland, Japan has virtually announced her policy toward the East Indies for all the world to hear.

At the time of my visit, the subject was under frank discussion in educated circles. Would the shortage of fuel permit the Japanese navy to wage a war of several months in the region of the Dutch Indies, four thousand miles from Japan? Probably not, they thought. The distances were enormous. Hongkong, if allowed to remain as a British base, would most certainly be troublesome. Its capture might take several days and allow the American fleet to arrive in the arena. No, the seizure of the rich Indies would have to be a sudden, quick coup, with a treasure-trove of oil waiting at the end of the venture to allow the warring vessels to engage any intervening powers and hold what they had already seized. Rumors that the Dutch could destroy their oil wells were not taken very seriously by the Japanese. Only one thing really worried them — the American fleet. It seemed to give them considerable pause; but whether their respect arose from a determination to be polite to me or from a spontaneous fear, I could not tell. Meanwhile, our chiding attitude toward Japan continued to hurt and puzzle her people. They could not easily forget that we were traditionally their close and honorable friends. Our disapproval struck a deep wound in their pride.

War-weary Japan certainly was; tired of the long-drawn-out China 'Incident,' beginning to lose the high faith she had put in Wang Ching-wei as providing the solution to all her troubles. But to say that she was, or is today, on the verge of internal collapse is merely another symptom of that familiar disease (and cliché), Wishful Thinking. Belt-tightening has just begun in Japan. She can take in many more notches without serious consequences. Her people are spiritually fashioned for long and loyal sacrifice. They do not love their country in the ordinary sense — they love and cherish each miniature village that they pass in the train, each range of mountains, each gaudy temple, each pool and garden, each flower. Their beauty spots are places of worship. They throng by hundreds and by thousands to famous shrines and scenic parks. Japan's nagging pleas for space in which to colonize her overflowing population run right into the simple fact that few Japanese can be torn from their own country. They will not colonize. Given any other surroundings, they are as bewildered as lost puppies in a city street. Their traditions are a fanatical part of their lives. And their nationalism has been carefully nurtured by government propaganda. It is strange to suppose that a people so emotionally in love with their land would actively turn against that land, would even admit its discrepancies and sins in the face of world censure, unless matters reached a stage far more acute than they are today. The people possess a resilience and ability to suffer not always recognized by the hopeful West, which assumes that any population so oppressed and put upon by their government and military must certainly revolt.

In the first place, the educated Japanese have our own sins on their fingertips. They know by heart each dubious act committed by the Western Powers, and they feel sublimely free to go and do likewise. Our wagging finger of disapproval only infuriates them the more. When the imperialism of the West forced its way upon Japan, it won a strong disciple — stronger, perhaps, than it bargained for. All the scolding on earth will not arouse her shame or cause her people to turn against their government. However, the very pride of the Japanese and their sense of divine superiority might some day work the necessary magic. Germans have long been disliked and looked down upon by the Japanese; German good-will missions which toured the country during my visit, to the sound of drums and national fanfare, were discussed with devastating scorn behind their backs. The alliance with the Axis in 1940 brought only a glum silence from the people. Should Japan be called upon to suffer and make sacrifices for the sake of Germany, the people's resentment, which is now confined solely to the length of the China 'Incident,' might swell and become a dangerous menace.

Japan's greatest protection has been in her censorship. Had the truth of her army's deeds in China become public property, the national shame would have been overwhelming, for next to the Emperor, the Army is the most worshipful institution in the land. But the people do not know. They are told day after day that Japan is helping China get rid of her war lords, is cleaning up her diseased cities, ridding her of skulking Communists, and becoming her greatest and most beloved savior. Wall posters are hung in every village and town showing, for instance, a portion of the Japanese army just entering a captured Chinese town; the streets would be lined with Chinese, all cheering and shouting and waving small Japanese flags, while in the background a group of dark-faced Communists slunk away in shameful retreat. Tell anyone this sort of thing for a few years and the very force of repetition will cause him to believe it.

I began to understand the mentality of the Japanese soldier in China who can be so needlessly brutal in his treatment of the Chinese. Filled with the glory of a sacred mission, the rescue of a victimized people, a boy will go forth to war in China, dreaming of the gratitude and joy with which the unfortunate populace will receive him, ready for any sacrifice in the fulfillment of his great and good cause. It is only a short time before his disillusionment is complete. All that he once believed in has collapsed and he is left bewildered, defensive, easily enraged. The constant strain of fighting unseen enemies, of facing each day the smoldering hatred of the Chinese who pass him by, is enough to turn him into a sadist, to make him work off his inward turmoil in physical and brutal action.

It was my job to do all within my power to shatter the illusions of the Japanese people. It was not an easy job to do. Especially among the student class, I found boys so violently loyal that they could not and *would* not believe their army capable of a single crime, although I backed up my statements with absolute proof. To others, the news was a horrible awakening.

'Our soldiers can violate women? *Our soldiers!*'

Every sleek black head in the room would be turned toward me, unmoving.

'Yes.' It was useless to elaborate. The silence would hang for slow seconds. No boy in the room would move or speak until I broke the spell.

They were strange little affairs, these lectures of mine. For obvious reasons I cannot divulge specific details, names, and places; but they told me more about Japanese public opinion than a year of official conversations might have done. Naturally I spoke almost entirely to groups already discontented with their government's China policy; who wished to know the truth without any sugar-coating. The great mass of the people had had no hint that all was not well in China, except for the fact that the 'incident' dragged on and demanded more and more sacrifice from them; they still took it quite for granted that their brave, selfless army was saving the Chinese masses from the heavy hand of Chiang Kai-shek and the terrible Communists; they still admired their army, felt very sorry for China, and hoped and prayed that the war would soon end. But among the intelligentsia, there was an underground current of unrest and suspicion — suspicion of their own military. Obviously the army was being extremely unsuccessful in China; the war debt threatened to snow them under at any minute; the whole venture was a mistake from start to finish. Many officials and professional men privately advocated withdrawal from China at once. The main reason for the resentment was not so much pity for China as pity for Japan. Their own military was threatening a national suicide. Why did the war have to start, anyway! Why could not everything have been settled without any fighting! It was all very annoying. In fact, it is safe to say that a large proportion of Japan's educated classes, even including her own officials, would like nothing better than to toss its military as diplomatically as possible to the wolves.

As a group, the intelligentsia took the fantastic newspaper reports of victories and more victories and infinitesimal casualty lists with a large grain of salt. The editors themselves chafed under the constant farce of publishing what they knew to be false. It became the habit to publish items which were probably true (but would not pass the censor) in the form of denials and indignant explanations. Readers, seeing such items, would know at once that here was something upon which they could probably rely.

Quite a lot of this national suspicion remained well hidden. Once, at a long and difficult session of mine, a certain old gentleman was especially persistent in standing up for the justice of Japan's actions in China. Later in the evening we were strolling home in a group together. As I turned up a road toward the home where I visited, the old scholar suddenly left the others and hurried after me. Speaking as rapidly as possible, he whispered:

'You must not believe what I have said this evening. I am forced to say such things by my pride and my fear of arrest. You must know that I hate this war. I hate it! I am ashamed....'

The interview took perhaps seven seconds. Then he turned and trotted down the path like an agitated ancient goat, and was gone.

I had but one way of reaching these people with my message from China. I must always first confess (and quite truthfully) that my own country and the nations of the West were guilty of many crimes; that I did not come to criticize and censure, but merely to tell them facts which were true and which were difficult to learn within the well-censored borders of Japan. At once the atmosphere would relax. All the defensive arguments they had been making up in the backs of their brains could be discarded. This was not to be a debate, merely a news session. And they were avid for the truth. The truth was not all misery and horror stories. I was able to tell them of the strange attitude of

Free China toward her enemies; the fact that Chiang was by no means the fanatic, seeking vengeance upon his Japanese foes, but rather a man capable of seeing many sides of a question, a man so wise that he was deliberately keeping bitterness out of the picture in the hopes of making possible a fair and lasting peace. I based my portrait of Chiang not upon sentimental faith but upon the internal evidence of his propaganda and treatment of prisoners. It was good to see the hope that came into the faces of my listeners when they heard such matter-of-fact and astonishing news.

Probably the most important work I was able to do in Japan consisted of certain private interviews which I had with Japanese officials, very high in their government, who were against their own military and eager to corroborate the details of their army's actions in China, as well as Chiang's attitude toward themselves. At these times, I was the one to be interviewed, to answer questions and give reports. Their own attitude sometimes astonished me. One internationally known Japanese (and he was not alone in his opinions) begged me to 'return to your country and implore your people to place a complete embargo on all war materials to our government. We who are fighting our own military do not have our people behind us, for they know nothing of our crimes against China. We fight alone and in secret. A physical restriction upon our "incident" may be the one weapon with which we could force our army out of power. Do not fear that we will wage war upon you for your act. My people are war-weary, in no mood for conflict with the United States. An embargo would really be an act of mercy to us as well as an act of justice to China.'

Most humble among my listeners were the Christians. The majority of Japan's Christians have backed their government's policies in China, partly through ignorance of the true situation there, partly through fear of persecution. They do not believe that it is a Christian's job to mix into political matters and let himself be executed for a cause which seems to him not to concern his church in the least. But there were a few — very few — who would not compromise their Christianity. They suffered private agony from the actions of their own people. They prayed for China's victory.

The work in Japan was over at last. Bill and I met once more for the long voyage home. But now that I was to go, I perversely did not want to leave Japan. Contrary to all traditional lovers of China, I also loved this odd, intense, graceful little country. True, the Japanese do not have the habit of frank self-criticism that I found in the Chinese, nor the devastating honesty, nor the passionate love of life, nor the sense of humor. But they have startling qualities of their own: an exhaustive patience and ability to learn from others, a quiet pleasure in almost everything beautiful, a natural efficiency and neatness of body and mind. More than all else, they have an ability to dedicate themselves to an ideal or an idea with a devotion so complete that it could accomplish the best or the worst deeds known to man. Probably no nation upon earth has such potential cruelty and such potential greatness. I kept thinking, 'It is the funny old game all over again — pin the tail on the donkey. Please, someone, turn Japan in the right direction, head her straight. She might one day become a natural leader of us all.'

The hour was long past midnight. Bill and I were sprawled out on our elbows on the after deck of the big trans-Pacific boat, not saying very much but watching the black shoreline and the dark, perfect cone of Fuji grow far away. I was wondering to myself what I should say about China when I reached home, what neat, profound interpretations I could conjure up in the manner habitual to travelers in the East. I muttered some experimental phrases to myself. They sounded foolish. China — queer old complex land — does not lend herself to generalizations. Must I crystallize my experiences, parse them and fold them into comfortable clauses in order that the public may admire my superior knowledge? The experiences themselves are the only certain truth. Better by far to give them honestly, without sensationalism or bias, and let the listener and the reader form them, if he must, into deeper stuff. . . .

Out there beyond the ship's rail the last faint horizons of Far Eastern shores dimmed, narrowed, and were gone. Suddenly Mr. Sun was at my elbow murmuring, 'I regret to say that they are mines.' And the harbor of Wenchow was wide and calm. That girl in the Changsha hospital — what was it she had said? Something about not wanting to die but death being part of the job. The wounded soldier in Hengyang hadn't wanted the extra blanket because it wouldn't have been fair, and in Kweilin a crowd of workmen told us, 'This is a water main, Hsien-sheng, for the fireproof buildings we will put up here,' and below the city wall a boy coolie lay with his head split open. Somewhere — Chungking it was, in January — a wounded girl nursed her baby on a stretcher. That boy, Jang Jin, had held the baby gently too. Caves and caves in the northwest, they were dim and cool, dusty. And the people — in Chihsien there had been five thousand lined up. They sang their songs pretty well, like the students who sang on the road to Yenan and the soldiers of Yen Hsi-shan beneath the moon's eclipse. There was Eva, looking distraught under her load, and Edward Bear wriggled warmly beneath my right ear. The family in Changpei had eaten their early meal squatting in a kitchen by the light of their burning home, and the dawn had been foggy that day when I sat in a cornfield and saw the crest of Chungking rise from a fogbank. Almost like a vision the way it rose.

But quieter still had been the moment on the long wild road to Sian when we dined in the courtyard of the temple, high on the slopes of a sacred mountain, and plum blossoms had filled the bitter air and somewhere beyond the outer courts a villager had played upon his flute. The low, twisted evergreens had grown protecting arms out over the tiled roofs and the gargoyles; and before the latticed doorways within our own small courtyard had stood iron statues, a lioness, a lean crane, a phoenix...

My thoughts focused abruptly. There was something I could not remember.

'Bill,' I said, 'what's that legend about the phoenix? About the sacrifice?'

'What? Oh, you mean the Arabian one.' Bill's eyes took on a satisfied expression. He liked legends. 'Every five hundred years,' he explained, 'the old worn-out phoenix flies to a certain shrine and burns himself upon the altar. Then the young phoenix is supposed to be born from the ashes. It rises up and flies away until the next five hundred years are ended.'

'The young phoenix...'

'Very strong bird with brilliant colors. It's a great story.'

'Mmm.'

Bill grinned at me.

'Yes, little fish, there's a Chinese phoenix too...'

Eastward, the edge of the ocean met a strip of pale blue light where the dawn was coming in. It was a clear quick dawn. It swept upward to the top of the sky, giving way to sunrise, moving onward toward the shores of China. In an hour or so it would be over Wenchow, bright on her guardian pagodas, then across the red hills of Chekiang, above the emerald river and the cocky sails of sampans. The ruins of Changsha would see it next, and the cold gorges of the Yangtze would let in a little of its light.

Pretty soon it would reach the place where two rivers meet.

THE END